Cornelius Castoriadis

ALSO AVAILABLE FROM BLOOMSBURY

Postscript on Insignificance, Cornelius Castoriadis, translated by Gabriel Rockhill and John V. Garner

Castoriadis, Foucault, and Autonomy, Marcela Tovar-Restrepo

Cornelius Castoriadis

Key Concepts

Edited by
SUZI ADAMS

B L O O M S B U R Y
LONDON • NEW DELHI • NEW YORK • SYDNEY

Bloomsbury Academic

An imprint of Bloomsbury Publishing Plc

50 Bedford Square   1385 Broadway
London   New York
WC1B 3DP   NY 10018
UK   USA

www.bloomsbury.com

Bloomsbury is a registered trade mark of Bloomsbury Publishing Plc

First published 2014

British Library Cataloguing-in-Publication Data
A catalogue record for this book is available from the British Library.

ISBN: HB: 978-1-4411-8164-0
PB: 978-1-4411-0290-4
ePDF: 978-1-4411-7290-7
ePub: 978-1-4411-6914-3

Library of Congress Cataloging-in-Publication Data
A catalog record for this book is available from the Library of Congress.

Typeset by Newgen Knowledge Works (P) Ltd., Chennai, India
Printed and bound in India

PERMISSIONS

CONTENTS

NOTES ON CONTRIBUTORS

Dr Suzi Adams is Senior Lecturer in Sociology at Flinders University (Adelaide) and External Fellow of the Central European Institute of Philosophy (Czech Academy of Science and Charles University, Prague). Her monograph, *Castoriadis's Ontology: Being and Creation* was published by Fordham University Press (New York, 2011), and she has published widely on Castoriadis's thought in international journals. Her research elaborates a philosophical anthropology of modernity from a cultural hermeneutic and phenomenological perspective.

Professor Johann P. Arnason is Emeritus Professor of Sociology at La Trobe University (Melbourne) and Visiting Professor at the Faculty of Human Studies, Charles University (Prague). He was editor of *Thesis Eleven* from 1987–2003. Key publications include: *Civilizations in Dispute* (Leiden, 2003); *The Roman Empire in Context: Historical and Comparative Perspectives*, edited with K. Raaflaub (Malden/MA and Oxford, 2011) and *The Greek Polis and the Invention of Democracy: A Politico-Cultural Transformation and its Interpretations*, edited with K. Raaflaub and P. Wagner (Malden/MA and Oxford, 2013).

Sophie Klimis teaches Philosophy at the University Saint-Louis in Brussels. She is one of the three founding members of the *Groupe de Recherche Castoriadis* at the University Saint-Louis, co-editor of the *Cahiers Castoriadis* (8 volumes) and member of the board of directors of the Association *Castoriadis* in Paris. She is the author of *Le statut du mythe dans la Poétique d'Aristote. Les fondements philosophiques de la tragédie* (Brussels, 1997) and *Archéologie du sujet tragique* (Paris, 2003).

Dr Jeff Klooger teaches sociology at Swinburne University of Technology (Melbourne). He is the author of *Castoriadis: Psyche,*

Society, Autonomy (Leiden and Boston, 2009) and has published on Castoriadis's thought in international journals.

Dr Angelos Mouzakitis (MA, PhD University of Warwick, UK) was a Jean Monnet Fellow at the European University Institute, Florence, Italy (2003–2004). His research and teaching expertise lie in the fields of social theory and philosophical phenomenology. He currently teaches social theory at the University of Crete and the Hellenic Open University. He is the author of *Meaning, Historicity and the Social. A Critical Approach to the Works of Heidegger, Gadamer and Castoriadis* (Saarbrücken, 2008).

Dr Anders Ramsay holds a PhD in sociology from the University of Lund. He has studied and published on Theodor W. Adorno, and Marx's critique of political economy, psychoanalysis and critical theory in general. He currently works as Lecturer at the Department of Sociology at the University of Örebro, Sweden.

Professor Mats Rosengren is Professor of Rhetoric in the Department for Communication, Media and IT at Södertörn University College, Sweden. He is member of the editorial board of *Glänta* and Vice President of the Swedish Ernst Cassirer Society. He has published widely on continental philosophy and is the author of *Cave Art, Perception and Knowledge* (Palgrave Macmilan, 2012).

Dr Jeremy Smith is Senior Lecturer and Associate Dean (Learning and Teaching) in the School of Education and Arts at the University of Ballarat in Australia. He has published in leading international journals and is the author of *Europe and the Americas: State Formation, Capitalism and Civilizations in Atlantic Modernity* (Leiden and Boston, 2006) and *Debating Civilizations: Interrogating Civilizations Analysis in the Global Age* (forthcoming).

Dr Karl E. Smith is Lecturer in Sociology at Victoria University (Melbourne). He is the author of *Meaning, Subjectivity, Society: Making Sense of Modernity* (Leiden and Boston, 2010). He has published in leading international journals on challenges of identity, subjectivity and religion in modernity.

Dr Ingerid S. Straume has a PhD in the philosophy of education with a thesis on Castoriadis (Oslo, 2010). She has published in several journals and anthologies, and is active in international networks of Castoriadis studies. Straume works as a subject specialist at Oslo University Library.

ELUCIDATING CASTORIADIS: EDITOR'S PREFACE

Cornelius Castoriadis (1922–1997) was a Greek-French thinker best known for his work on 'autonomy' and 'human creation'. Co-founder with Claude Lefort of *Socialisme ou Barbarie*, Castoriadis was a political activist, philosopher, political and social theorist, psychoanalyst and economist. The intricacies of pure mathematics were as important for his thought as the poetry of Athenian tragedy. Each served to deepen his elucidation of a politico-philosophical anthropology – a 'political ontology' as Dick Howard has called it. And if Castoriadis's image of the human condition was not strictly situated *in-the-world*, in the phenomenological sense, it was certainly not *without-the-world*. His philosophical reflections were not, however, for their own sake. They were always harnessed to the broader project of autonomy as a politics in the strong and explicit sense (*la politique*) that aimed to radically interrogate and transform the existing institution of society (especially its unquestioning obeisance to what Castoriadis calls the 'infinite pursuit of (pseudo)rational mastery'). Moving beyond Marx, but remaining a revolutionary, Castoriadis was tireless in his (sometimes controversial) engagement with the contemporary issues of the day – from the Hungarian Revolution to the Gulf War and the growing ecological crisis.

Notwithstanding the richness of his thought, Castoriadis's terminology can be idiosyncratic and challenging to understand. Most of the literature on Castoriadis's work is aimed at an audience already at least broadly familiar with his project. The purpose of the present book is different: it aims to make Castoriadis's thought more accessible to scholars who might be encountering him for the first time. It seeks to introduce and clarify the complexity of his conceptual framework through the elucidation of 19 key concepts that are fundamental to understanding – and grappling with – his intellectual project. The concepts have been selected to cover the most central aspects and periods of his thought. They range from 'autonomy', 'heteronomy' and 'the social-historical', to the very specialized notions of 'legein and teukhein' and 'ensemblistic-identiarian logic'.

The authors approached each key concept in the Castoriadian spirit of elucidation and interrogation. The seldom used philosophical term elucidation was central to Castoriadis's project. Elucidation presumes that we can only know the world 'in fragments', and only in cultural-historical contexts. But this does not presume a cultural relativism: the active acceptance of our historical situation allows us also to gain distance from historical horizons that can thereby open onto the possibility of critique. Underlying Castoriadis's usage of 'elucidation' was his criticism of the fallacy of 'general theory' as a totalizing system of absolute, de-contextualized knowledge. He was interested instead to provide an account of the human condition and the world as elucible not deducible. Interrogation of the socially instituted world was also a key aspect of Castoriadis's project – and his own work does not provide an exception to this. The concepts elucidated here are not reducible to exegesis or summary; rather they provide both articulation and interrogation of the idea under consideration. Like any other philosophical framework, Castoriadis's thought does not form a totalizing system of knowledge, but an open horizon for further problematization, elucidation and debate.

Recognized as one of the most important thinkers of the twentieth century, there is an ongoing interest in and burgeoning new literature on Castoriadis's thought. Yet his work tends to remain marginal to much contemporary philosophical and political debate. There are, no doubt, a variety of reasons for his outsider status; it is both more and less than an historical accident. He is at least in good company – for some time Maurice Merleau-Ponty's thought, too, remained on the margins.

Suzi Adams
Adelaide, 10 August 2013

ACKNOWLEDGEMENTS

This book would not have been possible without the support and input of a whole range of people. I would like to first thank all the authors who generously contributed their thoughtful – and thought provoking – entries to this project. I would like to also thank Johann Arnason, Zoé Castoriadis, Dick Howard, Gabriel Rockhill and Peter Wagner for their generous comments on various aspects of the project. Many thanks also go to Sarah Campbell from Bloomsbury (formerly Continuum) for recognizing the significance of this project, Rachel Eisenhauer from Bloomsbury for her great patience in seeing the book through to completion and Srikanth Srinivasan of Newgen Knowledge Works and the rest of the Production team for their patience and hard work in creating this book. Louise Coventry kindly gave her time and expertise in preparing the final manuscript for publication, for which I am very grateful. I would also like to thank Tejaswini Patil Vishwanath for her invaluable assistance with compiling the index. I would like to especially thank Ingerid Straume, who was co-editor in the early stages of the project. Without her dedicated enthusiasm this book would not have gone further than a brainstorming session or two.

CHAPTER ONE

Autonomy

Suzi Adams

The *project of autonomy* is central to Cornelius Castoriadis's intellectual and political work, especially after the mid-1960s. It aims at the radical transformation of society – dominated in modernity by the rational mastery of bureaucratic capitalism – by revolutionary activity. Literally meaning 'self-governing' or 'laws given by the self, for itself' (*auto-nomos*), Castoriadis's elucidation of autonomy builds on his articulation of socialism as workers' self-management and council communism (see *Socialism*), which he developed during his time in *Socialisme ou Barbarie* as part of the broader, non-communist Left in France. Autonomy for Castoriadis consists in the interplay of collective and individual aspects; an autonomous society presupposes autonomous citizens (and vice versa) and the participation of all in power (Castoriadis, 1991, pp. 168–169; see also Howard, 1988). It is a sociopolitical project that aims to illuminate society's 'instituting power and at rendering it explicit in reflection', on the one hand, and to reabsorb the explicit power of *the* political (*le politique*) into politics (*la politique*) in the strong sense, as the 'lucid and deliberate activity whose object is the explicit institution of society', on the other (Castoriadis, 1991, p. 174).

On Castoriadis's account all societies institute themselves; that is, they create their own political form of society, be that, for example, monarchy or democracy (see *Institution* and *Social-Historical*).

However, not all societies recognize that they are the source of their own form, customs, meanings and laws, and instead attribute them to an extra-social source, such as god or nature; such societies are *heteronomous* (see *Heteronomy*). An autonomous society in Castoriadis's strong sense presupposes three things: first, the recognition that society is the source of its own form, meanings and laws; second, the recognition that socially created laws and norms are not given once and for all, and as such can be collectively – and publicly – problematized, interrogated and altered; third, the acknowledgement that there are no pre-given limits to the human realm – apart from very general, existential limits, such as mortality – and, as such, the social collective must set its own limits. This is the task of self-limitation (see *Tragedy*, *Paideia* and *Democracy*).

Intellectually, the project of autonomy emerged in Castoriadis's thought during the second half of the 1950s as part of his 'roads beyond Marx'; it is not however reducible to his shift beyond Marx. The crucial transition to a sustained critique of Marx is to be found in his text 'Modern Capitalism and the Revolutionary Movement' (in Castoriadis, 1987). The concept of autonomy did not emerge fully fledged in his thought but was rather a concept inprogress. In all, four intellectual sources and connections can be identified: first, the rethinking of the meaning of revolution via a critique of Marxist historical materialism and of Leninist vanguardism; second, the incorporation of psychoanalysis as a way of rethinking individual autonomy; third, the significance of the ancient Greek breakthrough to democracy; fourth, the attempt to rethink democracy as the anti-capitalist aspect of modernity. Each of these will be addressed in turn. The chapter concludes by mapping some open questions concerning possible limitations to Castoriadis's elucidation of autonomy.

From the mid-1950s, Castoriadis began a critical engagement with Marx. More specifically, he set out to renew the revolutionary project via a critique of historical materialism in order to give self-determining human agency a central place.[1] He writes:

> Starting from revolutionary Marxism, we have arrived at the point where we have to choose between remaining Marxist and remaining revolutionaries, between faithfulness to a doctrine that, for a long time now, has ceased to fuel either

reflection or action, and faithfulness to the project of a radical change of society, which demands that we first understand what we want to change and that we identify what in society truly challenges this society and is struggling against its present form. (1987, p. 14)

Castoriadis identifies two aspects to Marx's work: the emancipatory and *praxis*-oriented, which was found especially in Marx's early writings, and the deterministic-reductionist, as found in Marx's later writings, but also as taken up by orthodox Marxism. Castoriadis seeks to retrieve the former as a way of rethinking authentic revolutionary activity.

Castoriadis begins his critique of Marx by considering his economic theory. Here he hones in on the primary contradiction of capitalism in Marx's eyes: the incompatibility of the development of the productive forces and the relations of production by shifting it to the level of bureaucratic organization (p. 15). His critique begins with an assessment of Marx's theory of history via the 'forces of production' – something that is clearly central in Marx's own thought – and later moved on to discuss the 'base' and 'superstructure' couplet – something that became more central in the later Marxian tradition than it had been in Marx's own thought. Castoriadis builds a critique of the notion of technological determinism that underpins historical materialism (Castoriadis, 1987). But the forces of production are, in the last instance, the technological moment – in the strong sense of 'technicist' – of social relations conceived in economic (capitalist) terms, and thus fall prey to technological determinism (see *Capitalism* and *Socialism*). However, historical experience reveals a different perspective. 'Technical progress' is historically instituted and is thus far from being autonomous, linear and continuous in its long-term development – sustained technological innovation was not a feature of Greek antiquity or the Middle Ages, for example (Castoriadis, 1987).

From the critique of technological determinism, Castoriadis identifies the centrality of meaning as a basic aspect of society and history (see Arnason, 2012, p. 51) (see *Social Imaginary Significations*). He does so through a reconstruction of the latent idealism underlying Marx's 'objective rationalist' philosophy of history (Castoriadis, 1987, pp. 41ff.). Castoriadis shows that Marx presumes a causal determinism in history, and, more importantly, in the 'second degree', that it is 'the bearer of meanings that are linked together in totalities which themselves are meaningful' (pp. 42–43), but in its abstraction to the regularities of behaviour as pure facts from which the concrete, lived content of actions and meanings has been jettisoned. On Castoriadis's account, Marx's did not supersede Hegelianism; rather, 'the cunning of reason' is also evident in Marx: 'there is a reason at work in history, guaranteeing that past history is comprehensible, that history to come is desirable and that the apparently blind necessity of the facts is secretly arranged to give birth to the Good' (p. 42). In contrast to deterministic conceptions, Castoriadis posits 'non-causal' elements to history (p. 44), of which the most important is human creativity. Human creativity in this strong sense is not merely a deviation from an already existing form or type but the positing of a new behaviour, the institution of a new social rule or the invention of a new social form. History is not dialectical but the domain of creation (p. 45). The importance of meaning to the human condition is central in this context; Castoriadis developed this further as *social imaginary significations*, for which his understanding of autonomy as a central social imaginary signification was a key complement to the dimension of autonomy as political doing/*praxis* (see *Magma*, *Creation* ex nihilo, *Social Imaginary Significations* and the *Social-Historical*).

Castoriadis's rethinking of revolution and Marx's theory of history included a (less systematic) critique of Leninist political vanguardism as a form of authoritarianism and self-alienation. On his account, Leninists are 'technicians of this rationality' and 'specialists of this [historical] theory' (p. 59). They are locked into the 'materialist conception of history' and disregard the autonomous activity of the revolutionary movement. Workers need to be directly involved in organizing and determining what is to be done, not informed of it, and required then to conform to it, by the vanguard party. Castoriadis argues that 'they [the revolutionary masses] alone can invent, create a solution to a problem of which today no one can have even a suspicion' (Castoriadis, 1988, p. 232). His opposition to political vanguardism formed part of his growing critique of bureaucracy, the rationality that underpinned it, its technical application and the apparent neutrality of such technique although it was employed for capitalist ends advocated by Lenin. In this vein, Castoriadis writes:

> The formation and training of a bureaucracy as the managerial stratum in production (with the economic privileges that inevitably go along with this status) was, practically from the beginning, the conscious, straight forward and, sincere policy of the Bolshevik party, headed by Lenin and Trotsky. This was honestly and sincerely thought to be a socialist policy – or, more precisely, an 'administrative technique' that could be put in the service of socialism, since the class of administrators managing production were to remain under the control of the working class, 'personified by its Communist party'. (1964, n.p.)

In the wake of these criticisms of Marx and orthodox Marxism, Castoriadis began to develop a positive account of autonomy by drawing on both Aristotelian and Marxian approaches to *praxis* as a creative and collective activity (Castoriadis, 1987). Instead of the means-end schemata, praxis, as a conscious and lucid activity, takes the autonomy of self and others as an end in themselves as primary: 'In praxis, there is something to be done, but what is to be done is something specific: it is precisely the development of the autonomy of the other or of others' (p. 75). But praxis – and concomitantly, autonomy – is not so much an end but a beginning (p. 75). In contrast to the phantasy of exhaustive and absolute knowledge of humanity as a technique – a technology – to achieve a given end, revolutionary praxis seeks to create a *new* society whereby 'its object is the real as such and not a stable, limited, dead artifact' (p. 77).

Castoriadis elucidated the *individual* aspect of autonomy through a psychoanalytic approach. His interest in psychoanalysis was already evident in the first half of the 1960s (see Castoriadis, 1987). He began training as a psychoanalyst in 1969 and started practicing in 1974. Castoriadis elaborated the creativity of the psyche through a rethinking of Freud. However, the importance of psychoanalysis for the project of autonomy has less to do with the specifics of Castoriadis's theory of the psychic monad, the radical imagination of the psyche or his reading of Freud (see the *Creative Imagination*), and more to do with a certain idea – trans-

Freudian and anti-Lacanian – of the overall goal of psychoanalytic therapy. (Castoriadis was not, however, advocating for universal psychoanalytic treatment!) Drawing on and radicalizing the ancient Greek tradition of self-examination, Castoriadis saw psychoanalysis as a way of incorporating critical self-reflection to formative psychical experiences and socializing institutions (see *Paideia* and *Psyche*). In this vein he writes:

> Psychoanalysis can and should make a basic contribution to a politics of autonomy. For each person's self-understanding is a necessary condition for autonomy. One cannot have an autonomous society that would fail to turn back upon itself, that would not interrogate itself about its motives, its reasons for acting, its deep-seated [*profondes*] tendencies. Considered in concrete terms, however, society doesn't exist outside the individuals making it up. The self-reflective activity of an autonomous society depends essentially upon the self-reflective activity of the humans who form that society. (2007, p. 151)

In this context we can posit a differentiation for Castoriadis between the 'subject' and 'self'. For Castoriadis, the 'autonomous individual' signifies the shift from 'socialized individual' to the 'autonomous subject', and reflects a broader distinction between 'self' and 'subject', whereby the former engages with societal meaning, but the latter explicitly problematizes and reflects upon the institutions and meanings of society, on the one hand, but, on a more individual level, also posits a new relation to one's psychical history and experiences, on the other (see *Psyche* and the *The Living Being*). This new relationship

> makes it possible for the individual to escape the enslavement of repetition, to look back upon itself, to reflect on the reason for its thoughts and the motives of its acts, guided by the elucidation of its desire and aiming at the truth. (Castoriadis, 1991, p. 164; see also 1997a, pp. 137–171)

The capacity for reflection and deliberation – instead of passivity – characterizes the autonomous subject towards his/her psychical life and the problematization of received meanings.

Castoriadis deepened his elaboration of autonomy through renewed engagement with the ancient Greeks, with particular reference to the ancient Athenian instauration of direct democracy that blossomed in the sixth century BCE. In his view, the project of autonomy has only emerged twice in human history, and even then only partially: in ancient Greece and with the onset of European modernity. Castoriadis stresses that the ancient Greek breakthrough to autonomy is to be understood not as a 'model' to be replicated but as a 'germ' requiring further collective creation and problematization (see *Democracy* and *Modernity*).[2]

The significance of the ancient Greek breakthrough to autonomy lies in its creation of a new, political form of society: democracy. Ancient Greece was the only society to institute political power directly into the hands of its citizens, despite long histories – both in Greece and surrounding areas – of rule by sacred kingship and tyrants. In Castoriadis's terms, the Greek invention of democracy was a self-creation *out of nothing*, as it could not be reduced to, or explained by, its antecedents (see *Creation* ex nihilo). The invention of democracy thus had weighty ontological consequences for Castoriadis. For him, autonomy and its elaboration as the concrete democratic *polis* signifies the creation of a new ontological form, and the very possibility of an autonomous society presupposes an ontology of human creativity and of society (the *Social-Historical*) as radically self-creating, on the one hand, and an image of being as not fully determined, as the interplay of chaos and kosmos, on the other.[3]

As Castoriadis understood it, the project of autonomy emerged as the dual instauration of *politics* in the strong and explicit sense (*la politique*) – as opposed to 'the political' (*le politique*) – and philosophy, also in a strong and interrogative sense (*la philosophie*) instead of what we might term 'the philosophical' (*le philosophique*). Autonomy is the 'co-birth' of politics and philosophy as 'con-substantial' (although he also affirms that 'philosophy cannot found a politics' (Castoriadis, 1991, p. 126)). Castoriadis gives an explicit meaning to the generally held view of the discovery of political freedom – or 'the political' in ancient Greece (see, for example, Vernant, 2000). The creation of 'politics' (*la politique*) in the strong and explicit sense 'puts into question the actual institution of society; it is the activity that tries to aim clearly at the social institution as such' (Castoriadis, 1991, p. 125). For him, this would ideally take place as part of a direct democracy with the free participation of citizens. Politics is thus not reducible to elections and voting. He writes: 'Politics [*la politique*] is a project of autonomy. Politics is the reflective and lucid collective activity that aims at the overall institution of society. It pertains to everything in society that is participable and shareable' (p. 169). 'The political' (*le politique*) in the weaker sense, however, refers to the particular arrangement and institution of patterns of power within a given society, which every social collective must institute in its own way.

The philosophical aspect of autonomy comprises 'the reflective activity of a reason creating itself in an endless movement, both as individual and social reason' (p. 164). It is the institution of philosophy in the strong sense (*la philosophie*) as the *explicit and unlimited interrogation* of the 'instituted representations of the world, the idols of the tribe' (p. 125). This can be contrasted with 'the philosophical' (*le philosophique*), in the weaker sense (see Adams, 2011).The strong sense of philosophy (*la philosophie*) as interrogation does not so much reflect on factual issues per se but on 'social imaginary significations and their possible grounding' (Castoriadis, 1991, p. 163). This allows the demos to ask: What is it that we ought to think? (p. 163). More concretely, it allows for such questions on the sociopolitical level as 'What is justice?' and 'Are our laws just?' On the intellectual level, it raises questions of truth.

Castoriadis discovers in the ancient Greeks a more radical dimension of the imaginary signification of autonomy, a particularly innovative *grasp of the world* (*saisie du monde*) that posits mortals confronted with partial order (*kosmos*) and ultimate chaos. Following Arnason (2012), in this context 'the meta-social dimension of imaginary significations becomes more fundamental than the social one'. This image of the world emerged in Homeric writings on the *polis* as an internal 'imaginary core' that informs the long-term historical innovations of Greek civilization, and prefigured the explicit institution of autonomy as the interplay of chaos and democracy in classical Athens (Castoriadis, 2004, pp. 70ff.). In this sense, Castoriadis saw the archaic period as a formative phase for the later blossoming of autonomy in the fifth century BCE.

Of all the philosophical distinctions to emerge in ancient Greece – such as Being/appearance; knowledge/opinion – the *physis* (nature) and *nomos* (human convention) problematic was the most central for Castoriadis's thought (Castoriadis, 2004). In his view, philosophy has been preoccupied with articulating the being of *physis*, but that, as he observed, there was no place for the being of *nomos* (Castoriadis, 1984). Although a contested term, for Castoriadis, *nomos*, in contrast to *physis*, was peculiar to the human condition and was a self-founding, self-altering order that gave philosophical expression to the possibilities of the *polis* (see *The Living Being*).

The final direction in which Castoriadis elucidates the project of autonomy is in connection with his theory of modernity (see *Democracy* and *Modernity*). Unlike approaches that reduce modernity to the Enlightenment – Habermas's account of modernity as the 'Unfinished Project of the Enlightenment' is the best-known example – Castoriadis elucidates modernity as instituted by two central social imaginary significations: 'autonomy' and the 'infinite pursuit of pseudo-rational mastery' (Castoriadis, 1997a, b). In modernity, these core imaginary significations have been concretely articulated as democracy, on the one hand, and a cluster of interlinked institutions – capitalism, the bureaucratic state and 'techno-science' – of which capitalism is the most significant, on the other (see *Capitalism*). This aspect of autonomy builds on both his earlier work on socialism (see *Socialism*), but also highlights modernity's dialogue with the ancients. Modernity's infinite pursuit of rational mastery through the nexus of techno-science and capitalism is perhaps most catastrophically evident in the devastation of the natural world. From the 1970s, Castoriadis draws attention to this aspect (Castoriadis and Cohn-Bendit, 1981). But he also sees in ecological movements a resurgence of the project of autonomy, especially in their call for self-limitation in human interactions with the natural world, which is at odds with the 'infinite pursuit of rational-mastery' that is characteristic of capitalism.

We have identified four key sources and connections for Castoriadis's elaboration of the project of autonomy. There is a further connection that is worth mentioning – the question of biological autonomy – although it is less a connection than a demarcation. While Castoriadis starts to articulate the living being

in terms of an ontology of creation from around the late 1970s to
the early 1980s, and thereby brings it more into continuity rather
than discontinuity with human modes of being, he nonetheless
baulks at the idea of biological autonomy. Castoriadis pursued the
question of biological autonomy as part of a longstanding debate
with Chilean biologist Francesco Varela. In the end, Castoriadis
reserved 'the project autonomy' for a human-only capacity for
politics and philosophy in the strong sense. The debate nonetheless
points to internal tensions in his thought between weaker senses
of autonomy as a self-directed mode of being resulting in the 'self-
constitution of a world', which he extends to the living being, and
the strong sense of autonomy as a political project, which he does
not (see *The Living Being*).

Castoriadis's elucidation of autonomy and his enduring
commitment to the revolutionary project brings both philosophical
and political aspects into rich dialogue. A range of criticisms have
been levelled at his work (see, for example, Habermas, 1991;
Honneth, 1991) but the following comments intend rather to open
horizons for further debate. It is interesting to note that although
Castoriadis recognizes that the ancient Greek breakthrough to
autonomy was only partial, he did not – as he does in his interpretation
of modernity – posit another core social imaginary signification
with which autonomy would be in conflict, and which would
represent heteronomous tendencies. Although the meta-institution
of religion, in general, and monotheism, in particular, is a common
basis for heteronomous societies, Castoriadis underestimates the
role of religion in the Greek *polis* and does not raise the question of
the specific character of that role in democratic Athens (Osborne,
2013) (see *Heteronomy*). As Christine Sourvinou-Inwood notes,
only citizens practiced and articulated religion in ancient Greece
and the *polis* provided a religious as much as a political setting
(Sourvinou-Inwood, 1990): their historical interlacing raises
questions about Castoriadis's polarization of autonomy and
heteronomy. In writings published during his lifetime, Castoriadis
seems to hesitate between a broad and a narrow conception of the
democratic transformation in ancient Greece. The former would
equate it with radical democracy in Athens and possibly a few other
places, whereas the latter would emphasize the degree of autonomy
inherent in the general structures of the *polis*. The broad conception
seems to prevail in the posthumously published seminars (see, for

example, Castoriadis, 2004). But for the argument to be completed, it would require a typology of different *poleis* with diverse ways of articulating the project of autonomy. Castoriadis hints at such a typology in the last part of *The Imaginary Institution of Society* (1987), where he refers to Athens, Sparta and Corinth as different versions of *polis* society. More generally speaking, autonomy can be instituted in ways that vary within and across traditions, and that have theoretical implications; Castoriadis's tendency to neglect this points to a tension in his thought between the project of autonomy that emerges from socialism as a universal and normative political project that aims to result in direct democracy, and imaginary significations as under-determined complexes of cultural meaning that by definition require interpretation and will, indeed, be interpreted and instituted in different ways in different social-historical contexts.

Notes

1 Whether his subsequent work can be termed post-Marxist or not, or whether there is a break between the early and late work of Castoriadis or not are questions that go beyond the scope of this short chapter (see *Socialism*).

2 Given the biological and developmental connotations of 'germ' it is perhaps an unfortunate term for such a central creation of and in human history.

3 Castoriadis elucidates his ontology of human creation in his magnum opus, *The Imaginary Institution of Society*, as a critique of the Western philosophical tradition which understands being as determinism (see *Creation* ex nihilo, *Magma*, *Ensemblistic-Identitary Logic* and the *Social-Historical*.)

References

Adams, S. (2011), *Castoriadis' Ontology: Being and Creation*, New York: Fordham University Press.

Arnason, J. P. (2012), 'Castoriadis im Kontext: Genese und Anspruchs eines metaphilosophischen Projekts', in H. Wolf (ed.), *Das Imaginäre in Sozialen: Zur Sozialtheorie von Cornelius Castoriadis*, Göttingen: Wallstein Verlag.

Castoriadis, C. (1964), 'The role of Bolshevik ideology in the birth of bureaucracy', www.marxists.org/archive/castoriadis/1964/ bureaucracy.html, accessed 12 July 2013.

—. (1984), *Crossroads in the Labyrinth*, K. Soper and M. H. Ryle (trans. and eds), Cambridge, MA: MIT Press.

—. (1987), *The Imaginary Institution of Society*, K. Blamey (trans.), Oxford: Polity; and Cambridge, MA: MIT Press.

—. (1988), *Political and Social Writings, Volume 1: 1946–1955. From the Critique of Bureaucracy to the Positive Content of Socialism*, D. A. Curtis (ed. and trans.), Minneapolis, MN: University of Minnesota Press.

—. (1991), *Philosophy, Politics, Autonomy*, D. A. Curtis (ed. and trans.), New York and Oxford: Oxford University Press.

—. (1997a), *World in Fragments*, D. A. Curtis (ed. and trans.), Stanford, CA: Stanford University Press.

—. (1997b), *The Castoriadis Reader*, D. A. Curtis (ed. and trans.), Oxford and Cambridge, MA: Oxford University Press.

—. (2004), *Ce qui fait la Grèce, t. 1: D'Homère à Héraclite*, Paris: Seuil.

—. (2007), *Figures of the Thinkable*, H. Arnold (trans.), Stanford, CA: Stanford University Press.

Castoriadis, C. and Cohn-Bendit, D. (1981), *De l'écologie à l'autonomie*, Paris: Seuil.

Habermas, J. (1991), *The Philosophical Discourse of Modernity: Twelve Lectures*, Cambridge, MA: MIT Press.

Honneth, A. (1991), *The Fragmented World of the Social: Essays in Social and Political Philosophy*, Albany, NY: SUNY.

Howard, D. (1988), *The Marxian Legacy*, Minneapolis, MN: University of Minnesota Press.

Osborne, R. (2013), 'Democracy and religion in classical Greece', in J. P. Arnason, K. A. Raaflaub and P. Wagner (eds), *The Greek Polis and the Invention of Democracy: A Politico-cultural Transformation and Its Interpretations*, Malden, MA: Wiley-Blackwell.

Sourvinou-Inwood, C. (1990), 'What is *polis* religion?' in O. Murray and S. Price (eds), *The Greek City: From Homer to Alexander*, Oxford: Clarendon.

Vernant, J.-P. (2000), 'The birth of the political', *Thesis Eleven*, 60, 87–91.

CHAPTER TWO

Heteronomy

Karl E. Smith

Heteronomy has a special place in Castoriadis's lexicon, standing as both a descriptor of (almost all of) human history and culture and as the opposite of *autonomy*. Both terms are built upon the Greek root *nomos*, which literally translates as 'law' but also means norms, rules, customs and so on. More particularly, for Castoriadis, *nomos* refers to *social* customs, conventions and institutions. *Auto-* and *hetero-* mean 'self' and 'other' respectively. In simple terms, then, we are making a distinction between self-rule and rule-by-the-other. As we shall see, however, the implications of this distinction are anything but simple. One important complicating factor is that 'self-rule' refers to both an individual's rule over him- or herself and to a society's or a social institution's rule of itself. Another important complication can be found in the origins of the concept *nomos*, which first appears in the ancient Greek distinction between *nomos*, rules made by society, and *physis*, things of 'nature' (including 'natural laws') (Castoriadis, 1997a, p. 331).

Autonomy is, as discussed in *Autonomy*, the objective of Castoriadis's political and philosophical project. Castoriadis's project of autonomy aims to create the kinds of societies that clearly and lucidly take responsibility for being the source and the grounds of their own institutions (Castoriadis, 1997b, p. 282). To be autonomous in this sense is to be the kind of society which self-reflexively creates its own social institutions – norms, laws, customs and practices – knowing that it has no grounds or foundations for choosing this particular form of institution over any other. It institutes these particular institutions because it chooses to, and remains open to calling them into question, to re-evaluation and re-formation, as experience accumulates and further evidence comes to light. Heteronomy, in contrast, is a closure to such questioning and a refusal to take responsibility for the creation of the institutions, attributing their creation instead to extra-social sources (e.g. gods, nature, reason, etc.) upon whose authority one relies to proclaim that these are the laws we have adopted because they are given by X and are therefore the only true and proper laws.

While this sense of heteronomy is our focus, it is important to remain cognizant of the distinction between *nomos* and *physis*. Whether describing or prescribing contemporary social institutions it is necessary to recognize that the self-rule of society always occurs in a context that forever remains outside of our (complete) control. To take only the most obvious examples, we cannot control tsunamis, earthquakes, hurricanes or floods. They are beyond our rules, laws, norms, etc. – and they impose certain minimal requirements upon us.

Castoriadis argues, however, that they do not *determine* social institutions (Castoriadis, 1987, p. 234). Societies, and individuals, must take *physis* into account (or suffer consequences), but how one takes it into account is not determined. This important distinction, Castoriadis argues, was covered over, lost or repressed for most of human history, as almost every human society has sought a determinant for its laws somewhere outside of itself (see 1997b, p. 314). These are what Castoriadis calls *heteronomous* societies.

For Castoriadis every social institution is at the same time instituting and instituted (Castoriadis, 1987, p. 370; 1997a, p. 8; Merleau-Ponty, 1963, pp. 106–107; Sheikh, 2011; Smith, 2010, p. 25); they are created and recreated as their members perform the roles, actions and practices which define *this* institution as itself (Castoriadis, 1987, pp. 234, 359). Society itself is such an institution, Castoriadis argues, instituted in and through the *social imaginary* by *social imaginary significations* (Castoriadis, 1987, pp. 135ff., 235, 359; 1997a, p. 313). As such it is not reducible to its individual 'members' for it institutes them, through socialization, to be the types of social individuals who institute *this particular society* (Castoriadis, 1987, pp. 105, 311ff.).

Castoriadis's core argument is that the institution is always the creation of the society in question, but almost every society has 'pretended' (has convinced itself, deluded itself into believing) that its institutions derive from something with 'stronger' foundations, and thus has greater authority than the collective itself, something like god, nature, history, etc. (Castoriadis, 1997a, p. 86). 'Stronger foundations' are believed to be necessary to ensure the survival of the institution. For example, the king rules in the name of his ancestors, or by heavenly decree, thereby reducing the legitimacy of any challengers to the throne.

'Heavenly decree' in this context is, of course, a synonym for god in particular, but also for religious justifications more generally. Religion, for Castoriadis is the most pervasive mode of heteronomy in human history (p. 316). He makes a sharp and clear distinction between 'mysticism' and 'religion' (p. 325), and then treats religion as nothing more than or other than social institution; a mode of social institution that credits the form and substance of this particular society and its particular ways of being to an extra-social source. We find every form of human cruelty and injustice somewhere sanctioned and justified on the grounds of it being the will of some god or another. Behaviours and practices that outsiders might find dubious cannot be questioned by insiders because they are prescribed by a higher power; as Castoriadis puts it, one cannot ask whether the law of god is just when 'justice is nothing other than one of the names of God' (p. 86).

Whether we justify, and thereby authorize, *nomoi* by some transcendental supreme being or in a more mundane source such as tradition, the ancestors, or some sort of natural law, at bottom, according to Castoriadis, 'the law never really is given by *someone else*' (p. 86): we are always and everywhere the authors, creators, justifiers and authorities of the laws and social institutions that define us, and which define us precisely as this particular society and no other. Here it is helpful to think of the alienation of social institutions from the people and practices that institute them (Castoriadis, 1987, pp. 108–110).

Sticking with the example above, monarchy is a human-made social institution, which is reproduced through honouring the role of the monarch. Each time a petitioner genuflects before the monarch s/he re-institutes this social institution. Yet we are alienated from this act of creation – or production and reproduction – by attributing the institution of the monarchy to heavenly decree, seeing the inhabitant of the monarch's role as anointed with divine right. This inverts the relationship, such that the generative qualities of the petitioners' action are occluded, or covered over: instead of recognizing that the genuflection creates (re-produces, re-institutes) the monarch, we are led to believe that some deity created the monarch, which in turn demands the genuflection. This is of course the same trick that underpins those holy scriptures that, although clearly penned by human hands, claim their authority from the supposedly direct intervention of a divine author or narrator. These 'tricks' are simply manifestations of a trend that we see throughout history, as time after time those who create new social institutions seek the authority of extra-social foundations to ensure the continuance of the institution. For Castoriadis, religion is both the epitome of this heteronomous tendency and its most persistent manifestation.

Once we accept that human beings, for both individual and species survival, must create social institutions – that each new member of the species must be institutionalized as the type of social individual that is appropriate for the particular society which is socializing him/her (Castoriadis, 1997a, pp. 315, 143, 155; Smith, 2010, pp. 96–97) – then we are unavoidably confronted by the questions 'what kind of institutions?' and 'where do we get them?' I have already indicated that for Castoriadis, the answer to the second question is 'we create them ourselves'. This gives us the responsibility to choose wisely – or at least, it gives us the burden of choice. Yet for most of human history we have chosen to abdicate responsibility for this choice – or rather, to deny our fellow citizens the freedom of choice – by denying that we create them ourselves, and attributing them instead to some extra-social source.

I mentioned that one of the complicating factors we must deal with is that 'self-rule' refers both to the individual's rule over him/herself and a society's or a social institution's rule of itself. It is therefore important to clearly distinguish between the level of the individual human *psyche*, the subject, the social individual[1] and the social institution, the anonymous collective, society and the social-historical.[2] As we have seen, Castoriadis argues that society is always the source of its own institutions, even when it attributes the source of *nomos* to an extra-social authority. This holds true for every level of institution, including the instituting which forms the psyche into a social individual. In a very real sense, the psyche is self-constituting, self-forming; hence, autonomous (Castoriadis, 1987, p. 320). Yet at the same time, it always forms itself, *can only form itself*, with and from the forms available to it in the social-historical world into which it has been thrown: a society; a world of others; a world characterized by the 'discourses of the other' (Castoriadis, 1987, pp. 102–103; see 1997a, pp. 155, 311); a world constituted by social imaginary significations (Castoriadis, 1987, pp. 135ff., 235, 359; 1997a, p. 313); a world which, in many and various ways, *imposes* particular forms, particular *nomos*, upon the individual psyche. It is not too much of a simplification to say, then, that socialization is an intrinsically heteronomous process: the psyche forms itself into a social individual in accordance with the discourses of the other (Castoriadis, 1987, pp. 311–312). Indeed, the discourses of the other, the magma of social imaginary significations that constitute *this* society's social imaginary,[3] is the only available source of the forms that are necessary for the psyche to form itself as a social individual.

So is autonomy even possible? It is paradoxical but clear that one can only become an autonomous individual in an autonomous society (p. 107), that one must be socialized to internalize the discourses of the autonomous others. In a sense (but not literally), the socialization of autonomous subjects is a two-stage process. First, in what we might call 'primary socialization', the discourses of the other must be internalized. Then, in a 'secondary socialization' the subject must call into question these internalized discourses of the other to form 'one's own discourses'. In other words, in all cases, the human psyche must form itself into a socialized subject, and can only do so through the internalization of the forms of being a social individual that are present in its surrounding environment. At this primary stage the human subject is a heteronomous social institution. But in an autonomous society, a crucial dimension of the discourses of the other is the injunction to 'call the discourses of the other into question'. From this perspective, what I have called secondary socialization is an internal dialogue, a critical inventory, a radical reflexivity, weighing and assessing those discourses that have been internalized and deciding which to keep, which to discard. It amounts to turning the discourses of the other into 'my own'. Yet, the ones that are kept, like the ones that are discarded, originate from 'outside', and thus always remain also 'discourses of the other'. Which is to say that Castoriadis's notion of autonomous subjectivity is radically different to the atomistic or monadic freedom that we find in classical liberalism – whereas liberalism posits an individual that is *free from* society, the autonomous subject can only exist within an autonomous society; that is, in a self-limiting society which creates self-limiting social individuals.

The institutions of an autonomous society, meanwhile, must be clearly and lucidly instituted as open institutions; as institutions that are self-reflexive about their self-instituting character; institutions which clearly and lucidly call themselves into question (Castoriadis, 1997a, pp. 190, 329). Castoriadis argues that this type of society has only appeared twice in history: first with the Ancient Greeks (or more accurately, in Athens ca. 500–300 BCE, whose participatory democracy is, for Castoriadis, the epitome of an autonomous society), and subsequently in Western Europe, where it initially emerged in the independent city-states of the Low Countries ca. 1100–1700 and hit its fullest manifestation ca. 1750–1950 before its more recent 'retreat into conformity' (pp. 36–37), or 'heteronomy'.

One useful way to think of this 'retreat into conformity', this new heteronomy, is to consider the rationalization that George Ritzer (2011) famously dubbed 'the McDonaldization of Society'. The ubiquity of this form of rationalization, with its corresponding irrationalities (Ritzer, 2011, pp. 16–18, 143ff.), is both symptomatic and representative of what Castoriadis calls the retreat into conformity. Like Weber before him, Ritzer observes that rationalization per se is value-neutral, and in many respects can produce genuine benefits; but highly rationalized systems and societies produce a myriad of irrationalities (p. 143). Ritzer elucidates some of the effects of this rationalization across a number of aspects of contemporary society. Of these effects, the two most relevant for this discussion are homogenization and dehumanization (pp. 153–157). Of the former, Ritzer says:

> Anywhere you go in the United States and, increasingly, throughout the world you are likely to find the same products offered in the same way. The expansion of franchising across the United States means that people find little difference between

regions and between cities. On a global scale, travellers are finding more familiarity and less diversity. Exotic settings are increasingly likely sites for American fast-food chains. (pp. 153–154)

Of the latter:

[R]ational systems are unreasonable systems that deny the humanity, the human reason, of the human beings who work within them or are served by them. (p. 143)

Castoriadis's analysis of the retreat into conformity, though, goes much deeper, identifying the driving force at the root of this modern phenomenon, which he calls the project of the 'unlimited expansion of rational-mastery' (Castoriadis, 1997a, pp. 15, 37). While he would largely concur with Ritzer's descriptions, for Castoriadis the problem is not so much that 'human reason' is denied, but rather that the creative imagination is suppressed, constrained within the quest for the unlimited expansion of knowledge and control, that is, rational-mastery. Creativity is sacrificed for predictability, and in the process, human agency becomes subordinated to the rationalized processes and techniques of the rationalized workplace. In this sense, what Ritzer calls McDonaldization is a *technique* of rationalized control. Its ubiquity in the globalized twenty-first-century world is perhaps evidence of its effectiveness in achieving the ends to which this particular technique is the means.

Although Castoriadis's work on *technique* is too extensive and detailed to fully explore in this chapter, a cursory consideration of its key dimensions can shed much light on our topic. Castoriadis observes that its earliest etymological roots (ca. 800 BCE) effectively meant 'to fabricate', 'to produce' and 'to construct' (Castoriadis, 1984, p. 231). A few centuries later, Aristotle depicts it as habituated practices of informed doing; the rational application of knowledge to manipulate the world (or parts thereof) (pp. 232–234). Importantly, while it 'puts knowledge into operation', Castoriadis stresses that technique is distinct from the knowledge per se and 'pays no heed to the ultimate ends of the activity in question' (p. 234). This is the critical point for our discussion: technique refers to 'know-how' – to produce, fabricate, construct, etc. – but it is 'separated from creation' which means that it is separated 'from questions about *what* is produced, and *for what*' it is produced (p. 235).

From this perspective, we can see why Castoriadis regards the culture that has produced the amazing technological development of the late twentieth century a 'retreat into conformity' – we are increasingly generating more efficient, predictable, calculable and controllable methods/techniques to produce things; we are educating ever-greater numbers of people with the skills and knowledge to operate new technologies; but fewer and fewer people have any say in terms of *what* they produce and what they are producing it *for*. Instead, these decisions are left to the 'invisible hand of the market', whose rationality can no sooner be questioned than can God's justice.

In sum, when 'rationalized systems' or techniques/technologies/ etc. become alienated from their creators, when all human endeavour is allocated to the project of the unlimited expansion of (pseudo-)rational-(pseudo-)mastery, when the pursuit of this project is so deeply embedded/interwoven into the institutional fabric of a society that it is not possible to ask why we pursue this project rather than another, then we are dealing with a heteronomous society, with heteronomous subjects who are alienated from their fundamental creativity.

Generally, it is in the 'nature' of institutions to become alienated from the societies and subjects that institute them: 'once an institution is established it seems to become autonomous, . . . it possesses its own inertia and its own logic, . . . in its continuance and in its effects, it outstrips its function, its "ends" and its "reasons for existing"' (Castoriadis, 1987, p. 110). It is perhaps somewhat confusing that in this use of the term 'autonomous' we find a dimension of alienation, and thus, of heteronomy. However, when institutions become autonomous *from* the instituting society, they become alienated from their makers, and in turn, become sources of heteronomous *inscription* or *instauration*. That is to say, they become heteronomous instituting-institutions, which institute the type of social individuals that sustain them.

Notes

1 These three terms, psyche, subject and social individual, are not interchangeable; each refers to distinct aspects of the singular human being. These distinctions are not, however, important for the present

discussion. See the chapter on the psyche for a discussion of their interrelationship.

2 As per the previous note, these terms are not interchangeable either, although their interrelationship is much closer and more intertwined. First, Castoriadis argues that we always mis-speak when we refer to society, for it is in fact the social-historical to which we refer (Castoriadis, 1987, pp. 167ff.). Society is in fact the historical and the continuing institution of the social. In a simple sense the social consists of the interrelationships within the anonymous collective. And the anonymous collective, consisting of living human beings, as we have just seen, must institute itself at every level of the spectrum between the largest collective and the individual, and beyond, into the realm of the psyche.

3 To be clear, although the language employed here might suggest a self-contained, bounded society, I am speaking also of the interconnected globalized society of the early twenty-first century.

References

Castoriadis, C. (1984), *Crossroads in the Labyrinth*, K. Soper and M. H. Ryle (trans.), Cambridge, MA: MIT Press.

—. (1987), *The Imaginary Institution of Society*, K. Blamey (trans.), Cambridge, MA: Polity Press.

—. (1997a), *World in Fragments*, D. A. Curtis (ed. and trans.), Stanford, CA: Stanford University Press.

—. (1997b), *Castoriadis Reader*, D. A. Curtis (ed. and trans.), Oxford, MA: Blackwell.

Merleau-Ponty, M. (1963), 'Themes from the lectures', in *In Search of Philosophy and Other Essays*, J. Wild and J. Edie (trans.), Evanston, IL: Northwestern University Press.

Ritzer, G. (2011), *The McDonaldization of Society*, Thousand Oaks, CA: Pine Forge Press.

Sheikh, S. (2011), 'Instituting the Institutions', *The Open Institutions: New Meeting Points of Culture and Citizens*, http://openinstitutions.net/2011/03/instituting-the-institution/, accessed 1 February 2012.

Smith, K. E. (2010), *Meaning, Subjectivity, Society: Making Sense of Modernity*, Leiden: Brill.

CHAPTER THREE

Social Imaginary Significations

Johann P. Arnason

Preliminary bearings

The concept of social imaginary significations (sometimes abbreviated to SIS) is arguably more central to Castoriadis's thought than any other theme or notion. It marks the most important turning-point in his intellectual biography, and there is no doubt about its key role in the unfolding – and unfinished – conceptual articulation of the project that took shape from the mid-1960s onwards, but was never presented in a systematic work. More precisely, four main reasons led Castoriadis to focus on the problematic of imaginary significations. It is, first of all, a logical outcome and a necessary completion of the critical reflections on Marxism, developed in the first half of the 1960s and later included in *The Imaginary Institution of Society* (Castoriadis, 1987, pp. 7–164). Second, above and beyond that, the concept of social imaginary significations revives basic questions inherited from classical sociology and responds to them in a way different but not disconnected from traditional arguments. Third, in so doing, it redefines the role of meaning in social life, and this puts it at the centre of Castoriadis's efforts 'to elucidate the question of society and that of history' (p. 167); to quote a subtitle in the last section of the same book, 'the mode of being of social imaginary significations' (p. 364) is a core theme for the ontology of the social-historical (see the *Social-Historical*). Finally, the need to develop a more comprehensive philosophical framework around the original field of inquiry is also to be understood in this context. The introduction of imaginary significations into the social-historical world raises problems and suggests perspectives with broader implications for ontological and cosmological levels of analysis. This last question is taken up in other entries; here we focus on the first three.

In addition to these substantive aspects, the concept of social imaginary significations – as it appears in the two parts of *The Imaginary Institution of Society* – reflects a more conjunctural factor. Castoriadis's break with Marxism and his simultaneous shift to a new intellectual project occurred at a time and place where the question of signification could not be raised without confronting the perceived challenge of structuralism. In retrospect, it seems more than doubtful that structuralism ever existed as a coherent intellectual movement, but in Paris during the 1960s, the dominant perception was of that kind, and there is no better expression of its apparent logic than a remark by Claude Lévi-Strauss in a conversation with Paul Ricoeur (quoted in p. 138). On that occasion, Lévi-Strauss described meaning as a certain savour experienced by consciousness, due to a specific combination of elements. This emphasis on the radically derivative, transient and elusive character of meaning was shared by a broader current, and it represented the polar opposite of the view that Castoriadis wanted to develop. For him, it became a fundamental tenet that significations were not reducible to combinations of signs. Significations are always already involved in the choice and organization of 'the signifiers that carry them' (p. 139). Two implications of this primacy of meaning should be noted. Against those who stress the changing but always determinate combinations of signs, Castoriadis insists on the originating and patterning capacity inherent in the configurations of meaning (or sense, to use an equivalent expression also employed in the English translation of *The Imaginary Institution of Society*); but to do justice to the dimension explored by the 'structuralists', he needs a concept that will encompass the networks of signifiers without reducing them to closed systems of unequivocal rules. The concept of social imaginary significations addresses the former issue, whereas the latter is dealt with through the concept of institution, suitably modified beyond its conventional sociological use.

Marx and the imagination

It would, however, be very misleading to explain these alternatives to structuralism as a direct result of engagement with its ideas. For Castoriadis, neither Lévi-Strauss nor any of the authors briefly lumped together with him (and later reclassified as post-structuralists) could ever merit interpretive efforts comparable to his dialogues with Marx and Freud, or – on another level – with Aristotle, Kant and German idealism (for further comments on Castoriadis's reading of Freud, see *The Creative Imagination*). With regard to our present topic, it can be shown that the concept of social imaginary significations grows out of the very thoroughly reasoned break with Marx's vision of history. Here we need not enter into the question whether Castoriadis neglected 'the other Marx', the less reductionistic, more praxis-centred but long-unknown and much less influential counter-current in Marx's work. The critical discussion in the first part of *The Imaginary Institution of Society* admits the presence of 'two elements' in Marxism, one of which was committed to the idea of a world-transforming historical praxis, and acknowledges Marx's youthful writings as the first evidence of this trend; there is no reference to Marx's *Grundrisse*. But for present purposes, what matters is the exceptionally illuminating critique of a conceptual scheme that took centre stage in Marx's work, became more markedly dominant in the Marxian tradition and affected the political destinies of Marxism in decisive ways.

The two key sections of the text in question deal with 'Marxist theory of history' and 'Marxist philosophy of history'; but the double focus on history and society is implicit on both levels of the critique, and the foregrounding of history is obviously due to the fact that, as the label 'historical materialism' shows, Marxists tended to put it first. The refutation of historical materialism can be taken as a starting-point for a reconsideration of meaning and its role in the constitution of a social-historical world. As Castoriadis shows, the fully articulated Marxian vision of history is vulnerable

to criticism on many counts: as economic reductionism, economic
determinism, objectivist rationalism and – last but not least – as
an exemplary case of theory aspiring to full knowledge and final
control of history. Castoriadis finds the common denominator of
these positions in assumptions about the autonomy and primacy of
technology. It is the Marxist view of the technological factor (and
its supposedly inherent progressive dynamic) that makes it possible
to see the economy as a determining aspect of social life, to posit a
universal developmental trend, and to translate the understanding
of history into a predictive theory based on laws. The Marxist
version of technological determinism has been criticized by other
authors; Castoriadis's next step is more distinctive. As he argues,
the privileged place attributed to technology is not merely a matter
of causal impact and relative weight. The avowedly materialist
conception of history is in fact based on claims about meaning: 'a
technical fact is held to have an immediate and full significance,
there is no ambiguity; it is what it "says" and it says what it is'
(p. 22). Against this a priori absolutization of a particular field,
Castoriadis defends a more de-centred view:

> That history is the domain in which meanings are 'embodied'
> and in which things become meaningful is certain beyond the
> shadow of a doubt. However, none of these meanings is ever
> complete and closed in on itself; each always refers to something
> else, and no thing, no particular historical fact can deliver
> a meaning that in and of itself would be inscribed on it. No
> technical fact has an assignable meaning if it is isolated from the
> society in which it is produced and none imposes a univocal and
> ineluctable sense to the human activities that it underlies, even
> these. (p. 23)

To put it another way, the attempted reduction of meaning to a
secondary aspect of social life presupposes a tacit privileging
and unfounded isolation of one particular meaning-dependent
domain.

The critique of historical materialism imposes certain requirements
on the alternative approach that Castoriadis has in mind. It must,
first and foremost, provide a better account of meaning in society
and history, and this entails a threefold task: to demolish the
notion of an objective and determining 'basis', to rethink cultural

and political formations in a way that would emphasize their irreducibility to 'superstructural' derivatives of the economy and to theorize the field that transcends all specific centres of meaning. For the very strong and broadly conceived interpretation of meaning thus envisaged, it was a priori plausible to bring in the imagination as a source of significations beyond the given, the useful and the established. But this is not to suggest that Castoriadis deduced his specific idea of the creative imagination from the logic of his social theory. Rather, the argument that was first outlined through the concepts of the institution and the imaginary drew on a variety of sources which Castoriadis read in light of his own emerging problematic. He was inclined to stress the particular importance of Freud's work, where the creative imagination was – as he saw it – acknowledged without being mentioned by its proper name. But here it is the Marxian background that should be highlighted. Castoriadis's critique of Marx was, as we have seen, qualified by references to insights that merit further thought. More specifically, closer examination of Marx's writings reveals three unmistakable but inconclusive encounters with the imaginary element in human affairs. Castoriadis's comments on them vary in length and level, but all three cases are important signposts for his road beyond Marx (see *Autonomy*).

The first and most fundamental example is Marx's analysis of the labour process, but Castoriadis only mentions it in passing. At the beginning of a section discussing the role of imaginary significations, he points out:

> human labour (in both the narrowest and the broadest sense) indicates in all of its aspects – in its objects, its ends, its modalities, its instruments – a specific manner of grasping the world, of defining itself as need, of positing itself in relation to other beings. (p. 147)

As he then argues, this web of significations, and not merely the prior mental representation of results to be achieved, stressed by Marx, sets human labour apart from the most purposeful activity of animals. But when he adds that prior representation could be added to the latter type without changing anything, it is hard to follow him: rather, the logic of the argument is that conscious anticipation cannot take effect without insertion into a web of significations, and that Marx was therefore taking the first step into a field which could not be explored without a more adequate grasp of significations as such.

The latent presence of the imagination becomes clearer in the second case. It has to do with the Marxian notion of reification, which Castoriadis links to a more general 'dehumanization of individuals of the exploited classes' (p. 140). Neither the definition of the slave as *animal vocale* (this should more properly have been *instrumentum vocale*) nor the reduction of labour power to a commodity can be understood as fully and purely objective transformations. In both cases, we are dealing with 'a new *operative signification*' and 'an *imaginary creation*' (p. 141) that affects history in a decisive way, but only through more or less effective imposition on a substratum that will always to some degree resist it. Here we may add that these two divergent patterns of class domination are particularly interesting because they exemplify the imprint of imaginary significations on power; this theme was otherwise not in the forefront of Castoriadis's thought during the period spanned by *The Imaginary Institution of Society* (from the early 1960s to the mid-1970s).

By contrast, the third example concerns the revolutionary project expected to put an end to class domination. The project in general is for Castoriadis 'the element of praxis'; as such, it is 'the intention of transforming the real', guided by 'a representation of the meaning of this transformation' (p. 77), but it does not presuppose exhaustive knowledge and should not be confused with a precisely determined plan. All that applies a fortiori to the project that aims at a reorganization of society by autonomous individuals, and to the extent that the revolutionary element is at least intermittently present in Marx's work, he can be credited with a pioneering insight into this matter. A meaning that transcends the given and is not translatable into knowledge is easily linked to imaginary significations. The fact that Castoriadis does not explicitly make the connection is clearly not unrelated to ambiguities surrounding his own rethinking of the idea of autonomy (see *Autonomy*). As an alternative to hitherto dominant ways of social life, the project of autonomy is a vision of possible new beginnings, and that would seem to put it into the category of imaginary significations. It is occasionally identified as such, but Castoriadis is markedly disinclined to pursue that line; his main emphasis is on autonomy as a more reflective stance towards significations.

Castoriadis, Weber and Durkheim

Castoriadis's critique of the basis-superstructure model was not the first of its kind. Max Weber and Emile Durkheim had, each in his own way, taken issue with the twin ideas of material determinants and derivative meaning. The overcoming of this misguided dichotomy may be seen as one of the main achievements of classical sociology. Castoriadis does not refer to these predecessors in his early 1960s writings on Marx, quoted above (it seems clear that Merleau-Ponty's critique of Marxist objectivism and rationalism was more important to him than any sociological sources); when he later considers their approach to the question that his concept of imaginary significations was designed to answer, he stresses basic disagreements. There is no reason to doubt the differences between him and the classics, but the picture is nevertheless more complicated than his account would suggest.

Castoriadis distinguishes social imaginary significations from the 'various types of signification or sense (*Sinn*)' (p. 367) thematized in Max Weber's work, and goes on to consider the two main versions. The subjectively intended sense of individual action is not an adequate key to the wider field of significations; individual attributions of meaning are, as Castoriadis insists, made possible by social imaginary significations. Here he is obviously invoking his basic conception of the socially constituted individual, and using it to highlight the social sources of individual meaning. The other Weberian way to theorize meaning is linked to the concept of the ideal type. Castoriadis accepts that Weber's ideal-typical constructs serve to grasp the social world, but to the extent that they depend on individualistic premises, the critical point just made applies to them as well; and when they have a more structural or institutional basis, there is another problem. Ideal types designed to reconstruct particular aspects or components of society do not do justice to the complementarity of the phenomena in question. For Castoriadis, 'the latter are in each case what they are and as they are only through their immersion in society as a whole' (p. 368), and this perspective brings us back to the web of significations that links different domains of social life to each other. The social dimension of meaning thus returns as a theme to be developed against or at least beyond Weber.

But before going on to discuss Castoriadis's attempt to rethink meaning and society with a view to clarifying their mutually constitutive relationship, there is more to be said on his reading of Weber. The individualistic theory of action, reinforced by corresponding theories of meaning and rationality, has had a strong influence on twentieth-century sociologists, and Weber's text on basic sociological concepts (Weber, 1994) has been one of its main sources; the premises of this approach have come under criticism from various points of view, but the concept of social imaginary significations adds a new angle. For one thing, its take on the question of meaning enables a more radical critique of individualistic assumptions than does the widely accepted reference to shared norms and rules. On the other hand, the analysis of individual action is not the only entry to the field of meaning in Weber's work. Among other indications, more compatible with the line taken by Castoriadis, the best known is the brief mention of 'ideas' playing the role of 'switchmen' with regard to the interests that determine action (Weber, 1991, p. 280). The ideas in question can only be understood as comprehensive frames of interpretation, linking self, others and world, and reflected in the orientations of human action. Their broad dimensions and their socially shared implications argue against derivation from individual intentions, and although Weber does not raise the issue, an institutional aspect – added by some later Weberians as a third component – seems inherent in the ideas as such. Another brief but suggestive formulation, found in an early text, defines the idea of culture – and a corresponding mode of inquiry – in terms of a human ability to lend meaning and significance to the world (Weber, 1969, p. 81). This reference to culture is not included in the later discussion of basic sociological concepts, but it is implicit in the notion of cultural worlds, which Weber uses to demarcate the historical units covered by his comparative studies; the final versions of the latter also belong to the last phase of Weber's work, and as late twentieth-century interpretations of his work were to show, they are more important for understanding his project than are the conceptual prolegomena (for pioneering arguments in this vein, see Nelson, 1974 and Tenbruck, 1980). And on that level, a basic continuity between Weber and Castoriadis seems undeniable. Weber's 'cultural worlds' are macro-social formations structured around constellations of meaning, and for Castoriadis society institutes itself in 'instituting a world of significations' (Castoriadis, 1987, p. 360). On the other hand, Weber's adumbrations of a broad view beyond subjective meaning remain vague, and, most importantly, he makes no reference to the imagination.

To better grasp the innovative aspects of Castoriadis's views on meaning, a brief comment on the other classical source is needed. In *The Imaginary Institution of Society*, Durkheim is treated more dismissively than Weber: in the concluding chapter, he is not even mentioned by name, but the allusion to 'certain sociologists', dealing with collective or social representations (p. 366), is unmistakable. For Castoriadis, such terms reflect a partial and inadequate understanding of the matter. He makes the same point as in relation to Weber: social imaginary significations are preconditions and sources of individual representations, and therefore not reducible to common or typical contents of the latter. The surplus meaning of the social imaginary element asserts itself on several levels. The web of significations constitutes a reservoir which is only partially activated in individual use; it posits presuppositions that remain in large part unarticulated in the individual context; and its ongoing changes are to a varying but always limited extent reflected in individual representing/saying. To cite an example often mentioned by Castoriadis, all this is thoroughly applicable to the significations embedded in language, no matter whether we think of language in general or of the particular languages through which its common characteristics are realized. But important and convincing as these points are, the preceding comments on Durkheim seem inadequate: they do not take into account the development of Durkheim's views beyond the first attempts to define a realm of shared meanings (see especially Durkheim, 1974, pp. 1–34). His various statements on the subject reveal a consistent trend: a growing emphasis on the autonomy of collective representations with regard to individual ones, while at the same time the notion of a collective consciousness is abandoned due to its misleading connotations of a macro-subjective dimension beyond the individual. The shift is, on a more specific level, accompanied and reinforced by Durkheim's gradual turn to religion as a supposedly foundational form of social life. This line of inquiry leads beyond the limiting assumptions of earlier writings. Durkheim's mature sociology of religion centres on a set of interconnected but also polarizing representations (notions relating to the sacred and the profane); their central role in the constitution of society transcends the experiences and horizons of individual actors involved in the process. Moreover, the primordial instituting of society through religion appears as the beginning of a very long-term differentiating trend that gives rise to other institutions (Durkheim, 1995, pp. 418–448). These genetic connections are grounded in representations, but they only become intelligible *ex post* at the collective level. Castoriadis did, as will be seen, draw some lessons from Durkheim's theory of religion, but not in a way that would have prompted new thoughts on collective representations. And in any case, the implicit affinities suggested above are limited by the absence – in Durkheim's as in Weber's work – of a properly thematized imaginary element. Castoriadis's turn in that direction leads him to associate collective meaning with significations rather than representations. This point takes us to the next stage of the discussion: a closer analysis of the imaginary component in instituted meaning.

Imagination, signification, institution

As argued above, the concept of social imaginary significations should be understood in light of a double genealogy: the direct and explicit grounding in a dialogue with Marx and the more latent links to classical sociology. But this survey of sources and prefigurations must be complemented by a more structured analysis of interrelations within Castoriadis's own problematic, and the most appropriate point of transition between the two contexts is the critique of functionalism. It begins as a generalizing twist to the polemic against Marxism, gains added significance through the encounter with structuralism (seen as a transient fashion of the same intellectual family, but not as a tradition of the same calibre as functionalism) and grows into a distinctive conception of the social-historical world. The starting-point (Castoriadis, 1987, pp. 116–117) is the observation that although human societies indisputably have a functional component, they are not reducible to systems with given needs; cultural definitions always enter into the making of societal needs, and the defining patterns most familiar to the human sciences, at the time of Castoriadis's writings, were symbolic networks. When their dependence on underlying meanings is established, the ground is prepared for Castoriadis's specific version of the reorientation often described as the greatest sea change in twentieth-century philosophy: the shift from the question of knowledge to the question of meaning. The first step is to introduce a tripartite typology of significations: they can 'correspond to the *perceived*, to the *rational* or the *imaginary*' (p. 139). These categories are introduced in a seemingly abrupt fashion, but it is not difficult to reconstruct the background. It is, first and foremost, a Kantian one: the distinction between the perceived and the rational recalls the Kantian duality of perception and understanding, and the third type brings us back to the foundational role of the imagination in the first edition of the *Critique of Pure Reason*. Castoriadis was very familiar with that text and refers to it elsewhere, but his project is incompatible with a mere return to the transcendental imagination. On the one hand, he goes beyond the Kantian framework and links the recovery of the imagination to the questioning of a traditional ontological postulate which Kant's critical turn had left untouched: the equation of being and determinity. As a result, the philosophical theme of the creative imagination can be brought to bear on the sociological problem of creativity, forcefully raised but not developed by Durkheim and intermittently revived by later authors. Castoriadis takes the issue further by merging the social and the historical dimensions of the human world more closely than any other theorist has done. History, understood as the emergence of new forms, thus becomes the self-unfolding of society. On the other hand, the insertion of the imagination into the social-historical field must – by the same token – bring it into contact with other forces at work in that field, and this interconnection rules out any claim to transcendental primacy. The imaginary element in the social-historical complex is to be distinguished from the components based on perception (in the broad sense of more or less explicit awareness of the given) or rationality (defined in terms of basic rules applying to coherent thought and behaviour). But the next step is to recognize permanent interaction with these two aspects (or, to put it another way, with experiential data and rationalizing efforts) as the modus operandi of the imaginary source, and therefore also of the significations which it brings into being. And the picture becomes even more complicated when we add that the interaction is not a matter of contacts between clearly demarcated domains: rather, the three factors interpenetrate in complex and often ambiguous ways. Imaginary significations shape patterns of perception as well as frameworks and horizons of rationalization, even when the specific imaginary content appears to merge with a model of rationality and/or fade into a levelling notion of reality (as it does in the case of the distinctively modern visions of infinitely expanding rational mastery). Conversely, inputs from perceptual experience enter into the making of imaginary significations, and the imagination cannot articulate its themes without an admixture of rationalization. Finally, the intertwining of imaginary and functional aspects, with which Castoriadis's critique of functionalism began, can be understood in light of the tripartite division: A functional institution or activity is, or would be, a rational and therefore generalizable response to a uniformly perceived problem; the critical point is that the imagination intervenes on both sides, in the definition of the problem as well as in the elaboration of the response.

All this adds up to a relational conception of the imagination and its role in the constitution of society. To put it another way, the creativity of the imagination is expressed in configurations and transformations involving a broader context, not in self-contained mutations. That point is further supported by the particular examples that Castoriadis uses to introduce the concept of imaginary significations: the key cases are also noteworthy as illustrations of the approach that works through criticism of established views, but remains open-ended enough to allow for further shifts of emphasis and changes of direction. With these implications in mind, let us look at the relevant passages in *The Imaginary Institution of Society*. The first discussion of specific imaginary significations deals with two very different instances. At one extreme, 'God [capitalized in the original] is neither a signification of something real, nor a signification of something rational' (p. 140); the imaginary content attributed to the idea of divinity transcends both perceived realities and rational patterns. This is not to say that the perceptual or the rational dimension is unimportant. Perceived and, more specifically, iconic aspects of divine presence played a crucial role in the history of the religious imagination; the reaction against them was a later one (part of the reorientation known, somewhat misleadingly, as the monotheistic turn), and contested even within the traditions rooted in that same source. Rationalizing elaborations of notions about the divine realm have a long history, not limited to the record of theology in the strict sense, and with the emergence of negative theology, a high level of rationalization turned on itself. A brief analysis of the idea of god thus shows not only that the imaginary element combines with the perceptual and the rational; it also reveals that relations between these components vary historically in ways that can be conducive to self-problematization. To round off our reading of this passage, however, we must note a limiting assumption: Castoriadis refers to 'God' as the centre of 'every religion' (p. 140). This claim runs counter to key arguments in the sociology of religion; notions of god or divinity have, in line with Durkheim's seminal work, been subordinated to the more basic category of the sacred. Castoriadis later adopted that line of argument and gave it a very distinctive twist. For him, the sacred became a 'simulacrum', an imaginary signification that reflects and simultaneously occludes the chaos or abyss beyond all approximative order. This view raises questions about the supposedly fundamental but non-foundational notion of the chaos: it is most plausibly seen as an imaginary signification in its own right, but Castoriadis also wants to present it as the fruit of critical reflection on the philosophical mirage of fully determined being, and at the same time, he identifies it as a crucial component of the ancient Greek world view that predated the emergence of philosophy. If we try to trace the origins of the last-mentioned version, it is tempting to go back to the experience of an unusually thoroughgoing civilizational collapse between the Mycenaean and archaic periods of Greek history (for a summary of the evidence now available, see Morris, 2006). As Castoriadis argues in his posthumously published interpretation of ancient Greece (Castoriadis, 2004, p. 121), the Homeric epics were probably preceded by a religious revolution. If so, the historical background must have left its mark on the new imaginary. In short, this case seems to re-open the question of imaginary significations in a way that has yet to be clarified.

If the choice of God as a starting point reflects the role of encompassing significations in the constitution of society, the other example used in the same context is of a different kind. The generalized notion of reification, understood as an imaginary de-humanization of the exploited, has to do with the processes traditionally seen as the material side of social reproduction. We have already discussed this part of the argument as a comment on Marx's encounter with the imagination; but it also exemplifies the survival of certain Marxist models in Castoriadis's thought, even after the turn taken in the early 1960s. The connection between slavery and wage labour presupposes a continuum of class domination, familiar in the Marxist tradition but less compatible with the variety of social forms (and their respective patterns of social power) emphasized in Castoriadis's post-Marxist work. If we replace the one-sided focus on class rule with a more diverse spectrum of relationships between hierarchy and equality, allowing for mixtures of cultural values and power structures on both sides, the scope of imaginary significations can be defined in broader terms. Castoriadis's later essay on ideas of equality (Castoriadis, 1986) offers suggestions to that effect. As he explains, equality has been envisioned and demarcated in different ways, not invariably convergent; religious versions do not necessarily translate into social or political ones. Castoriadis's own vision of equality is inseparable from the project of autonomy, and in that sense coupled with freedom; since it transcends given realities and disclaims rational foundations, its imaginary dimension is beyond doubt.

To sum up, the main point emerging from Castoriadis's first approach to imaginary significations is that the argument reflects a limiting background, but lends itself to further nuancing and development. The same applies to the more structured survey in a later section of the chapter (Castoriadis, 1987, pp. 146–158). This bird's eye view of 'the role of imaginary significations', the only one of its kind in Castoriadis's writings, highlights four principal fields of imaginary articulation. The first is 'the being of the group and of the collectivity' (p. 147); in view of the fact that collective identity has been a rather underdeveloped theme in the sociological tradition, it is all the more noteworthy that Castoriadis's analysis begins here. Another strong point to be noted is the vast range of historical cases taken into account, from the imaginary identification with ruler or city to the modern nation; Castoriadis's comments on the imaginary character of national identity preceded later debates on 'imagined communities' (Anderson, 2006). But the unqualified emphasis on 'the institution . . . that *posits* the collectivity as existing' (Castoriadis, 1987, p. 148) leaves a key question unasked: to what extent is the instituting aspect of society incorporated into the collectivity? The world-historical change that took place in and through the Greek *polis* depended on a shift of that kind; a strong collective identity of the citizenry was a precondition for the capacity to question and transform institutions. That claim is not contradicted by the Greek experience of civic conflict; this was a frequent but not ubiquitous feature of *polis* society, and the very intensity of the division reflected the integrative powers of the community that it tore apart. This aspect of the Greek constellation was certainly not unfamiliar to Castoriadis, but in his later discussions, it is overshadowed by the self-reflexive project of autonomy. Another example in point is the compatibility of modern nationhood with varying forms of statehood, even though some allowance has to be made for cases of national identity linked to specific institutions (the US constitution is the most frequently mentioned one). This institutional openness has been a major factor in the development of modern democracy, and the prospects for transnational democracy are still uncertain; but such issues were, to say the least, not prominent in Castoriadis's discussions of the subject.

The second point to be noted is the ability and propensity of every society to create an image of 'the universe in which it lives, attempting in every instance to make of it a signifying whole' (p. 149). This integrative 'grasp of the world', as Castoriadis was to call it in his seminars on ancient Greece, is always based on the abovementioned three dimensions of meaning: it draws on rational elaborations of experience, but subordinates them to imaginary significations that go beyond the given and the grounded. Here the key to further questioning and conceptual development is the reference to a 'signifying whole'. This apparently unproblematic term conceals a variety of responses to the paradox of the world as an under-determined but inexhaustible horizon of cultural interpretation. A tacit totalizing intention may be attributed to the 'savage mind', most memorably analyzed by Lévi-Strauss, and even more so to the mytho-poetic and mytho-speculative thought of archaic civilizations. But comparative scholarship seems to have shown that an explicit thematization of the whole first occurred in Greek thought, together with a new awareness of cosmic fragility and an ability to envisage alternative models of order. On the other hand, a paradigmatic way of relativizing the 'signifying whole' emerged during the same epoch, that is, the 'axial age'. S. N. Eisenstadt's interpretation of this historical period (Eisenstadt, 1986), defined as the middle centuries of the last millennium BCE, centres on a radical division of the world into a transcendental and a mundane sphere (the monotheistic turn in ancient Israel and the emergence of Buddhism in ancient India may be seen as exemplary but vastly different cases; whether the Platonic moment in Greek philosophy belongs in the same category is still a matter of debate). Discussions so far suggest (Arnason et al., 2005; Bellah and Joas, 2012) that while Eisenstadt's model is less easily generalizable than he liked to think, the notion of a radical ontological division is one of the principal innovations of the axial age, and it was of major importance for later cultural transformations. A comparative history of its interpretations has yet to be written; one of the key themes would be its interaction (sometimes mutually reinforcing, sometimes more disruptive) with visions of a signifying whole. Both this particular aspect and the broader debate around axial legacies are obvious fields for testing the analytical potential of Castoriadis's ideas on the imaginary.

The third focal point is introduced as a link between word image and social self-image: 'the definition each society gives of its needs, as this is inscribed in its activity, its doing' (Castoriadis, 1987, p. 149). Definitions of needs are intertwined with definitions of values; both needs and values enter into the context of 'doing', and although Castoriadis's comments are very brief, we can link this set of themes to broader horizons outlined elsewhere in his work. At the beginning of the second, more systematic part of *The Imaginary Institution of Society*, the question 'what *doing* means, what the being of doing is' (p. 168) is posed as a challenge to inherited ways of thinking, comparable to and inseparable from the rethinking of the social-historical. However, neither the following chapter nor later writings pursued the problematic of action to the same extent as the problematic of meaning. There is no doubt that the overcoming of individualistic preconceptions was one of Castoriadis's main concerns in this field as in others, but theories of action cannot do without a clear-cut understanding of the individual, and that requirement in turn raises the question of the psyche and its social-historical transformations. Castoriadis's reflections and indications on that subject do not add up to a full integration of his revised psychoanalytical paradigm with his ontology of the social-historical (see the *Psyche* and the *Social-Historical*). And most importantly, Castoriadis's last essays and – even more – his seminars signal a major shift in his view of the relationship between the two levels. Social imaginary significations now appear as a structuring link between 'the representations, the affects and the intentions dominant in a society' (Castoriadis, 2007, p. 231), and this perspective is explicitly modelled on traditional psychological notions. Castoriadis does describe the application of this scheme to society as a metaphor, but then it is all the more necessary to spell out the implications; it seems significant that he places particular emphasis on the tripartite distinction in regard to the understanding of markedly different cultural worlds, such as the Christian societies of the European past, where the central role of faith is taken to represent the affective dimension. The idea of interconnected representations, affects and intentions at the social-historical level is certainly not a radical break with Castoriadis's earlier arguments, but it is undeniably a major innovation. It constitutes one of the most challenging openings in his later work.

Finally, imaginary significations are involved in the formation of 'a structure, or an articulation of a society' (Castoriadis, 1987, p. 150); but although it is made clear that this general statement also applies to pre-state and pre-class societies, the discussion is exclusively concerned with the articulation that divided society into antagonistic classes and transformed the whole framework of social life on that basis; against the 'materialist' explanations of this change, Castoriadis insists that it presupposes a new signification, a new self-image of society as divided in a radically asymmetric way. But as the reference to slavery as the first form of class domination shows, this analysis is still dependent on residual Marxist assumptions. More recent scholarship has changed our picture of the transformation in question. It is now widely accepted that the emergence of the state represents a more fundamental and more comprehensive change than the formation of classes (for forceful versions of this thesis, see Clastres, 1977 and Gauchet, 1999); this is not to say that the accumulation of wealth and the social asymmetries arising on that basis are unimportant, but the evidence suggests that wealth was more dependent on power than the other way around. On the other hand, the emerging power centre – the early state – takes shape in close connection with transformations of religious life and claims an exclusive relationship with the sacred.

These new insights have put paid to the traditional Marxist account of early class societies, but they have reinforced Castoriadis's general claim and made it more separable from the particular formulation quoted above. The formation of archaic civilizations, marked by new divisions within society and fundamental changes to cultural orientations, presupposes new visions of power and corresponding rearticulations of its divine foundations; this new understanding of the most decisive watershed in human history allows us to grasp the role of imaginary significations on a broader scale than did the references to early class societies.

It will be obvious from the preceding discussion that social imaginary significations are not reducible to language. But although linguistic articulation is only one aspect of their mode of being, it is an essential one. To conclude, a few words should therefore be said about Castoriadis's analysis of significations in language (Castoriadis, 1987, pp. 345–353). It would be very misleading to describe his reorientation of philosophical reflection as a version of the linguistic turn (his substantive focus on the social-historical cannot be understood in such terms), but it did incorporate a specific approach to language and a recognition of its central role. He writes: 'Being in language is accepting to be in signification' (p. 350), and vice versa, as being in signification entails being in language. The preconditions for more complex social-historical domains of signification must be identified at this level. For Castoriadis, the most basic mode of being in signification and language is an interplay of determinacy and indeterminacy, or – in other words – of closure and creation.

> It is essential that language always provide the possibility of treating the meanings it conveys as an ensemble formed by terms which are determined . . . And it is equally essential that it always provide the possibility of new terms emerging, that the relations between existing terms be redefined. (p. 353)

The reference to essential features is contextual rather than functional: the argument relates to language as a component of the social-historical, and the concepts of system and function are inapplicable to the latter. A bipolarity of the kind highlighted by Castoriadis underlies the different uses and applications of language in social life, from everyday communication to the macro-articulations discussed above. But Castoriadis is not simply invoking an otherwise undefined creativity of language. He distinguishes three dimensions of meaning and criticizes the linguistic and philosophical approaches that have, in one way or another, oversimplified the issue. Linguistic expressions acquire meaning through the 'bundle of referrals starting from and surrounding them' (p. 345); through relations to and differences from other signifiers, and through their links to 'the representations of individuals, whether actual or virtual' (p. 346). None of the three aspects, variously foregrounded by selective conceptions of meaning, can be identified with one component of signification in social life, as defined above. Reference is obviously not reducible to perception; as understood by Castoriadis, it includes a more or less explicit use of rationality to organize experience, and the 'bundle' opens up imaginary horizons. The unfolding and underdetermined web of differences and interconnections that constitutes a language (emphasized but misrepresented by the structuralists) is anchored in perception; without that basis, there would be no relation to the world, articulated up to a point by rational rules and embedded in imaginary fields. As for representations, the point is too obvious to require further comment. In other words: each of the fundamental aspects of linguistic meaning turns out to involve a fusion of the three layers first distinguished at the level of social imaginary significations. This very complex pattern is Castoriadis's framework for a theory of meaning. His later writings did not develop such a theory, but the programmatic indications are among the most valuable parts of his work.

References

Anderson, B. (2006), *Imagined Communities: Reflections on the Origins and Spread of Nationalism*, London: Verso.

Arnason, J. P., Eisenstadt, S. N. and Wittrock, B. (eds) (2005), *Axial Civilizations and World History*, Leiden and Boston: Brill.

Bellah, R. and Joas, H. (eds) (2012), *The Axial Age and Its Consequences*, Cambridge, MA: Harvard University Press.

Castoriadis, C. (1986), 'The nature and value of equality', *Philosophy and Social Criticism*, 11, 4, 373–390.

—. (1987), *The Imaginary Institution of Society*, K. Blamey (trans.), Oxford: Polity; Cambridge, MA: MIT Press.

—. (2004), *Ce qui fait la Grèce, t. 1: D'Homère à Héraclite*, Paris: Seuil.

—. (2007), *Figures of the Thinkable*, H. Arnold (trans.), Stanford, CA: Stanford University Press.

Clastres, P. (1977), *Society against the State*, Oxford: Blackwell.

Durkheim, E. (1974), *Sociology and Philosophy*, New York: Free Press.

—. (1995), *The Elementary Forms of the Religious Life*, New York: Free Press.

Eisenstadt, S. N. (ed.) (1986), *The Origins and Diversity of Axial Age Civilizations*, Albany: SUNY Press.

Gauchet, M. (1999), *The Disenchantment of the World: A Political History of Religion*, Princeton: Princeton University Press.

Morris, I. (2006), 'The collapse and regeneration of complex society in Greece, 1500–500 BC', in G. J. Schwartz and J. J. Nichols (eds), *After Collapse: The Regeneration of Complex Societies*, Tucson: University of Arizona Press.

Nelson, B. (1974), 'Max Weber's *Author's Introduction* (1920): A master guide to his main aims', *Sociological Inquiry*, 44, 4, 269–278.

Tenbruck, F. H. (1980), 'The problem of thematic unity in the works of Max Weber', *The British Journal of Sociology*, 31, 3, 316–351.

Weber, M. (1969), *The Methodology of the Social Sciences*, New York: Free Press.

—. (1991), *From Max Weber*, H. H. Gerth and C. Wright Mills (eds), London: Routledge.

—. (1994), *Basic Concepts in Sociology*, New York: Citadel.

CHAPTER FOUR

Creative Imagination

Johann P. Arnason

The theme of the creative imagination is widely associated with romantic currents in modern thought and culture. Castoriadis does not often use this term, but some of his formulations presuppose it as a background concept. The limits to Kant's discovery of the imagination are summed up in the statement in which he called it 'productive and not creative' (Castoriadis, 1987, p. 199); Castoriadis's point is that the reference to production implies an a priori subordination to determinate and stable forms. This seems to contradict an earlier description of history as 'impossible and inconceivable outside the *productive or creative imagination*' (p. 146), where no distinction is made between production and creation. The difference can be explained as a result of growing emphasis on distance from the philosophical tradition and on a fundamental break with the assumptions that blocked understanding of human creation. In a later text, first presented in Stanford in 1981, he mentions key examples of social imaginary significations, from the religious to the economic, and adds: 'I call these significations imaginary because they do not correspond to, or are not exhausted by references to "rational" or "real" elements, and because they are posed by a creation' (Castoriadis, 1997a, p. 8) (see *Social Imaginary Significations* and the *Social-Historical*). This may be taken as a confirmation of the link to traditional debates on the creative imagination, and that connection is crucial to the understanding of Castoriadis's arguments; but he transforms the terms of reference and develops a new conceptual framework.

The basic conceptual innovations are spelled out in the last chapter of *The Imaginary Institution of Society* (1987). The general concept of the radical imaginary covers both the social-historical and the psychic/somatic dimension. 'As social-historical, it is an open stream of the anonymous-collective; as psyche/soma, it is representative/affective/intentional flux . . . That which in the psyche/soma is positing, creating, bringing-into-being for the psyche/soma, we call radical imagination' (Castoriadis, 1987, p. 369) (see the *Psyche* and *Social-Historical*). On this view, the radical imagination would be the radical imaginary seen from a certain angle, that is, in its capacity as an ongoing emergence; and the term appears to be a synonym for the creative imagination. If we recall the short comment on history, quoted above, it seems clear that a similar distinction could be made within the social-historical domain: its creative power – *vis formandi*, as Castoriadis calls it elsewhere (Castoriadis, 2007a, p. 71) – can also be singled out for conceptual focus. But to approach the problem from a properly broad perspective, we must first consider the shift from the imagination to the imaginary, which is Castoriadis's most distinctive move, then try to clarify the role of his principal interlocutors, especially Marx and Freud and on that basis, the question of a specific understanding of the imagination – distinguished from the imaginary in the way outlined above – can be reconsidered.

Castoriadis did not explain at length why he preferred to thematize the imaginary rather than the imagination. A late text on 'Imaginary and the imagination at the crossroads' (pp. 71–90) seems to take the difference between the two concepts for granted. But a closer look at this very text suggests that the main reasons for adopting it have to do with perceived limitations of the philosophical tradition and envisaged ways of overcoming them. Aristotle is credited with the discovery of the imagination; his principal insight in this regard is that the soul never thinks without recourse to imaginary representations. This could, in principle, be understood as a reference to an imaginary dimension or element as well as to an imaginary capacity. In fact, it was the notion of the imagination as a capacity that prevailed in the tradition. The focus was at first psychological, but Kant shifted it to the transcendental level, and although that line of argument found no systematic continuation, echoes of it include Heidegger's attempt 'to return imagination to a central position in the way human beings relate to the world' (p. 72). That attempt is also central to Castoriadis's rethinking of the whole issue. But as he sees it, the traditional framework – the conceptual space between the empirical and the transcendental subject – is inadequate. The underlying definitions of the subject belong to the set of categories that he wants to problematize as a whole, and the decision to foreground the imaginary – without an accompanying reference to the subject – serves to gain distance from the tradition. In substantive terms, it reorients the inquiry towards a trans-subjective field, and more precisely in a direction that helps to question the 'basic hyper-category of determinacy' (Castoriadis, 1997a, p. 4). In the final instance, this enables Castoriadis to reverse the traditional thrust of ontology: 'the imaginary, that is human, mode of existence' (p. 5) can be taken as a starting-point for a reflection on being as such, encompassing organic as well as inorganic nature. But the first and most decisive step, most extensively developed in Castoriadis's work, is an ontological reinterpretation of the social-historical. (The approach to that domain is discussed in the entry on *Social Imaginary Significations*.)

The discussion of social imaginary significations also shows that this concept grew out of Castoriadis's long and complex engagement with Marx. It is true that he tended to stress another source. He often referred to Freud's analysis of the unconscious as an epoch-making but paradoxically unacknowledged rediscovery of the imagination (Castoriadis, 1987, p. 281), and as a direct impulse to his own reflection on the same subject. On the level of intellectual biography, there is no reason to doubt this account. But the logic of the work does not necessarily coincide with the personal history of ideas. Even if the encounter with Freud triggered a new approach to the question of the imagination, closer examination of the texts shows that the conceptual articulation of this field was primarily achieved through a critical reading of Marx. Castoriadis's writings contain no discussion of Freud that can be compared to the systematic critique of Marx's historical materialism in the first part of *The Imaginary Institution of Society*. As noted above, this critique is, in general terms, linked to the idea of the creative imagination, but it is developed with reference to the imaginary as a dimension, to significations as the master key to a non-reductionist (i.e. neither empiricist nor rationalist) understanding of meaning, and to the social-historical as a distinctive level of reality, constituted through the imaginary element of meaning. In the second part of the book, this framework is then expanded into a more comprehensive ontology of the social-historical world.

In contrast to the move beyond Marx, Castoriadis's most sustained interpretation of Freud – the sixth chapter of *The Imaginary Institution of Society* – presupposes prior arguments and basic assumptions about the social-historical context. The title of the chapter refers to individuals and things, but the preceding chapters already showed that the individual must be understood as a social creation, and that the division of the world into determinate things involves the elementary institutions of *legein* and *teukhein* (see Legein *and* Teukhein). In other words: if the unconscious is to be brought into an anthropo-ontological frame of reference, the line of interpretation is prefigured by ideas developed at another level. Here I need not discuss the details of Castoriadis's revised psychoanalytical paradigm (see *Psyche*), but the ideas most relevant to his idea of the radical imagination should be noted. The starting-point is Freud's description of the unconscious as a domain beyond time and contradiction.

Neither naturalistic nor Marxian readings could make sense of this notion, and for Castoriadis the approaches inspired by linguistics – exemplified by the attribution of metaphoric and metonymic patterns to the unconscious – are fundamentally misconceived: instead of assimilating the unconscious to the institution of language, with its higher level of determinacy, we should grasp the former as a guide to questions and perspectives that help to problematize conventional views on the latter. The factor that makes it possible to ignore time and contradiction is the unbounded omnipresence of representations in the psyche. 'Representation has no borders, and any separation that is introduced into it can never be held to be pertinent – or rather, it will always be certain to be non-pertinent in some essential aspect' (Castoriadis, 1987, p. 276). It gives us 'a type of being which not only is both one and many, but for which these determinations are neither decisive nor indifferent' (p. 277). In this context, all demarcations of identity and difference are blurred, and Freud's comment on the absence of time and contradiction may be read in that light. The evanescent character of boundaries and distinctions affects all possible domains of meaning, from temporal order to logical relations.

Castoriadis credits Freud with having at least begun to understand the all-important role of representations in mental life. But he did not reflect on philosophical implications, and could not link his discoveries to an explicit grasp of the imagination. For Castoriadis, the test case is the question of the origin of representation. Freud wants to answer it in terms of drives and their vicissitudes, but finds it difficult to establish a plausible link 'between the soul and the body' (p. 282). His most revealing formulation is the reference to 'delegation through representation' (*Vorstellungsrepräsentanz*); Castoriadis interprets it as a retreat from causal explanations and reductionist interpretations. The irreducible specificity of representations is implicitly recognized, but it remains to show that this move must, if taken to its logical conclusion, bring the creative imagination into play. The psyche is endowed – indeed, in the last instance, identical – with 'an original capacity to make representations arise' (p. 283). This ability is an elementary form of creativity.

> The psyche is a forming, which exists in and through what it forms and *how* it forms; it is *Bildung* and *Einbildung* – formation and imagination – it is the radical imagination that makes a 'first' representation arise out of a nothingness of representation, that is to say, *out of nothing.* (p. 283)

The creative imagination thus becomes a basic component of mental life, and at the same time a source of further transformations beyond the psyche. Representation is 'the first matrix of meaning, the operating-operated scheme of bringing into relation or connection' (p. 299); but this prefiguration of the *signitive relation* – the co-belonging of sign and object – is also, and inseparably, a 'proto-meaning that realizes by itself, just where meaning obviously cannot yet exist, total meaning, the universal and unbroken bringing into relation which will tend to encompass even that which denies it' (p. 299). On this view, the elementary articulations and the most ambitious projections of meaning can be traced back to the same root. It would, for Castoriadis, be very misleading to limit the semantic potential of the radical imagination to the more specific imaginary aspect of social significations. Rather, the critical point is that the imagination – through its incessant creation of representative fields in flux – intervenes also on the empirical and the rational side. The link between representation and experience is established through a critique of the 'prejudice of perception'. As Castoriadis sees it, the traditional notion of representation as an 'imitative and defective' (p. 329) offshoot of perception stood things on their head, and it is the emergence of perception from the representative flux that should be subjected to closer examination. But if this turn appears at first to deprive perception of its long-assumed primacy, the outcome is a new understanding of the creative imagination at work. Perception becomes a prime example of creation in response to a triggering but not determining contact with external reality (in later writings Castoriadis uses Fichte's term *Anstoss* to characterize this infra-causal impact), and the aspects often dismissed by philosophers as secondary impressions – notably colours – are the most striking manifestations of this creative surge. Moreover, the creation of new patterns is inseparable from the opening of new horizons. If representation is 'that in which and through which at a given moment a world arises' (p. 331), perception is obviously of key importance for this breakthrough, and in that sense, the loss of its misconceived foundational status is matched by gains at another level.

As for the rational side, the unity of reason – 'the rational use of the form of the One, which allows access to the world which exists only as one *and* as the *other* than one' (p. 299) – is rooted in the totalizing proto-meaning and the initial autism of the psyche, and although not reducible to that source, it is not immune to temptations inherent in the origins. A more or less explicitly defined regulative idea of reason is a constitutive feature of thought in pursuit of knowledge, but it lends itself to conflation with '"the idea of the One", which would simply be a form of Identity' (p. 300), brought about by the imposition of institutional forms. The institution of the individual appears as a bridge between the mutating monad and a broader field of meanings and forces. From another point of view, and with reference to the Freudian framework, the opening and the reorientation of the monad represent the social-historical aspects of sublimation. This vast topic is explored from various angles in Castoriadis's writings, but many questions remain open; the overall argument can, however, be seen as an attempt to historicize the main insights of psychoanalysis. It differs from other projects of that kind (the main examples are Marxian readings of Freud, notably those of the Frankfurt school, and Norbert Elias's translation of psychoanalytical models into the language of historical psychology), most significantly in that it entails a radical rethinking of basic concepts. Further discussion of this approach to psychoanalysis is beyond the present scope of this chapter.

With regard to themes and problems traditionally associated with the creative imagination, Castoriadis's most important innovations are encoded in the concept *of social imaginary significations*. The concept of the radical imagination and the specific questions linked to it should be set against that background: they relate to human sources of social creativity, and to the need for an anthropological perspective that would complement the ontology of the social-historical. But there is yet another side to the issue. If the radical imagination feeds into significations on the social-historical level, it does not seem far-fetched to ask whether there is – within the social-historical domain – a particular dimension where it becomes more markedly creative than in other contexts. Reflections in that vein, revolving around culture in general and art in particular, can be found in some of Castoriadis's essays. Although they do not go beyond tentative formulations, the points made are clear and weighty enough to constitute one of the most interesting frontiers of Castoriadis's thought. The first step is a definition of culture as

> all that, in the public domain of a society, goes beyond that which is simply functional and instrumental in the operation of that society and all that introduces an invisible – or, better, an unperceivable – dimension invested or 'cathected' in a positive way by the individuals of that society. In other words, culture concerns all that, in this society, pertains to the imaginary *stricto sensu*, to the poietic imaginary. . . . (Castoriadis, 1997b, p. 339)

The *poietic imaginary* sounds like another synonym for the creative imagination. In his critique of functionalist conceptions (including historical materialism), Castoriadis had stressed that imaginary significations enter into the social-historical definitions of needs and goals. In more conventional terms, this is to say that the meaning and the criteria of functional utility depend on cultural interpretations. If culture is now to be understood in contrast to the functional and utilitarian dimensions of social life, we are obviously dealing with a more specific and circumscribed domain of creation, and presumably one where the imaginary component becomes more pronounced than it is on the level of core institutions and organizational principles. And since the collective anonymity of instituted significations is clearly in the line of Hegel's Objective Spirit, it is tempting to associate the more transcending patterns of cultural creation with the Absolute Spirit.

But this analogy runs into problems. The Absolute Spirit was the realm of art, religion and philosophy, with a markedly privileged position reserved for philosophy and a more elusive role attributed to religion as a realm of meaning to be rethought by philosophy (this point was important enough to become a lasting source of disagreement among interpreters of Hegel's work). Art is of much more limited significance. If we compare Castoriadis's views to the Hegelian model, the differences are obvious. For Castoriadis, religion is directly involved in the institution of society: it represents the very core of the heteronomous framework that has characterized most human societies throughout history. Philosophy is defined primarily in opposition to that mode of life and thought, that is, as an effort to problematize instituted meanings, and a reasoned questioning of accepted presuppositions. This entails a certain tendency to neglect other aspects commonly regarded as defining achievements of philosophy, such as the articulation of cosmological visions or the conceptualization of symbolic and/ or narrative forms. To put it briefly, religion and philosophy are defined in relatively narrow and mutually polarizing terms. What does this mean for the position and the understanding of art? Some of Castoriadis's later essays contain at least the outline of an answer. The idea of art as a window on the chaos (developed in Castoriadis, 2007b), a way of looking beyond cultural models of the human world and getting a closer view of its underlying existential problematic, obviously requires further development; but some implications suggest themselves. If aesthetic creation can, in its own fashion, problematize established ideas and visions, this throws new light on the crucial distinction between autonomy and heteronomy. The way of art differs from the ways of philosophy and politics. And if it is – as Castoriadis clearly implies – the hallmark of great art that it can call the values of its own society into question in and through the very act of affirming them (for one thing, that applies to Homer), this double-edged relationship is not confined to modern culture. The whole line of argument is too tentative for any key concepts to emerge from it. But that is not a reason to dismiss these beginnings of aesthetic reflection as a marginal part of Castoriadis's work; they relate to its most fundamental themes.

References

Castoriadis, C. (1987), *The Imaginary Institution of Society*, K. Blamey (trans.), Oxford: Polity; Cambridge, MA: MIT Press.
—. (1997a), *World in Fragments: Writings on Politics, Society, Psychoanalysis, and the Imagination*, D. A. Curtis (ed.), Stanford, CA: Stanford University Press.
—. (1997b), *The Castoriadis Reader*, D. A. Curtis (ed. and trans.), Oxford and Cambridge, MA: Oxford University Press.
—. (2007a), *Figures of the Thinkable*, H. Arnold (trans.), Stanford, CA: Stanford University Press.
—. (2007b), *Fenêtre sur le chaos*, Paris: Seuil.

CHAPTER FIVE

Creation *ex nihilo*

Angelos Mouzakitis

As Castoriadis explains in the preface to *The Imaginary Institution of Society*, the concept of creation *ex nihilo* is one of the key concepts introduced in the 1964–1965 publication of 'Marxism and Revolutionary Theory' in *Socialisme ou Barbarie* (Castoriadis, 1987, p. 2). Linked to the concept of creation *ex nihilo* are the concepts of the social imaginary, the social-historical, instituting and instituted society, etc., all of which, in Castoriadis's view, are 'unrecognized' (and arguably also inaccessible) by inherited thought (see *Social Imaginary Significations*, the *Social-Historical*, the *Creative Imagination* and *Institution*). These concepts later became 'starting points' for his reflections, which, in my opinion, shows *inter alia* their *dynamic* character (p. 2).

Castoriadis formulates the concept of creation *ex nihilo* in contradistinction to that of *production* and in close relation with the creative imagination. Indeed, the importance of creation *ex nihilo* for the development of Castoriadis's distinctive approach to the theorization of the social-historical could hardly be overemphasized. Of great significance is Castoriadis's claim that humanity has thought creation almost exclusively in the guise of the creation of *matter*, therefore disregarding the workings of creative imagination (p. 199). Castoriadis argues that creation *ex nihilo* is a unique characteristic of social-historical formations and uses this notion in order to defy teleological and causal conceptions of history and society. Castoriadis's interpretation of creation *ex nihilo* rests ultimately on the distinction between (mere) *difference* and (radical) *otherness*. For Castoriadis *difference* is tantamount to the production of the same within what is already given both on the level of 'extant' being and on the level of meaning. *Otherness* points to the emergence of unprecedented modes of being(s), which cannot be traced back – or explained with regard to – to pre-established nexuses of relations, meanings, etc. The social-historical is then seen as the field of the creation of otherness, since history is 'precisely our authentic *otherness*, other human possibilities in their absolute singularity' (p. 163). The incessant creation of otherness that characterizes social-historical formations thwarts speculative attempts at an 'exhaustive understanding and explanation of societies of other times and other places' and the 'speculative project of total history' (p. 163). Importantly, Castoriadis argues that the explicit acknowledgement of the *creative* dimension of the social-historical is the condition sine qua non for revolutionary change (p. 164).

At first glance it is striking that creation *ex nihilo* almost automatically suggests some reference to the Judaeo-Christian theological tradition. Castoriadis, however, argues that his application of the term borrows nothing from theology and that rational theology's application of the term creation is no more than a misnomer for mere *production* or *reproduction* of already existent forms. As he emphatically puts it, creation 'in theology is obviously merely a pseudo-creation; it is producing or manufacturing' (p. 196).

Castoriadis seems to wish to base his argument on the grounds that in Judaeo-Christian theology creation is attributed to a divine creator and is understood as taking place once and for all. He argues that in theology the 'created' world is conceived as a necessary world, since creation 'itself is predetermined and entirely determined starting from the elsewhere and the atemporal always of God; it takes place once and for all, once and for always' (Castoriadis, 1987, p. 196; 1999, p. 121). In this way, Castoriadis argues, not only does theology ultimately deprive the human being of any creative agency by postulating an extra-social source of creation but it also denies the emergence of any radically new element in the totality of being through the unfolding of time.

As I have attempted to indicate elsewhere (see Mouzakitis, 2008, p. 56, n. 73), mainly in relation to Max Scheler's interpretation of the Judaeo-Christian understanding of creation, the accuracy of Castoriadis's argument is debatable. This happens insofar as we can find in the various aspects of this ontotheological tradition at least fragmentary conceptions of the human being as co-creator. However, Castoriadis argues that even conceptions of 'continued creation' based on theological discourses are pseudo-conceptions of creation, since they rely on 'the indispensable support that the only true being-a-being, God, grants to created beings in order to maintain them in this minor mode of being . . . and which they owe to him' (Castoriadis, 1987, p. 196). It follows that the 'created world' is postulated as 'not ontologically autarchic' as leaning 'upon the sole being which "lacks nothing for its existence"' (p. 196).

It is important to note in this context – and especially for the benefit of scholars who do not read modern Greek – that in a work dedicated to the assessment of Castoriadis's *oeuvre*, Ramphos understands Castoriadis's conception of creation *ex nihilo* as representing a *reversal* of the Judaeo-Christian conception of this term. According to Ramphos the main reversal consists in the attribution of indeterminacy to historical *praxis* rather than to a divine being as in the case of theological discourses, and it is also shaped by Castoriadis's interpretation and critique of the Marxist conception of history (Ramphos, 2002, p. 172). Stavrakakis (2007, pp. 42–48) seems to agree on the issue – even if his own epistemic perspective and political agenda differ radically from Ramphos's – and claims that Castoriadis gives a *subjectivist* twist to the theological conception of creation due to the emphasis he places on the unconscious of the individual human psyche. He furthermore argues that by so doing, Castoriadis develops an account of human creativity that owes much to the philosophical tradition of romanticism and ultimately fails to do justice to the destructive dimensions of human creation. Now, although this is, in my view, a far-fetched and one-sided interpretation of Castoriadis's *oeuvre* it is still of interest to scholars as it points our attention to certain *aporiae* that follow from Castoriadis's conception of creation. More specifically, it calls our attention to such themes as the possible relationship between individual and collective creation (to which by no means Castoriadis gives a simplistic subjectivist solution as Stavrakakis argues), the inability to safeguard human societies from undesirable and/or destructive creations, the possible affinities between Castoriadis's own understanding of creation *ex nihilo* and the theologico-philosophical tradition he wishes to overcome, etc.

At any rate and irrespective of whether one accepts or rejects these interpretations, it is difficult to deny the force, novelty and uniqueness of Castoriadis's conception of creation. His overall conception is premised on a radical – and to some, perhaps audacious – re-interpretation of the Platonic concept of *eidos* (form) and could be best understood in the light of his critique of various philosophical conceptions of creation, and consequently also of inherited notions of time and history. In effect, it seems as though his critique of the theological understanding of creation is performed on two grounds: the wider rejection of religious discourses as the most heteronomous and alienating instances of the social-historical (see, for example, Castoriadis, 1997a, p. 319) and the unhappy wedding of Greek philosophy and Christian monotheism, as exemplified in the writings of St. Augustine on time (see pp. 380ff.).

Castoriadis argues that in the long history of philosophical thought, creation has been understood exclusively and invariably in terms of production or of reproduction of the given. He traces the inception of this tradition in the works of Plato and especially in the *Timaeus*. Castoriadis detects an intimation of a radical understanding of creation in Plato's dialogues and especially in Plato's assertion that creation or *poiesis* is the 'cause of passage from non-being to being', leading thereby 'a former non-being to a subsequent beingness (*ousia*)' (Castoriadis, 1987, p. 197). However, Castoriadis claims that Plato abandons this radical insight and that in the *Timaeus* he advances instead an understanding of creation in terms of *imitation*. In this dialogue, the divine demiurge, that is, the creator of all being, is conceptualized as a craftsman imitating a prototype, since the cosmos is declared to be by necessity 'the image of something', that is, of an eternal, extra-temporal paradigm (p. 198). In Castoriadis's view this gesture is basically repeated by Aristotle who once more defines creation (in the guise of *poiesis*) as *imitation* (p. 198).

In this context, Castoriadis's attack on the modern philosophical tradition takes an interesting twist in his drawing a parallel between the Platonic *chora* and Kant's treatment of space and time as pure forms of intuition in the first *Critique*. Castoriadis claims that there is an astonishing similarity between the positing of a *chora*, a receptacle partaking at the same time of the intelligible (indestructible) and the sensible (destructible) worlds and the understanding of both time and space 'as containing *nothing* at all (not even pure figures)' (p. 189). In this manner, Castoriadis argues, space and time become inseparable and ultimately time gets conflated with space in the works of both Kant and Hegel (p. 189). Apart from the objection that an 'empty space' is unthinkable, the identification of space with time ultimately robs time of its creative dimensions. It mystifies the existence of 'another time for each category or class of otherness', as the time of 'Flaubert's *Education Sentimentale* is not the same as the time of Becket's *Endgame*' (Castoriadis, 1997a, p. 395). Interestingly, Castoriadis interprets even Heidegger's elaborations on temporality and the so-called epochality of being as a result of this inability to clearly separate space from time, of the mystification of time as creation proper, of time as emergence of radically new forms (*eide*), while arguing that the postulation on Heidegger's part of *one* authentic temporality is absurd (p. 401).

In effect, Castoriadis argues that inherited thought from Plato to Heidegger has suppressed the emergence of the essential characteristic of time by conceptualizing time in terms of space. This attitude finds its most explicit expression in the representation of time 'by means of pure non-time, that is, by means of a line' in a series of important thinkers from Aristotle to Hegel (Castoriadis, 1987, p. 189). Simultaneously, 'being' in general is thought as determinacy and as atemporality. Inherited thought obscures the essence of time as 'absolute creation', that is, as a state-of-affairs where '*what* emerges is not *in* what exists, not even *logically* or as an already constituted *potentiality*' (p. 190). This 'logic-ontology of the same, of repetition, of the forever intemporal (*aei*)' is in Castoriadis's view incapable of grasping 'the emergence of otherness', the 'ontological genesis, that brings about beings as *eidos*' (p. 181). When 'being' is thought as determinacy it is represented as determined succession of events *in space*. However, pure succession 'has never been thought, and could never be thought, except as a modality of the *co*existence of the terms of a series' (p. 191). Castoriadis detects a reciprocal relation between the formulation of an understanding of being within 'the horizon of determinacy and of the atemporal always, as an indubitable *self'* and the neutralization of temporality that becomes but a faint reflection of the atemporal always (p. 191). For Castoriadis traditional philosophical discourse fabricates the unity of being through the sublation of multiplicity via the 'application' of a rule that operates at 'a deeper level', and which can be formulated in the maxim 'do not multiply the meanings of being; being *must have* a single meaning' (p. 168). In other words, in the context of traditional philosophy the multiplicity of the modes in which beings emerge has to be traced back to an *origin*, to a being proper, allegedly inalterable and imperishable, while all other beings are conceptualized as *deficient* in this respect, namely as subject to change and ultimately to demise, always incapable of maintaining an absolute identity with themselves. On these grounds, Castoriadis places Heidegger's questioning of the meaning of being within the discourse of the inherited philosophical tradition of determinacy, and argues that the Heideggerian conception of the *ontological difference* is 'impossible to maintain', and that it merely exposes 'the limit of inherited thought' (p. 182).

Now there are important implications following Castoriadis's critique of inherited ontology. On the one hand he seems to champion the idea of there being some dimension (or dimensions) of being that are not amenable to unification. In this sense we could arguably speak of being as something unified only insofar as we have in mind its ensidic-identitary dimension. It is impossible, however, to speak of being as forming a unitary whole as long as we allow for the existence of a *magmatic* dimension. This happens insofar as the opposite of identity, difference, inscribes the different parts again in the pre-existing whole, while the product of the *magmatic* dimension is *otherness proper*, irreducible to identity (see *Magma* and *Ensemblistic-Identitarian Logic*).

Although Castoriadis maintains that both dimensions (i.e. the ensidic and the *magmatic*) are to be found in both nature and society, he explicitly states that the paradigmatic domain of this *magmatic-creative* dimension is the domain of human beings. Castoriadis defines an object as *magmatic* when it cannot be 'exhaustively and systematically' reduced or explained with recourse to the ensidic dimension, when it is not 'reducible to the elements and the relations' that emerge 'exclusively' in a way that belongs to the ensemblistic-identitary logic (Castoriadis, 1997b, p. 214). Even more explicitly put, the *magma* is defined as that 'from which one can extract (or in which one can construct) an indefinite number of ensemblist organizations but which can never be reconstituted (ideally) by a (finite or infinite) ensemblist composition of these organizations' (Castoriadis, 1987, p. 343). Although Castoriadis believes that it is easy to convince oneself that the *magmatic* character belongs to any object, be it 'a galaxy, a city, or a dream' (Castoriadis, 1997b, p. 214), he traces two notable exceptions to this state-of-affairs. Artefacts considered solely in their instrumental, non-ontological aspects (like machines) and the branches of mathematics, seemingly exclusively exemplify an ensidic dimension. However, even in this case it would be almost impossible to eliminate the *magmatic* dimension, since artefacts are at the end of the day products of human imagination as are the *axioms* of mathematics. Actually, this reliance of mathematics on axioms is what allows Castoriadis to characterize the history of mathematics as 'the history of the creative imagination of mathematicians' (pp. 214–215).

In another text Castoriadis attempts to illuminate the relations between human and non-human regions of being, through an interpretation of Aristotle's concept of *physis* and a critical discussion of the concept of self-organization in contemporary biology (see *The Living Being*). Castoriadis distinguishes two distinctive understandings of *physis* in Aristotle: First, a 'finalistic' one, which he is quick to explain has no validity nowadays, since finality is now attributed mostly to artefacts and especially to *machines* and not to nature, and second, an understanding of *physis* as the origin of movement, in the sense that every living being has the origin of its movement within itself. Although he argues that through the concept of *entelecheia* these two conceptions come ultimately together, Castoriadis traces in the second conception mentioned above an understanding of movement that is not confined to that of Galilean physics. He therefore argues that the Aristotelian understanding of movement is not confined to spatial movement but it also includes change – in general, transformation. Thus according to Castoriadis in movement we should include 'the change of form', alteration and transformation 'considered in the strictest sense', which should include 'the emergence [and] the creation of form' (Castoriadis, 1997a, p. 335). With this move Castoriadis is able to pronounce *physis* to be 'in itself principle and origin of creation', something that in his opinion was inconceivable for Aristotle for whom forms were allegedly 'determined in advance and from all eternity' (pp. 335–336).

Moreover, Castoriadis argues that the uniqueness of humanity lies in that – as Aristotle himself acknowledged – the human being does not only have the principle and origin of movement within itself, but it is rather 'principle and origin of what *will* be' (p. 336). Arguably, this formulation aims at highlighting the unique creative power of the human being, which does not simply follow a *telos* set by its 'inner' nature, but rather freely generates movement in the sense defined above. Castoriadis notes that being is 'defined by *alloiosis* in the strong sense of the term', that is, by 'self-alteration, self-creation'. He furthermore argues – in relation to Varela – that the living being in general 'self-constitutes itself, it is for itself; it creates its world', or it constitutes 'each time, a *proper world*' (p. 338). At the same time, the living being is said to pose itself 'as self-finality' and this 'implies a minimal *intention*, at least the intention of self-preservation' (p. 338). Castoriadis distinguishes four types of living being: the living being by and large (*le vivant*), the human psyche, the always socially fabricated individual and each particular instituted society. It is easily observable that three of the four types of living being 'known to us', correspond to the human domain proper.

Importantly, Castoriadis maintains that the creation of the world proper to a given society entails *closure*. This closure is primarily premised on the existence of a world of significations that remain largely unchallenged and is reinforced by the fact that each society creates its individual members in such a manner that they would almost invariably conform to its overall institution. Indeed, this closure is at times so compelling and inescapable that Castoriadis compares it with the closure produced by Newspeak in Orwell's *1984* where it would be impossible to even say that 'Big Brother is ungood' since this would not be an option in the artificial language produced by the monstrous imaginary state of Orwell's novel (p. 339).

True to his wider conception of autonomy and heteronomy, Castoriadis argues that there are only two historical exceptions to this closure, two moments of 'rupture' in a series of heteronomously instituted societies: the first such moment is the emergence of the Greek *polis*, followed by that of European modernity (see also *Autonomy, Heteronomy* and *Modernity*). In Castoriadis's view, what these exceptional creations have in common is their being premised on autonomy, on the explicit acknowledgement of society's being the origin and creator of its laws, and concurrently the commitment to the relentless *questioning* of the established institutions, which is of course inextricably linked with the concurrent emergence of philosophy and democracy (see *Democracy*). It is only on these rare occasions of autonomous creation – which is creation *ex nihilo* par excellence since neither democracy nor philosophy are necessary results of pre-established modes of being – that societies spare themselves of the 'blind' self-creation characteristic of heteronomous societies (pp. 339–340).

We encounter here in yet another guise Castoriadis's deep-seated conviction that human history is essentially creation *ex nihilo* that time in its not-identitary, imaginary dimension, is but the emergence of the radical kind of *otherness* characteristic of human creations (p. 392). However, according to Castoriadis only in the case of *autonomous* societies this creation is fully acknowledged and also liberated from the confines of the always already instituted dimension of the social-historical. It should be noted in this context that the emergence of autonomous societies, of the central imaginary signification of autonomy itself presents us in some respects with a riddle. In effect, like every other imaginary signification, autonomy springs from the *magmatic* unconscious dimension of the psyche and it is therefore *creation proper*. This means that as far as we lack a clear and detailed understanding of the workings of *magmas*, a 'new logic' or a 'logic of *magmas*' the necessity of which Castoriadis explicitly championed (Castoriadis, 1978, pp. 276–277, n. c; for a detailed discussion on the issue see Mouzakitis, 2010), the emergence of autonomy can be at best conceptualized as a happy accident. Although the same is true of any other form of signification, the problem posed by the emergence of autonomy is arguably much more important in the context of Castoriadis's works, since for him it is with the emergence of autonomy that humanity explicitly acknowledges itself as *creative* concurrently of its 'world' and of *itself*. In other words it bears at the same time ontological, anthropological and political significance.

Being the outcome of human activity, the various aspects of human history, the history of science and the history of thought by and large, could be but instantiations of the creative powers of human beings; they *are* the emergence of *other* 'figures of the thinkable' (Castoriadis, 1999). These figures are *creations proper* of the philosopher or the scientist; they are not discovered as it is often assumed (Castoriadis, 1978, pp. 18, 22). Far from simply not being a (re)production of already existent figures or forms, history – and the history of thought – is said to be even more than *simple ontological* creation, that is, than the positing of new forms (*eide*). Castoriadis speaks of a complex creation of *types of eide* of a dehiscence (*déhisence*) between background and figure, of yet another 'solidarity/difference of its component parts' (p. 25).

Music – and art in general – is perhaps the paradigmatic field of creation, since there it is easier to observe its emergence out of silence, or out of nothing. It is there that we freely encounter a dehiscence (*déhisence*), where figure and background *are* concurrent, 'each through the other and in its relation to the other' (pp. 25–26). Importantly, Castoriadis argues that if we fail to think history and the history of thought as creation, it becomes nothing more than sheer tautology (p. 19). This hardly means that this creation is completely unrelated to being or even to history, be it the history of philosophy, of science, of art or of history by and large. Castoriadis has repeatedly noted that when speaking of creation *ex nihilo*, he does not mean creation *cum* nihilo or *in* nihilo (e.g. Castoriadis, 1997a, p. 392; 1997b, p. 212). At first glance this conception looks rather intriguing, however it merely points to the fact that creation cannot be explained with reference to what already is. Or, we could say that creation is *conditioned* to various degrees by being but never *determined* by it. As he writes, the new *eidos* posited each time by human creation is not merely 'unforeseeable, unpredictable' or 'undetermined', but rather a form that is 'neither producible nor reducible to other forms' and which posits itself 'new determinations, new laws' (Castoriadis, 1997a, p. 392). Thus humans create the 'world of meaning and signification, or institution upon certain conditions', but they create it *ex nihilo* in the sense that both the 'level of being' of the social-historical and its 'particular contents' *cannot be derived* from these conditions (pp. 392–393). A helpful metaphor that Castoriadis offers us in order to depict this state-of-affairs and which is related to the *creative* dimensions of *thought* is that of a distance or gap (*écart*) between thought and its object, which for him is not *given* or even posited once and for all but always created and *re-created* by thought itself (Castoriadis, 1978, p. 20).

It is certainly no accident that in defining society as *magma* – or even more emphatically as *magma* of *magmas* – Castoriadis explains that his use of the concept of *magma* does not signify chaos but 'the mode of organization belonging to a non-ensemblistic diversity, exemplified by society, the imaginary, or the unconscious' (Castoriadis, 1987, p. 182). With this move, creation proper, that is, the incessant emergence of radically new institutions and forms of life is pronounced to be the attribute of humans and humans only, premised as it is on the enigmatic combination of the creative powers of the psyche and the institution. Indeed, in his thought the primary act of creation is the self-creation of society without which the individual human being is unthinkable and which Castoriadis calls the 'primary institution of society' (Castoriadis, 1999, p. 124). It is therefore hardly surprising that in his interpretation of Greek tragedy and especially of the *Antigone*, Castoriadis traces in Aeschylous's play an early intimation of his own insight that the essence of the human being is 'self-creation' (Castoriadis, 2001, p. 151). Far from being tranquil and harmonious, this creation is always endangered by the emergence of destructive imaginary significations, or to put it in the parlance of Greek tragedy it is always shadowed by *hybris* (see Klimis, 2006, p. 11), by transgression and catastrophe, as Castoriadis time and again warns his readers of the dual character of human creation, both potentially liberating and destructive.

References

Castoriadis, C. (1978), *Les Carrefours du Labyrinthe*, Paris: Seuil.
—. (1987), *The Imaginary Institution of Society*, K. Blamey (trans.), Cambridge: Polity.
—. (1997a), *World in Fragments*, D. A. Curtis (ed. and trans.), Stanford, CA: Stanford University Press.
—. (1997b), *Fait et a Faire*, Paris: Seuil.
—. (1999), *Figures du Pensable: Les Carrefours du labyrinthe VI*, Paris: Seuil.
—. (2001), 'Aeschylean anthropology and Sophoclean self-creation of anthropos', in J. P. Arnason and P. Murphy (eds), *Agon, Logos, Polis: The Greek Achievement and its Aftermath*, Stuttgart: Franz Steiner Verlag.

Klimis, S. (2006), 'Explorer le labyrinthe imaginaire de la creation grecque: un projet en travail . . .', in S. Klimis and L. Van Eynde (eds), *L' Imaginaire selon Castoriadis. Themes et enjeux, Cahiers Castoriadis, 1*, Bruxelles: Publications des Facultes Universitaires Saint Louis, pp. 9–46.

Mouzakitis, A. (2008), *Meaning, Historicity and the Social. A Critical Approach to the Works of Heidegger, Gadamer and Castoriadis*, Saarbrücken: Dr. Mueller Verlag.

—. (2010), 'What is Knowledge? Castoriadis on Truth, Signification and Symbolism', in *Cahiers Castoriadis, n. 6 Castoriadis et la question de la vérité*, Bruxelles: Publications des Facultés Universitaires Saint-Louis.

Ramphos, S. (2002), *Μαρτυρία και Γράμμα: Απόλογος για τον Μαρξ και λόγος για τον Καστοριάδη* [Witness and Letter: Afterward on Marx and Word on Castoriades], Athens: Armos.

Stavrakakis, Y. (2007), *The Lacanian Left*, Edinburgh: Edinburgh University Press.

CHAPTER SIX

Magma

Mats Rosengren

Magma (from ancient Greek, μαγμα) was originally a geological term. It signifies a blend of molten or semi-molten rock, volatiles and solids found beneath the surface of the Earth. Besides molten rock, magma may also contain suspended crystals, dissolved gas and sometimes gas bubbles. It may seep into adjacent rocks, extrude onto the surface as lava or in explosive ejections.

For Castoriadis, all of these senses of the term are important. On his account our whole world is magmatic. Not just the natural world, but also artefacts, societies, cultures, institutions, traditions and so forth. Opposing the traditional 'thing-ontology' in Western thought – that is, the tendency to think of our world as a ready-made, inert thing-ish substance and not as a process in constant motion – Castoriadis claims that what *is*, is structured as an ever-changing, stratified magma (which, in turn, may contain a multitude of magmas) (see *Creation* ex nihilo).

One may discern two intimately connected, interlaced and mutually dependent chief senses of magma in Castoriadis's philosophy. Taken as a primarily *ontological concept*, magma designates a world that is not completely determined, a world that is heterogeneously stratified and processual. Taken as a primarily *social concept*, Castoriadis uses magma to designate the complex modes of being of our human societies, traditions and institutions, that is, of the ways in which we make sense and create meaning in and for our world (see *Social Imaginary Significations*).

In what follows I will try to make these two meanings of magma in Castoriadis's philosophy a bit clearer. However, it should be noted right away that, for Castoriadis, social sense-making is always and inevitably world-making in an ontological sense: first, we organize our world so that we can orient ourselves in it – from spatial conceptions and simple objects to more complex and abstract 'things'. Then we try to make sense of this world that is always already there, which is one important aspect of Castoriadis's idea about us humans as always being *downstream* (see below). The first kind of sense-making is directly related to our bodies and our specific embodied existence – our *Umwelt*. The second is of a more hermeneutical kind, and relates to our *Lebenswelt*. (For all this, see the preface to Castoriadis, 1987, especially p. xxiv.) Thus it would be a mistake to think of the ontological use of *magma* as more fundamental, or more basic in relation to the social. It is not. But there is a difference in emphasis in the alternative ways in which Castoriadis uses the concept that I will try to bring out and elucidate.

Castoriadis uses magma in the *ontological sense* to articulate an alternative to the view that everything that *is* is fully and exhaustively determined, that everything that is can be completely explained in causal terms and that everything that *is* ultimately can be reduced to the same essence or substance (see the entry on *Ensemblistic-Identitary Logic*). Castoriadis criticizes this traditional and predominant way of thinking in Western thought. Instead, he discerns a form of being that has previously not been noticed in science or philosophy: magma. First discovered through his reflections on the human psyche and the unconscious in *The Imaginary Institution of Society* (Castoriadis, 1987, p. 281), the notion is expanded to include the mode of being of the social imaginary significations.

> Thus, the social imaginary significations in a given society present us with a type of organization unknown until now in other domains. This type is what I call a 'magma.' A magma contains sets – even an indefinite number of sets – but is not reducible to sets or systems, however rich and complex, of sets. (This reduction is the hopeless endeavour of functionalism and structuralism, causalism and finalism, materialism and rationalism in the social-historical domain.) Neither can it be

reconstituted 'analytically,' that is, by means of set-theoretical
categories and operations. (Castoriadis, 1997a, pp. 12–13)

In claiming that our world is magmatic through and through,
Castoriadis uses the image of the heterogeneously stratified magma
in order to make a place both for explanations of the world that
rely on ensidic logic (i.e. for ensidic explanations relating to
and functioning within specific strata or layers of the world)
and to make a place for the creation of new forms and things.
According to Castoriadis, each stratum of our world, each layer
in the magma, has its own specific mode of being. So even though
each layer is constantly influenced by other layers in the magma,
no layer can be completely reduced to another one. Castoriadis
chooses the example of colours to clarify what he means: In
the physical strata of our world we find light (or more precisely
radiation) of different frequencies but we find no colours. In the
strata of the lived human world, we do find colours as important
parts of the human experiencing of the world. A common way of
explaining human colour perception, that draws on ensidic logic,
would be to note that, for example, red is the equivalent of light
of a certain frequency – that is, that the colour red *is* light of this
specific frequency. For Castoriadis, this would be an example of
an unwarranted reduction from one stratum (the lifeworld, the
colours) to another stratum (the physical stratum, the frequencies
of light). Why unwarranted? Because the experience of red as it
appears in human perception is simply not identical to light waves
of a certain frequency. The colours of the life world are, in fact, a
new form in and for being that has no equivalent in the physical
strata. Castoriadis writes:

> The imagination begins with the sensibility; it is manifest in the
> most elementary data of the sensibility. We can determine a physico-
> physiological correspondence between certain wavelengths of
> light and the color red or blue; we absolutely cannot 'explain'
> either physically or physiologically the sensation red or blue as to
> its *quality*. (Castoriadis, 1997c, p. 104)

The three strata of the magma of the world involved here – the
physical stratum, the biological (the living being) and the cultural –
are of course all interacting, in the sense that if there were no light

waves or radiation at all, there would not be any perception of colour by a living being, nor would there be an understanding of the specific sense of what a colour-perception is (see *The Living Being*). But to claim that light waves are causing the perception of red or blue, or that each perception of red is reducible to the presence of radiation of a certain frequency would be to jump to conclusions. What we can say is that the radiation *conditions* the perception of colour, but it does not *determine* the quality, nor the sense of the experience it thus conditions. Consequently, according to Castoriadis, the form colour is a creation, and even more specifically a *creation out of nothing* (see *Creation* ex nihilo). This kind of relation between the strata in the magma of the world is a relation, in Castoriadis's terms, of 'leaning on' (see Anlehnung): Each stratum conserves its own identity while constantly leaning on, that is, being affected by and affecting other strata. There is no common foundation from which all of these strata spring forth or to which they can be reduced. Together they form a heterogeneously stratified magmatic universe in constant motion, no one stratum being more original or more real than another. Castoriadis writes:

> To the question 'Why do certain classes of living beings grasp certain electromagnetic waves as colours and as these colours?' there is no answer, [. . .]. This faculty of making be, of bringing out of itself modes of being, determinations and laws [. . .] is what I call radical creation. (Castoriadis, 1997b, p. 404)

Thus, the ontological form of being that Castoriadis discerns, magma, allows for an unsaturated, that is, not deterministic, universe that makes place for creation as part of the way the world is.

Let us now move from the primarily ontological use of magma to the other central function of the concept within Castoriadis's philosophy – the *magma of social imaginary significations* (see also *Social Imaginary Significations*). By way of transition, it should be noted that even though Castoriadis talks about the mode of being of the world as *a* magma, this does not exclude the existence of an infinite numbers of magmas. In fact, as I understand it, a magma or magmas may be constructed within a magma, and two or more magmas may be interlaced so as to form new magma in an ever ongoing stratified process. Some of these magmas are dense, slow and sluggish, while others are liquid, fast and fluid as water. All are interacting. Castoriadis writes: 'The mode of being of the magma signifies simply that the object under consideration is neither reducible to [. . .] ensidic organizations nor exhaustible by them' (p. 379). (Castoriadis even made an attempt to construe a specific logic of magmas, but it seems as if he eventually abandoned this idea. In any case, it was never fully developed in a systematic way (pp. 290–318).)

Among the magmas that make up our world, the *magma of social imaginary significations* is arguably the most important and encompassing of them all. It embraces many specific magmas connected to specific social, historical and institutional settings and situations. In this it resembles concepts like *common sense, doxa, paradigm*, etc. Thus the notion of a *magma of social imaginary significations* may be seen as a specific contribution to the general upsurge of constructivist epistemologies and ontologies of the late twentieth century. The notion also contributes to the growing interest in embodiment (magma is, after all, a very concrete notion, emphasizing that no meaning is possible without being embodied in some kind of material support) as well as to the contemporary field of philosophical anthropology and contemporary theories of meaning. Counting on the suggestive force of the metaphor, Castoriadis uses the expression 'the magma of social imaginary significations' to suggest – or this is at least how I understand him – social processes of instability, volatility, destructive outbreaks and of cooling down and of formation of layered new ground (institutionalization). Hence its central place in Castoriadis's way of conceptualizing and elucidating society, the social institution of thought and the processes of institutionalization themselves. This becomes clear in the following quotation:

What is the source, the root, the origin of this magma [i.e. of a specific magma of social imaginary significations MR] and of its unity? Here, we can see clearly the limits of the traditional ontology. No 'subject' or 'individual' (or 'group' of subjects and individuals) could ever be this origin. Not only is the amount of ecological, sociological, psychoanalytical, etc., knowledge, both theoretical and applied, necessary to engineer the organization of a primitive tribe, for instance, of such a complexity that it defies imagination and is, at any rate, far beyond our grasp; but, more radically, 'subjects,' 'individuals,' and their 'groups' are themselves the products of a socialization process, for their existence presupposes the existence of an instituted society. Neither can we find this origin in 'things'; the idea that myths or music are the (however roundabout) outcome of the operation of the laws of physics is just meaningless. Nor, finally, can we reduce the various institutions of the known societies and their corresponding significations to 'concepts' or 'ideas' {Hegel}. We have to recognize that the social-historical field is irreducible to the traditional types of being, that we observe here the works, the creation of what I call the social imaginary, or the instituting society (as opposed to the instituted society) – being careful not to make of it another 'thing,' another 'subject,' or another 'idea'. (Castoriadis, 1997a, p. 8)

This quotation may be read as spelling out, on a different level than before, Castoriadis's refusal to accept a reduction of one stratum of being to another. It emphasizes that the magma of social imaginary significations of a specific society cannot be traced back or reduced to individual or collective intentions. Not only because of the sheer complexity and vast amount of information and data such an intention would have to master but, more interestingly, because each individual (and hence each group or collective) is shaped by the always already instituted magma of social imaginary significations of the specific society in question. Moreover, this shaping occurs long before he or she (or them) can have any intentions at all. Without an instituted society, there would be no individuals at all, nor any intentions to institute anything – hence it would be as meaningless to go looking for a founding moment or an original intention to institute the social imaginary of a society as it would be to try to explain it in causal terms. We have to allow for the possibility of genuine creation and of magmatic relations between its strata if we are to grasp the social-historical in its specific mode of being. Castoriadis writes:

> The socialization process is at work and at stake in and through the process of bestowing signification. Society is primarily a magma of social imaginary significations that make collective and individual life meaningful. Consequently, socialization is nothing other than entering – and functioning within – that instituted magma of social significations. (Castoriadis, 2007, p. 216)

Thus, from the point of view of the individual, the magma of social imaginary significations is always already instituted. As individuals we are in a position that Castoriadis describes as always already 'downstream' (e.g. see Castoriadis, 1997a, p. 270). And the waters in which we wade are the *magmas* of social imaginary significations that were instituted by those who came before us. They are transmitted, conserved, transformed and communicated to us through different kinds of institutions: language and habits, ways of being in the world, practices and traditions – but also by political systems, schools, laws, trade-agreements, economies, city planning, communications, etc. These social imaginary significations form a stratified magma that is embodied in institutions of all kinds, they are the forms in and through which the individuals in a society live. The magma presents human beings with a world that makes sense to them, and in which they can make sense of themselves and their life. Castoriadis states:

> There is thus a *unity* of the total institution of society; and, upon further examination we find that this unity is in the last resort the unity and internal cohesion of the immensely complex web of meanings that permeate, orient, and direct the whole life of the society considered, as well as the concrete individuals that bodily constitute the society. This web of meanings is what I call the 'magma' of *social imaginary significations* that are carried by and embodied in the institution of the given society and that, so to speak, animate it. Such social imaginary significations are, for instance: spirits, gods, God; *polis*, citizen, nation, state, party; commodity, money, capital, interest rate; taboo, virtue, sin; and so forth. But such are also man/woman/child, as they are specified in a given society; beyond sheer anatomical or biological definitions, man, woman, and child are what they are by virtue of the social imaginary significations which make them that. (p. 7)

Castoriadis's idea of magma is, when seen in retrospect, in many ways typical for his times, that is, for the period between the end of the Second World War and the end of the twentieth century. From the *paradigm* of Thomas Kuhn (1962), the *discourse* of Michel Foucault (e.g. Foucault, 1972) and the uses of *ideology* in the 1970s, to the *doxa* of the theorists of rhetoric, most post-war schools and thinkers engaged in the wide field of philosophical anthropology have tried to devise concepts to deal with the same kind of problems as addressed by Castoriadis. But no one, I would claim, has done this as successfully as he. In order to bring out the force of the concept of magma even more clearly, let me compare it to the most salient aspects of some other concepts that have been suggested.

The magma of social imaginary significations differs from *ideology*, in that it has none of the latter's connotations of false consciousness. It is true that the magma of social imaginary significations, and the institutions, rituals, habits and language through which it is embodied, is permeated by social struggles and conflict and that it may close in upon itself in the same way as a dominant ideology might do. But contrary to the common understanding of ideology as false bourgeois consciousness, there is no way in which the insurgents of a society simply can eradicate the magma of social imaginary significations and replace it with a new one, supposedly more just or more true. The only way to change the magma of a society is to change it from within, through intellectual and conceptual critique as well as through collective action in order to change and transform the institutions of the society. One advantage with the concept of magma is thus that it takes heed of the inertia of the institutions of society. It gives any revolutionary project a more realistic basis in that it does not promise radical or quick changes. Magma allows for change through the digging of new channels, through blocking or diverting streams, through the breaking up of barriers – but not through getting rid of the existing magma altogether.

On another, more disciplinary and academic level, magma differs from *discourse* in that it does not give unwarranted precedence to language and speech (nor to semantic, linguistic meaning) over all other kinds of sense-making in society and within the academic disciplines. The magma of a society is formed around certain central social imaginary significations, and these significations may be expressed through art, architecture, city planning, social and political institutions and technologies as well as through discourses and statements. Thus the notion of magma allows for discussing the embodiment of knowledge and meaning in other and perhaps more encompassing terms than do semiotics, semiology or linguistically based philosophies of language.

Magma differs from the notion of *paradigm*, too. It does not imply, as does arguably the concept of Kuhn, that there are normal periods when development within society and or the sciences follows one paradigm that will eventually turn out to be insufficient; unrest and doubt will result for a while, and then the old paradigm will be replaced by another. There is no inherent order in magma; nor are there any guarantees against sudden eruptions or explosions – or against sedimentation and petrification. Thus, as a metaphor magma allows for the unforeseen. It does not imply any specific direction (neither in the sciences, nor in society) or give us any clue as to how we are to institute our society. Hence it works well with Castoriadis's cherished project of autonomy.

Finally, I would like to point out some promising affinities between *magma* and the *doxa* of modern rhetoric, as well as the notion of *symbolic forms* as found in Ernst Cassirer's philosophy (1955–1957). Within the broad strands in Western thinking that may be called rhetorical and sceptical philosophy respectively, that come together in the work of Chaïm Perelman and Lucie Olbrechts-Tyteca (1969), the term *doxa* has played more or less the same role as magma in Castoriadis's thought. *Doxa* is interesting in this context, since it has never been highly rated within philosophy. Instead of dealing with *doxa* (i.e. with opinions, habits, ways of being in the world) philosophy has typically sought a truth that cannot be doubted and a knowledge that never changes. Consequently it has developed techniques for separating the true from the false, the real from the illusory – in short, for separating *episteme* from *doxa*. This division is the hub around which the conflict between rhetoric and philosophy evolves. It is interesting to see that Castoriadis, in his philosophy of magma, takes a clearly doxic stance. In his philosophy, change is the condition of possibility for both knowledge and for truth. Thus, in this respect, he bridges the gap once created by Plato between rhetoric and philosophy, and may consequently be very useful for contemporary rhetorical attempts to make a case for a doxic notion of knowing, knowledge and truth. I think there are great mutual benefits to be won from approaching Castoriadis's philosophy of creation and magma to contemporary attempts within the field of rhetoric to formulate a doxic take on sense-making and knowing. Another concept, apart from the *doxa* of rhetoric, with which Castoriadis's concept of magma has great affinity, is the notion of symbolic forms as developed by the philosophical anthropologist Ernst Cassirer. Cassirer's work presents an open-ended and non-dogmatic philosophical anthropology that in many ways can be seen as a forerunner of Castoriadis's (even though the latter never, to my knowledge, referred to Cassirer). The different symbolic forms that Cassirer investigates in his philosophy – language, myth, religion, art, science, technology – are all important parts of what Castoriadis would call the magma of social imaginary significations of any known society. Working with the notions of both symbolic forms and magma, and to connect Castoriadis's philosophy of radical creation to Cassirer's wrestling with the question of human sense-making will, I have no doubt, prove to be very fecund both in the domain of philosophical anthropology and within philosophy in general.

References

Cassirer, E. (1955–1957), *The Philosophy of Symbolic Forms*, Vols 1, 2 and 3, New York: Yale University Press.

Castoriadis, C. (1987), *The Imaginary Institution of Society*, K. Blamey (trans.), Cambridge: Polity Press.

—. (1997a), *World in Fragments*, D. A. Curtis (ed. and trans.), Stanford, CA: Stanford University Press.

—. (1997b), *The Castoriadis Reader*, D. A. Curtis (ed. and trans.), Oxford: Blackwell.

—. (1997c), 'Anthropology, philosophy, politics', *Thesis Eleven*, 49, 1, 99–116.

—. (2007), *Figures of the Thinkable*, H. Arnold (trans.), Stanford, CA: Stanford University Press.

Foucault, M. (1972), *Archaeology of Knowledge*, New York: Pantheon.

Kuhn, T. S. (1962), *The Structure of Scientific Revolutions*, Chicago: University of Chicago Press.

Perelman, C. and Olbrechts-Tyteca, L. (1969), *The New Rhetoric: A Treatise on Argumentation*, Notre Dame: University of Notre Dame Press.

CHAPTER SEVEN

Psyche

Karl E. Smith

The importance of the psyche to Castoriadis's work cannot be underestimated. Although he posits autonomy as a sociopolitical project, he also observes that it must be achieved at the level of the social individual in each instance (Castoriadis, 1987, pp. 101–102; 1997a, p. 129). While society is by definition a social-historical institution, the structures of a society (whether an autonomous one or not) are 'threatened by individual transgressions, a result of the fact that at the core of each human being is to be found a singular psyche, irreducible and indomitable' (Castoriadis, 1997a, p. 85; see Gauchet, 1997, p. 49). The centrality of the psyche is nowhere clearer than in Castoriadis's observation that the question which has long driven sociology – the question of the 'relationship between the individual and society' – is the wrong question. The focus, he argues, should instead be on the relationship between the psyche and society, for these are the two irreducible poles of the relationship. The individual, in contrast, is the always already socialized psyche (Castoriadis, 1987, pp. 102–107; 1997a, p. 134) and, as such, is in a very real sense a social-historical institution – an artefact of society, so to speak. That is, there is no sense in discussing a 'relation' between the individual and society when there is no individual without society having already imposed itself upon the singular psyche – and been internalized by the psyche.

There are two very important points to make as a prelude to any discussion of the psyche, one methodological, the other historical. Methodologically, it is essential to recognize that no one has ever 'seen' a psyche – our observations and conclusions are limited to inferences drawn on the basis of its effects. On this point, Castoriadis observes that despite a lifetime ambition to establish psychoanalysis as a positivist science, in the end Freud acknowledged that even if one day our technology could reveal 'a direct relation between psychic life and the nervous system', as fMRI (functional magnetic resonance imaging) and other devices seem to be getting very close to doing, this would 'at the most afford an exact localization of the processes of consciousness, and would give us no help in understanding them' (Castoriadis, 1984, p. 4). Indeed, recent developments in neuro-plasticity have revealed that any 'exact localization' of these processes is problematized by the fact that the locations of neurological functions are fluid and dynamic – they can relocate to different areas of the brain as required to compensate[1] for acquired brain injuries as well as changes elsewhere in the neural system (e.g. the loss of a limb, or an organ) (see Doidge, 2007). The point here is that our understandings of psychic life continue to depend upon inferences drawn from observations of effects, rather than from direct observations of sources and processes.

Historically, etymologically, the term *psyche* (*psuchē*) is the ancient Greek term for the 'soul' (Castoriadis, 1997a, p. 150). Hence, for most of Western history it has been understood in religious terms, as something of the spirit world, independent of corporeality and materiality, something 'belonging to the realm of God or the gods' (Gauchet, 2002, p. 17). In this sense, one can think of psychology, psychoanalysis and their derivatives as efforts to develop a 'science of the soul' (Castoriadis, 1984, pp. 3ff.), after science displaced religious interpretations of human life. Freud, for example, sought the somatic bases of psychic activity, linking eros, or libido, with the pleasure-principle and the self-preservation instinct. In this rendering, the soul is no longer drawn towards the divine; rather, a wholly somatic psyche is reduced to evolutionary functions of biological self-preservation or species reproduction.[2]

One of Castoriadis's most important contributions to understanding the psyche (as well as the social individual and the social-historical) is his observation that the formation and functioning of the human psyche is not determined by mere biological imperatives, but has been defunctionalized such that 'representational pleasures' become dominant over 'organ pleasures' (Castoriadis, 1987, p. 314; 1994, pp. 145–146; 1997a, pp. 150–151, 161–162, 180). The psyche, Castoriadis says, is an 'unlimited and unmasterable representative flux, a representational spontaneity that is not enslaved to an ascribable end' (1997a, p. 151), which means that it exceeds the minimal requirements for – and the rationalities of – self-preservation and species-reproduction, as well as exceeding any simple reflection of the natural or objective world; it is irreducible to any rationality or ends-means logic.

Ontologically, however, it is clear that the *living being* must also fulfil those self-preservation functions, at least most of the time and to a more or less significant extent (depending on 'life opportunities', etc.). Castoriadis identifies the psyche as one of the four regions of being that can be understood as modes *for-itself* (along with the living being, the social individual and society/social-historical; Castoriadis, 1997a, pp. 143, 150–154; see also *The Living Being*). The 'essential attributes of the for-itself', according to Castoriadis, are 'the finality of self-preservation, self-centeredness, and the construction of a proper world' (Castoriadis, 1997a, p. 143). The for-itself is discussed in detail in the entry on *The Living Being*, so I will not elaborate on the development of Castoriadis's idea that self-finality entails creating a 'world of one's own' (p. 145); for our purposes what is important is that the for-itself creates a proper world of its own, *in and from* a world external to it; a world that is already there before it, and one which remains beyond its capacity to know and control. Importantly, Castoriadis is adamant that this 'external world' is itself a socially constituted reality: for humans 'there is no reality outside of that over which society and its institutions "reign", . . . there is never any reality other than socially instituted reality' (Castoriadis, 1987, p. 312). The psychical for-itself constructs an imaginary world of its own; the psyche is this capacity for imagining a world, for imaging a world external to itself and ordering it into meaningful representations. The dominance of representational pleasures means that the human subject can take pleasure from its efforts to modify the world around it; s/he finds pleasures

in making an object, in talking with others, in hearing a story or a song, in looking at a painting, in demonstrating a theorem or in acquiring knowledge – and also, in learning that others have a 'good opinion' of him [or her] and even in thinking that he [or she] has 'acted well'. (p. 315)

Here it is worth noting that we are dealing with an embodied agent – an actor intentionally taking on the world, actively responding to her/his situation, actively engaged in sustaining particular social institutions. Indeed, Castoriadis argues that there cannot be 'any essential ultimate distinction between . . . psyche and soma' (Castoriadis, 1997a, p. 177); 'the body is always, in a sense, psychical and the psyche always, in certain regards, somatical' (p. 180). We are discussing an embodied being who takes an intentional stance towards the objects and the subjects that it encounters in the world. At the level of the psyche, the idea of defunctionalization serves to disconnect the pleasure principle from the self-preservation instinct; as Castoriadis observes, it is not only possible but quite conceivable that someone might commit suicide for the 'pleasure' of preserving their self-image (p. 151).

Literature, art, music, theatre, etc. serve no evolutionary or biological functions; they provide pleasure for pleasure's sake. They do, however, serve important social purposes – including defining, recording, being a culture's collective expression of norms, values and distinctions, etc. – that is, expressions of a cultural world. These are particular expressions of what Castoriadis calls the radical social imaginary.

At the level of the psyche, Castoriadis calls the capacity to visualize, or conceptualize – to *imagine* – that which is not there the *radical imagination* (Castoriadis, 1987, p. 369). With the radical imagination comes the ability to create: to bring into being things which have never previously existed. For Castoriadis the radical imagination demands meaningful explanation of the representations, affects and intents it generates/perceives. 'What is most human is not rationality but the uncontrolled and uncontrollable continuous surge of *creative radical imagination* in and through the [psychic] flux of representation, affect and desires' (Castoriadis, 1997a, pp. 127–128; see the *Creative Imagination*). Contrary to the dominant trend in the history of Western thought, we find that 'reason' is but a creation of the radical imagination. Although deployed by *legein*, reason goes beyond *legein* in becoming autonomous reflection (see Legein *and* Teukhein). However, reason (and thus the psycho/social individual) frequently becomes trapped in the particular *ensemblist-identitarian (ensidic) logics* of the social-historical (see *Ensemblistic-Identiarian Logic*). This occurs when the institutions of the social imaginary become alienated from the instituting subjects (see *Heteronomy*).

The implications of the creative radical imagination lead to a controversial aspect of Castoriadis's work, for he contends that, contrary to all previous philosophy, the human animal has the capacity of *creatio ex nihilo* – to create something from nothing. It is, he argues, 'the radical imagination that makes a "first" representation arise out of a nothingness of representation, that is to say, out of *nothing*' (Castoriadis, 1987, p. 283). Clearly most human creations are made manifest *with* things (materials, objects, symbols) that already exist, and all are made *in* a pre-existing social and physical context. But Castoriadis is especially interested in those new creations which come from nothing other than the radical social imaginary. The great cultural works – works of art, but also and especially new forms of social organization – are not mere adaptations or interpretations of their predecessors; they are wholly new creations of the radical social imaginary (see *Creative Imagination*).

What is important for our purposes is that the radical imagination *is* the psychic flux. The psychic flux, Castoriadis argues, is 'the emergence of representations accompanied by an affect and inserted into an intentional process' (p. 282). These three 'essential determinants'[3] – the representation, the affect and the intention – are indissociable, both in fact and in theory (p. 282). The energetic field, the psychic upsurge, has the characteristics of a *magma*, which means that its constituents, or determinants, intermingle, flowing together in such a way that even to say 'accompanied by' or 'inserted into' as Castoriadis does in the previous quotation, is what he would call an 'abuse of language', which arises from the need to impose the structures of language into our discussion of this 'thing' which is not a 'thing' in any conventional (ensemblistic-identitarian) sense of the term; a thing which is beyond the structures of language, perpetually failing to (fully) con-*form* to its forms.[4]

The psychical is continuous – a flux of forms, but a formless flux: chaos. This flux is not just a temporary developmental condition, but continues for the life-span of the individual; it can be formed and is in constant need of being formed, but is beyond control, beyond conscious cognition. For the individual human being to survive, order must be imposed upon this chaos; the forms must be structured, so to speak. But the psyche has no intrinsic resources for constructing order of the world around it beyond its own capacity to 'distinguish-choose-posit-assemble-count-speak' (p. 223) (see Legein *and* Teukhein). Thrown into a world not of its making and beyond its control, the newborn child begins to search for meaning (order, structure) outside of itself, through significant others in the process known as socialization.

Most importantly, for Castoriadis, the psyche is itself the source, the genesis of emergent representations (Castoriadis, 1987, p. 276; 1997a, p. 273). These representations are independent of, and quite distinct from, social imaginary significations. The psyche is a formlessness which forms itself, yet forms itself in accordance with forms that it finds in social imaginary significations (this will become clearer in the discussion of socialization below). Here Castoriadis provides a correction to the history of philosophical thought about sense data (an issue at the heart of epistemology and a fundamental problem in the philosophy of mind): How do sensory impressions of what is external to the perceiving subject come to be internal to the subject? Castoriadis's response is that the external does not become internal, but rather that the psyche generates its own representations, both independently and in response to its sensory experience (Castoriadis, 1987, pp. 283ff.). But in order to make sense of these representations, to make them meaningful, it must draw upon and incorporate the social imaginary significations that are available in its particular social-historical milieu. Perceiving is representing, and 'representation pertains to the radical imagination; it is radical imagination manifesting itself and taking shape [*le figurant*]. It is so just as much when it is perceptual representation and when it "leans" . . . on a being-thus of the sensible' (Castoriadis, 1997a, p. 273). Furthermore, Castoriadis argues, it is not sufficient 'to say that perceiving presupposes imagining. To perceive is to imagine, in the literal and active sense of this term. To perceive (as well as to remember) is a species of imagining, perception a variant of representation' (p. 273).[5] This is the basis for the earlier claim that the psychical for-itself constructs an imaginary world of its own; its sensory perceptions of the external world are every bit as imaginary as its phantasms and dreams. The genesis of representations is an autopoietic psychic activity, an activity that remains beyond (complete or total) rational self-control, objective knowledge, etc. Another way to say this is that these processes remain *unconscious*, which I will discuss in more detail later.

Despite its autopoiesis and self-constitution, the psyche *can only* constitute itself with and from the forms available to it in the social-historical world. This world includes a society: both significant others and the generalized others of the anonymous collective. It is a world instituted by social imaginary significations (Castoriadis, 1987, pp. 135ff., 235, 359; 1997b, p. 313) or the 'discourses of the other' (Castoriadis, 1987, pp. 102–103; see 1997b, pp. 155, 311). While representations, affects and intentions may be seen to be 'internally' generated by the psychic flux, they must also be seen to be 'externally' stimulated – but not determined – by the *shock*[6] (*Anstoss*) of the subject's encounter with the external world. The psyche must distinguish-separate-order-choose – that is, it must *create* a world, making sense of the chaos, constructing a world of its own *with*, *from* and *in* the flux of representations, affects and intentions that it generates (Castoriadis, 1987, pp. 149, 300). This representing, this imaging/creating, is always an activity (not always an intentional activity, but always an activity) of an embodied subject immersed in a world of embodied subjects, physical objects and so on. These subjects and objects, etc., precede the world constructed by the psyche, and are thus present to the psyche in what we might think of as pre-imagined forms, what Castoriadis calls *social imaginary significations*. Social 'institutions and social imaginary significations are creations of the radical social instituting imaginary', which is, in turn 'the creative capacity of the anonymous collectivity' (Castoriadis, 1997a, p. 131). Here, the anonymous collectivity is a synonym for the social-historical which, as mentioned, has the characteristics of the for-itself. As we have seen, this entails the characteristics of self-finality and constructing a world of its own. Which is to say that the newborn psyche enters a world that has already been constructed in social imaginary significations by the particular society in which it finds itself, and must find (construct) its self.

Society, as for-itself, must institute itself, form itself, create social institutions and then protect and sustain those institutions. Self-preservation demands that new members of the collective are instituted in conformity with the prevailing social institutions: the social individual is itself a social institution. In many and various ways, the social-historical – society – imposes particular forms, particular norms, upon the individual psyche. The psyche forms itself into a social individual through intercourse with the radical social instituting imaginary (Castoriadis, 1987, pp. 311–312). Of course, this does not mean that every social individual is in conformity with all social norms and institutions; and the situation is clearly far more complex in globalized, cosmopolitan, multicultural and multi-faith mass societies than in smaller monocultures. But even in the most dynamic postmodern megalopolis, the individual must internalize – sublimate – some set of values, norms, institutions, etc., in order to create a place from which to take a stand while resisting or negotiating the demands of competing/imposing social forces.

In its initial state, the psyche is incapable of distinguishing between self and other, or self and world. It can only, and must, refer everything to itself *as* itself. Castoriadis therefore takes issue with Freud's choice of the term 'primary narcissism', a preference for the self 'to the exclusion of all others'. Instead, Castoriadis argues, we must think of a *totalitarian inclusion* (p. 294); a psychic form (or, more precisely, a preformed psyche) that precedes the ability to distinguish self from other; a psyche which represents itself to itself as undifferentiated, omnipotent and self-sufficient. Inevitably, however, this phantasy of totality is ruptured by desire; by the *absence* of the object of desire (the infamous 'absent breast' is the most obvious example here). This absence brings the other – and then another – into focus (the mother and then the father in the stereotypical psychoanalytical scenario). Castoriadis calls this encounter with the others the 'triadic phase' (p. 300), arguing that fragmentation of the psychical flux is inevitable and necessary, and yet the phantasy of monadic closure, the phantasy of totality, never dissipates. It remains a driving force throughout life (Castoriadis, 1997a, p. 128).

Hence there is a tension between openness and closure that appears to be imposed upon the psyche by its necessary and inevitable immersion in a social-historical world (p. 154). The theory of a 'psychic monad' that is fragmented in a 'triadic phase' implies that the newborn psyche is perhaps potentially satisfied as an undifferentiated, homogeneous flux. But this potential disappears with the appearance of the others. In the fragmentation, as the psyche moves from a monadic to a triadic condition, the primordial condition is fundamentally changed, altering the ontological ground (pp. 311–312). That which generates and forms – the psyche – has been transformed; re-constituted in the forming. And hence the perpetual desire for monadic closure ultimately cannot be satisfied; there can be no return to the primordial, preformed, psychic monad.

According to Castoriadis, the primary form(less-ness) of the psychic flux is chaos. The chaotic flux must be formed into images that are meaningful in the tension between self and other, between opening and closure. Socialization is the process of forming the psychic flux by sublimating social imaginary significations (Castoriadis, 1987, pp. 311–312; 1997b, pp. 154–155). Socialization/sublimation is the process through which the psyche/society institutes form, constructing a world of its own even while constituting itself as a socially instituted individual (Castoriadis, 1987, p. 311).[7] The human subject comes into being in the process of instituting form in and from the psychic flux (pp. 105–106). But the institution of the psychic flux is neither a simple external imposition, nor merely an autopoietic expression of an innate organization. As we have seen, it is a multifaceted interaction between the radical imagination of the singular psyche and the social instituting imaginary of the anonymous collective. 'It is the produced and productive union of the self and the other (or the world)' (p. 105). Society (attempts to) impose(s) various institutions and the psyche *must* institute meanings for itself with reference to these social institutions. The two processes are mutually irreducible.

The new psyche enters the world as an unformed, chaotic psychic flux of indistinct representations and a drive towards closure, but the need to create meaning drives an opposite move towards openness. In other words, although the unformed psyche has an insatiable desire for instituted closure, it is always and at the same time intrinsically open to new meanings, institutions and norms with which to form that closure. The demand for meaning creates a need for resources that the radical imagination cannot supply for itself; it does not have the resources from which to affect the closure it desires. Paradoxically, the psyche must actively open itself to the other to satisfy its need for the materials from which to construct its own closure. 'The psyche is a *forming*, which exists in and through *what* it forms and *how* it forms, it is . . . formation and imagination' (p. 283). The unformed psyche *must* form itself, but can only form itself as a self through being-with-others: other socialized individuals who are the bearers (instituting-institutions) of *a* particular society's social imaginary significations. Only through being-with-others can the psyche acquire the representations, norms and meanings, etc. that are necessary for it to construct itself as a self (p. 108).

Castoriadis frequently returns to Freud's famous phrase: 'Where Id was, there Ego shall be' (Castoriadis, 1987, p. 102; 1997a, p. 421 n. 4). Among the problems with this formulation, he points out, is that even if we could clearly distinguish the Id from the Ego, it would be an impossibility to bring all of Id into consciousness (Ego). A better expression of this poetic practice, he argues, comes if we turn this around and say: 'Where Ego is, Id should also emerge' (Castoriadis, 1997a, p. 128) – to bring the unconscious into the light; to distinguish between psychical phantasies and perceptions; to achieve greater lucidity and clarity about the particular relationship between the radical imagination at the core of the human psyche and the radical social instituting imaginary; and to change the relationship between the representation, the affect and the intentions. These are not all the same thing, yet they are inseparable. On the one hand we are invoking a 'different relationship' between the unconscious and consciousness – bringing more of the unconscious into consciousness, and thus enabling the individual to have greater control over their responses to the affects and intentions of the psychic flux (i.e. one cannot control the flux per se, but can to some extent control how one responds to the flux). On the other hand, we are discussing a different relationship to the internalized 'discourses of the other'. Discussions of the political project of autonomy tend to focus on this latter development; the institution of autonomous subjects requires first that they internalize the discourses of the other, and then self-reflexively make these discourses their own. Yet Castoriadis observes that this new relationship with the discourses of the other is contingent upon the social subject also developing a different relationship with its unconscious phantasies and drives. The similarities between the philosophical 'man of reason' from Plato to Descartes are obvious here – we are certainly discussing what Descartes referred to as the need to acquire control over the passions. What Castoriadis makes clear, though, is that this control is never once-and-for-all, never final or complete. The genesis of phantasms (of passions, drives, etc.) is interminable and ultimately irrepressible. Furthermore, and most importantly, the reason of inherited thought is presented as a faculty internal to the thinking subject; whereas, for Castoriadis, what has traditionally been called reason is in fact a plurality of ensidic logics – a magma of logics which is particular to a culture or society – which have been internalized by the psyche during the institution of the social individual. Put this way, the traditional view maintains that the person of reason is one who has managed to control his/her passions (drives, phantasms) in accordance with the magma of social imaginary institutions peculiar to his/her particular culture. Castoriadis's radical breakthrough is to see that autonomy can only be achieved when this magma of social imaginary significations is also called into question – by each autonomous individual, and thus by the collective anonymous itself.

He therefore defines the aim of the project of autonomy at the level of the psyche as 'instaurating another kind of relationship between the reflective subject (of will and of thought)' – that is, the socially instituted individual – and his or her 'Unconscious – that is, radical imagination', the pre-instituted/pre-formed flux of representation, affects and intentions (Castoriadis, 1997a, p. 132) (see *Autonomy*). Each psyche enters the world anew, unformed, needing form and forming itself in and with the forms present in the social imaginary. The social subject is thus this particular social individual, an embodied and psychical being that has formed itself, created a world of its own in and from the world in which it is immersed. Castoriadis understands the psyche to be compelled to make meaning, to make sense of its encounter with the world. But we must also recognize that in many, if not most instances, form is imposed upon the psyche by the social imaginary; that is, the social-historical, the other. In short, con-*form*-ance is often compulsory, demanded by significant and generalized others, by the anonymous collective.

Yet Castoriadis is also clear that the psychic flux is unquenchable, unmasterable; the forms it assumes are not 'once-and-for-all'; and therefore all psychic formations – whether imposed, compelled or voluntarily internalized – are at least in principle always potentially under threat from within the psyche itself. In the same way, the institutions of society are also in principle at least threatened by the perpetual dynamics of the individuals' psychic flux. Yet it is these same dynamics that render possible the instauration of autonomous modes of being; autonomous societies and autonomous subjectivities. For these institutions (societies and subjects) to be autonomous requires critical self-reflexivity focused upon the forms of the institutions themselves; an acceptance that the forms that have been instituted are self-generated, self-instituted and can be re-formed by this form that is simultaneously a forming. From this perspective, the place of psychoanalysis in Castoriadis's project of autonomy is to enable social individuals to more clearly elucidate their own self-forming in order to re-form it (pp. 128–129). As discussed in *Autonomy*, Castoriadis chooses to pursue a project of autonomy, which entails creating autonomous social institutions. At the level of the psyche this entails becoming increasingly cognizant of the instituted forms, the processes of institutions and the capacity to re-form. It also entails recognizing that the forms serve a function but cannot be reduced to these functions, and are certainly not inherently optimally functional.

Notes

1 Not always adequately, of course; perhaps all too frequently, pathologically.

2 Of course, it would also be overly simplistic to reduce Freud's body of work to this characterization. Nevertheless, as I will discuss later, Castoriadis and others have observed that Freud's desire to establish psychoanalysis as a robust, positive science produced various distortions in his interpretations of his data.

3 The term 'determinant' seems rather unfortunate, and should perhaps be replaced or avoided. I prefer constituents, or components – but must emphasize the *magma*-like characteristics of this flux: these are not 'separate' or even separa*ble* components, but three intermingled and co-dependent aspects of the psychic flux.

4 One of the techniques of some psycho-therapies, however, is to effect an effective separation between the affect and the intention and the representation. I will return to this later in discussing the role of psychoanalysis in the political project of autonomy.

5 A thorough discussion of the issue of perception would take us too far off-track from our focus here. For a more detailed discussion see 'Merleau-Ponty and the weight of the ontological tradition' (Castoriadis, 1997a, pp. 273–310).

6 This seems to be an unfortunate choice of term, implying unpleasantness, or even violence, which is not necessarily always a part of the encounter with the world. I would prefer a term with rather less 'shocking' implications (Smith, 2010, p. 98, n. 5), but I retain Castoriadis's choice of term here in the effort to more accurately reflect his thought.

7 Note that whereas conventional psychology understands sublimation to be the transformation of socially unacceptable impulses into socially acceptable actions or response, and Freud understood sublimation to be the conversion of sexual drives into other forms of cultural expression, for Castoriadis, sublimation is synonymous with socialization: the formation of the psychic flux in accordance with social institutions and imaginary significations (Castoriadis, 1987, pp. 311–316).

References

Castoriadis, C. (1984), *Crossroads in the Labyrinth*, K. Soper and M. H. Ryle (trans.), Cambridge, MA: MIT Press.

—. (1987), *The Imaginary Institution of Society*, K. Blamey (trans.), Cambridge: Polity Press.

—. (1994), 'Radical imagination and the social instituting imaginary', in G. Robinson and J. Rundell (eds), *Rethinking Imagination: Culture and Creativity*, London and New York: Routledge, pp. 136–154.

—. (1997a), *World in Fragments*, D. A. Curtis (ed. and trans.), Stanford, CA: Stanford University Press.

—. (1997b), *Castoriadis Reader*, D. A. Curtis (ed. and trans.), Oxford: Blackwell.

Doidge, N. (2007), *The Brain that Changes Itself: Stories of Personal Triumph From the Frontiers of Brain Science*, New York: Penguin.

Gauchet, M. (1997), *The Disenchantment of the World: A Political History of Religion*, O. Burge (trans.), New French Thought, Princeton: Princeton University Press.

—. (2002), 'Redefining the Unconscious', *Thesis Eleven*, 71, 4–23.

Smith, K. E. (2010), *Meaning, Subjectivity, Society: Making Sense of Modernity*, Leiden: Brill.

CHAPTER EIGHT

Social-Historical

Angelos Mouzakitis

Of all Castoriadis's concepts it is his elaboration of the *social-historical* that led critics like Habermas (1987, p. 330) to the conclusion that Castoriadis's view of society is but a continuation of earlier attempts to wed Marxism and phenomenology, or a modification of Heidegger's fundamental ontology. Habermas argues that by introducing 'a unique linguistic turn' to earlier attempts at formulating a philosophy of *praxis*, Castoriadis enlivens an intellectual tradition inaugurated by the young Marcuse and earns a central place among the philosophies of *praxis* that evolved 'since the mid-1960s, especially in Eastern Europe' (p. 327).

Although it seems difficult to establish a direct relationship with Heidegger's fundamental ontology, it is equally difficult to fail to acknowledge an indirect Heideggerian impact on Castoriadis's writings of the period of his so-called ontological turn, in the sense that these writings are informed by a relentless critique of key Heideggerian concepts like those of ontological difference and authentic historicity. However, the existence of an 'ontological turn' in Castoriadis's philosophy in the 1970s seems undeniable, even though the origins of his 'ontology of the social-historical' should be primarily sought in his long dialogue with the French phenomenological tradition and especially with Merleau-Ponty and Ricoeur rather than Heidegger (see Adams, 2011, pp. 2–3).

Castoriadis introduces the term *social-historical* in *The Imaginary Institution of Society* in an explicit reworking of his own meditations on the issue in the 1964–1965 article 'Marxism and revolutionary theory' published in *Socialisme ou Barbarie* (Castoriadis, 1987, p. 2). Castoriadis aims in this manner to overcome what he considers to be a fallacious distinction between society and history, since, as he writes, history *is* nothing but the 'unfolding in time' of the social-historical itself (p. 112). In this sense he believes that it would be mistaken to even define history as a *dimension* of society, since history is not something 'external' to society, but the very 'self-deployment of society' (Castoriadis, 1999, p. 262). He argues that the inability of inherited thought to grasp the belonging-together of society and history, results in theories that essentially misinterpret society and history and which fail to acknowledge the social-historical's proper mode of being (Castoriadis, 1987, pp. 167–169). Indeed, he holds that a clear-cut distinction between these aspects of human life could at best only serve analytical purposes.

The tension between a synchronic and diachronic analysis of societies looms large in sociology and modern social theory ever since August Comte's introduction of the dichotomy between social *statics* and social *dynamics* (Mazlish, 2006, p. 412). Despite the potentially positive effect of this distinction for the development of sociological research, Castoriadis is critical of its ossification that may ultimately result in the mystification of the mode of being characteristic of human societies.

Thus, the very concept of the social-historical suggests that all human societies – even so-called cold traditional societies – have their respective modes of historicity. It is exactly this difference in the *mode* of historicity exemplified in the case of each historical society that in Castoriadis's view has misled some authors to speak of historically 'cold' and 'hot' societies, a distinction originating in the writings of Lévi-Strauss (Castoriadis, 1987, p. 185). Castoriadis attempts to conceptually grasp the enigmatic mode of being of societies in general (i.e. the social-historical) when he defines the social-historical as 'the anonymous collective whole, the impersonal-human element that fills every given social formation but which also engulfs it', or as 'the union and the tension of instituting society and of instituted society, of history made and history in the making' (p. 108).

Arguably, this definition already contains both the main insights and the fundamental *aporiae* that his conception of society entails. Castoriadis conceptualizes the social-historical as a field which 'can never be grasped in itself but only in its "effects"' (p. 144), or even more emphatically as 'a non-being that is more real than any being' (p. 111). This conception arguably challenges the very notion of determinacy on which rests the whole edifice of Western metaphysics, or of 'inherited thought' in Castoriadis's terminology.

In Castoriadis's view the mode of being proper to the social-historical is not only obscured by traditional thought, but it is even inaccessible to it. This happens insofar as traditional thought is caught up in the confines of what Castoriadis calls *identitary logic*, while he describes the mode of being of the social-historical with the aid of a geological metaphor, as that of *magma* or of *magma of magmas* (p. 182; see *Ensemblistic-Identitarian Logic* and *Magma*).

Identitary logic is an umbrella term encapsulating the logical processes underlying mathematics, philosophical logic and scientific discourse in general. It represents the kind of logic underlying the entire development of the Western civilization, which is premised on a conception of being and thought as determined (see *Ensemblistic-Identitarian Logic*). Although he states that he is aware of 'the anachronism and the stretching of words' involved in this conception, Castoriadis declares the theory of mathematical sets to be the best exemplification of this logic, since it rests upon well-defined and therefore easily identifiable individual elements, the relations between which can be in principle extrapolated (p. 221). On the one hand, Castoriadis acknowledges the validity of identitary logic – and of the 'ontology that is homologous to it' on a specific level of being, which he calls 'first natural stratum' (p. 175), but challenges its adequacy for providing a non-reified explanatory model of social life (see Anlehnung and *The Living Being*). On the other hand, the very choice of the term '*magma*' for the description of the social-historical exemplifies Castoriadis's attempt to grasp both the collective and individual dimensions of human life as fluid, restless, potentially explosive and essentially indeterminate (see *Magma*).

Furthermore, this *magma* is likened to 'a web of meanings' that are 'carried by and embodied by the institution of the given society and that, so to speak, animate it' (Castoriadis, 1997a, p. 7), while Castoriadis offers by way of example a host of different imaginary significations on the basis of which the fabric of meaning of historical societies is woven, such as 'spirits, gods, God; *polis*, citizen, nation, state, party; commodity, money, capital, interest rate; taboo, virtue, sin; and so forth' (p. 7).

This conception entails that the mode of being of the social-historical is considered identical with the mode of being of *imagination* (Castoriadis, 1987, p. 172) and that therefore the social-historical is *essentially* indeterminacy (p. 199), since imaginary significations neither 'correspond to' nor are they 'exhausted by, references to "rational" or "real" elements' but are rather posited through an act of *creation* proper (Castoriadis, 1997a, p. 8).

Now, Castoriadis is certainly not the first thinker to underline the *creative* character of the faculty of imagination, and among the important precedents one could mention romanticism or more recently even Marcuse's interpretation of Novalis and Freud in his *Eros and Civilization*. However, Castoriadis is arguably the only contemporary thinker that turned creative imagination into *the* central theme of his theoretical construction (see the *Creative Imagination*).

In effect, Castoriadis thinks of the social-historical as existing in two main modes of being, namely as *instituting* and as *instituted*. First and foremost, this conception entails the identification of society, history and institution, which is yet another way of expressing the indissoluble bond between the social-historical and the generation of *meaning* (see *Institution* and *Social Imaginary Significations*). This marks the radical differentiation between social and natural formations as Castoriadis readily admits already in his early writings in the context of his discussion of Weber and Marx (Castoriadis, 1988, pp. 48–49).

Of course Castoriadis's mature conceptualization of *meaning* as the fundamental aspect of human life radically departs from Weber's perspective which in his view remains imprisoned in the rationalistic and individualistic confines of neo-Kantian epistemology (p. 365). As with every dichotomy, there is certainly a difficulty in relation to the postulated dichotomy between the instituting and the instituted moments of the social-historical, as it seems to introduce an irreconcilable dualism at the very heart of sociohistorical processes.

Although it has been rightly suggested that the dichotomy between the instituted and the instituting moments should not be overemphasized and that consequently the social-historical should be seen as an *event* considered in the totality of its modes of being (Delcroix, 2006, p. 229), it is undeniable that Castoriadis understands the social-historical on the basis of this essential dichotomy, or as the *unique* unfolding of the interplay between those two 'moments' that occurs each time.

Thus, the 'instituting' moment refers to the dynamic creation of unprecedented forms of life, their introduction to – and subsequent establishment in – the common social world. On the contrary, the 'instituted' moment is the moment of the mere re-production of already created forms of life. As mere 'reproduction' it entails a certain degree of self-alienation of the social-historical institution that is concurrent with the *reification* of the various institutions of which a given sociohistorical formation is made up. In other words, societies become self-alienated or *heteronomous* (Castoriadis, 1987, p. 372) whenever individually and collectively they are oblivious to the fact that they create-institute themselves and their corresponding 'worlds' (p. 370), or to put it in yet another manner when they *refuse* to acknowledge that they institute themselves (p. 214; see *Heteronomy*).

This conception has important repercussions for the very manner in which the social-historical is elaborated. Consequently, the instituting moment is elucidated as the *essential* mode of being of the social-historical and as such it is directly linked with the '*magma*' – like character of radical imagination and with the political aim of collective and individual *autonomy*. Based on an essentially indeterminate level of being, that of the unconscious/imaginary, the social-historical *creates* itself in ways that lie beyond the grasp of identitary logic. Or, to be more precise, the *instituting* moment of the social-historical defies the rules of inherited logic (see *Creation* ex nihilo). Castoriadis's attack on traditional conceptions of historical change, and especially on the Hegelian and Marxian attempts to grasp history in terms of a necessary, immanent and at bottom logical unfolding of spirit or matter, respectively, rests on this assumption (Castoriadis, 1987, pp. 112–113).

We encounter therefore a conception of history as essentially incessant *creation* – and self-creation – of radically new forms (*eide*) from the level of primary significations, of a creation *ex nihilo*

(p. 361). Or, to be more precise, Castoriadis theorizes history as society's incessant 'self-alteration' which entails *both* the creation and destruction of forms. It has to be noted in this respect that *destruction* is of equal importance with creation proper insofar as it points to a radical difference between nature and society. More specifically, Castoriadis argues that human creations are properly destroyed; they are not simply de-composed nor can they serve as components of a new form of being after their initial decomposition, as happens in nature (Castoriadis, 1999, pp. 262–263).

This position would be obviously one-sided – and perhaps even unsustainable – if it were not for the postulation of the instituted moment of the social-historical. This instituted moment suggests that social life has already taken some distance from its creative dimension and therefore the social practices associated with this mode of being are not alien to identitary dimensions of being and thinking. To this, we should add Castoriadis's important insight regarding the necessity of a fundamental compliance between nature and society, which he calls society's *leaning on* (*étayage/Anlhenung*, a term borrowed by Freud), *the first natural substratum* (see p. 120; see also Anlehnung). In other words, Castoriadis maintains that *society leans* on nature so as to create a rich nexus of significations, which is not determined by what is usually thought under the guise of 'nature' insofar as society's mode of being is radically different from that of the first natural substratum (p. 270). Again, we encounter in this formulation the problem of a theme that traditionally occupied the meditations of almost all important sociologists and social theorists, namely the question concerning the dependence of social formations on their natural environment (systems theories – especially those of Parsons – being particularly emblematic).

Now, it has to be noted that by insisting on society's *leaning on* nature Castoriadis pays heed to the complex relationship between indeterminate and determinate social processes, determination being both linked to the biological dimensions and prerequisites of human life *and* to the mere reproduction of already established patterns of collective and individual being. Such re-production is never mere repetition but rather involves a dynamic expansion of the already established themes, which however does not attain the level of *creation* proper, that is, it is not tantamount to the introduction of radically new *eide*, or forms of life (p. 262).

At the same time, the very mentioning of the *first* natural substratum could be interpreted as pointing both to the essential multi-dimensionality of nature and to Castoriadis's idea about the need to think of being in general in its multiplicity, or to think of being in terms of 'no-identity' (see *The Living Being*). In the same vein, this conception introduces a new ontological level and the need to reinterpret the very distinction between the so-called natural and social realms, which is also expressed as the difference between *nomos* and *physis*. Indicative in this respect is Castoriadis's insight that identitary logic might have limited access even to the world of nature, as quantum physics seem to indicate (p. 264).

However, in Castoriadis's view the most important attribute of the social-historical is that its 'ontological form' is auto-reflexive. In other words, he maintained that the mode of being of the social-historical allows it to put itself into question, to put into question the very 'laws of its existence' (p. 264; see also *Autonomy*). Importantly, the social-historical creates a 'closure of meaning'; it creates its own 'world', which is at the same time 'natural', 'supernatural' and 'human'. In other words the social-historical creates the entirety of meanings, practices and worldviews one encounters in the context of a given society (p. 265).

In his attempt to define closure of meaning or the kind of closure characteristic of significations, Castoriadis draws a parallel with mathematics in *Fait et a Faire* (Castoriadis, 1997a). In this field, the notion of closure indicates that all solutions to the equations produced with the aid of elements belonging to a given 'set of elements', belongs also to this same 'set'. He therefore maintains that closure of meaning represents a state-of-affairs where all questioning is limited to the very confines of the existent *magma* of social significations characterizing a given social formation. Indeed, Castoriadis takes a step further to argue that a society that is completely closed in terms of meaning is by definition *heteronomous*, since it is a society that is ultimately incapable of radically questioning its own foundations (see *Heteronomy*). Castoriadis traces the reason of this inability to the postulation of a supra-historical entity or realm as the alleged source of the institution, a process that he understands in terms of collective misrecognition or self-alienation, although he used the term far less frequently after the publication of *The Imaginary Institution of Society* (Castoriadis, 1987). In Castoriadis's view this alienation characterizes human history by and large with the

notable exceptions of the Greek *polis* and of European-American
modernity (see *Modernity*). In these two instances such radical
questioning of established institutions becomes the very essence
of collective life, making possible the rekindling of politics proper
(Castoriadis, 1997a, p. 271).

In an essay entitled 'The imaginary: Creation in the social-
historical domain' (Castoriadis, 1997b), Castoriadis draws
a distinction between the concept of closure in biology (and
especially in the work of Varela) and closure in relation to the
social-historical field. He argues that social-historical closure
differs from biological closure in several essential ways. First,
social-historical closure does not have a 'physical basis' in the
same way that the genetic code provides a basis for the closure
of the biological organism. Second, society creates its closure in
terms of *meaning*, that is, everything that occurs in the context
of a given social formation should fall under the categories of
meaningful or meaningless but it can never be merely understood
as 'noise'. Third, the 'fabrication of information' characteristic of
sociohistorical formations is never reducible to functional aspects
while being 'virtually limitless' at the same time. Fourth, the kind
of 'finality' pertaining to social-historical formations is different
from the finality ruling the development of biological organisms at
least in one essential respect, namely the fact that what is at stake
in the case of social-historical formations is the preservation of a
complex nexus of arbitrary attributes, that is, of 'social imaginary
significations'. Fifth, in contrast to biological organisms, societies
create ontological forms 'without physical correlates in a massive
and wholesale way'; and finally, societies 'create a new type of self-
reference: it creates its own metaobservers (and all the awkward
problems they create)' (Castoriadis, 1997a, pp. 9–10).

This juxtaposition between the biological and the social
significance of closure allows Castoriadis to further elaborate his
conception of (collective and individual) autonomy by contrasting
his use of the term with that of Varela. In Varela's work autonomy
is synonymous with the 'organizational, informational, cognitive'
closure of a biological organism; it means 'the functioning of the
living self' as a prerequisite for its relations with everything that lies
outside its proper 'self'. However, as mentioned above, for Castoriadis
this is a *heteronomous* state-of-affairs when it refers to the social-
historical domain (see *Heteronomy* and *The Living Being*). There

closure would entail complete and unchallenged conformity with already established 'laws, principles, norms, values, and meanings' in general. It becomes therefore apparent that autonomy is linked not with closure but with *openness* (pp. 16–17). Far from being a mere attack on biological determinism, Castoriadis's point should be interpreted as a thinly disguised assault on sociological accounts premised on biological and functionalist conceptions and perhaps most notably against Luhmann's appropriation of Varela's notion of *autopoiesis* and his subsequent discussion on systemic autonomy and openness (see, for example, Luhmann, 1995, pp. 10–11).

Importantly, Castoriadis acknowledges two fundamental institutions for the social-historical, namely the institutions of *legein* and *teukhein*. These terms which Castoriadis borrows from Greek language encapsulate the main ways in which human beings concurrently express and create themselves, viz. through *logos* (meaning at the same time speech, analogy, logic) and through *doing* (*teukhein* being derived from the word *teukhos* (Castoriadis, 1987, p. 180), meaning the small knife, the primordial human 'tool'; see also Legein *and* Teukhein).

This conceptualization entails that *legein* and *teukhein* form the basis on which the complex institutional edifice of a given societal formation is erected. Indeed, here Castoriadis traces again an 'identitary' and a signitive (creative) dimension. More specifically, *teukhein* is seen as primarily expressing the identitary dimension of doing, doing in the guise of *technique*. However, Castoriadis is adamant that this dimension hardly exhausts human doing, thus leaving room for creative aspects of individual and collective action that are not determined by technical interests and especially for creative political *praxis*. In the same vein, Castoriadis detects a signitive/creative dimension behind – and beyond – the ensidic/ systemic dimension of *legein* that is expressed in language as a system (pp. 360–361).

This creative dimension is understood as the proper *source* of signification in general, of which the system of language is but an aspect. Indeed, the departure from the basic tenets of structuralism could hardly be more radical, since Castoriadis maintains that 'imaginary significations' are responsible for the construction of the 'world' and of 'reality', since 'reality' is always 'socially instituted, not only as reality in general, but as a specific reality, as the reality *of this particular society* (p. 263). One has to be careful here not to attribute a merely 'mental' sense to imaginary significations. Rather, imaginary significations 'create a proper world' for a given society, 'in reality they *are* this world' (Castoriadis, 1997a, p. 272). He argues that the signs of a given language do not produce meaning by virtue of systemic difference or of some reference to 'real' entities but rather that meaning is generated on the fundamental level of signification, or to put it in another manner, language as a 'code' is only the identitary dimension of *legein* (Castoriadis, 1987, p. 264). Thus, 'God', 'gods', 'spirits', '*polis*', 'bourgeois', 'serf', etc. are not merely words corresponding to a given reality but social imaginary significations that at once *create* and represent this reality (Castoriadis, 1997a, p. 7). This conception shows an attempt to avoid privileging either idealistic or material aspects of human existence and makes plain how erroneous it would be to see Castoriadis's position as a – unique – variant of the 'linguistic turn' as Habermas (1987, p. 327) argues.

The postulated homogeneity between the mode of being of significations and the social-historical allows Castoriadis to argue that the mode of being of society is not that of an 'object'. It follows that any attempt to treat society as an object is bound with indissoluble *aporiae*, concerning, for example, the 'limits' of a given society or the 'turning' points in the process of its – ultimately incessant – self-alteration.

Castoriadis argues that the mode of being of sociohistorical entities is each time *posited* through the act of social-historical creation, and consequently the 'limits' of the various cities of ancient Greece and the peculiar ties between them are part of the institution of Greek society and nation-states and the whole nexus of relations between them are part of 'modern capitalism' (Castoriadis, 1987, pp. 359–360). Indeed Castoriadis even speaks of a fundamental *historicity* of significations, which entails that apparently similar institutions radically differ when they belong to different social formations (p. 368). However, and perhaps inevitably, Castoriadis's own position generates its own questions the most acute of which is the enigmatic convergence between the individual and collective aspects of signification, which according to Castoriadis has given rise to 'illegitimate' metaphors or misnomers, like the 'collective unconscious' or 'collective consciousness', etc. (pp. 179, 366).

Since the social-historical is theorized from the perspective of creation it should hardly come as a surprise that, in his discussion of the social-historical, Castoriadis explicitly tackles the problem of time. Indeed, his discussion of time is guided by the need to attain a conception of time that could do justice to the fundamental connection between society and history, the latter being thought of in terms of *creation*. Thus Castoriadis maintains that time is 'either creation or it is nothing' (Castoriadis, 1997a, p. 3).

Castoriadis furthermore argues that thought should liberate itself from the age-old habit of thinking of time in terms of space. Time does not form the abstract spatial dimension 'in' which historical events take place but it is rather these very events; it is human history. All other dimensions of time (i.e. its ensidic dimensions of calendar time) derive from this fundamental human temporality which is tantamount to creation proper. It is in the 'Hyppocratic concept of *kairos*' (which is also a concept we find in Aristotle and in the book of Ecclesiastes) that Castoriadis finds some traces of an understanding of time *qua* doing. In other words, the notion of *kairos*, of 'a time for something' contains in a concealed form the awareness of the essentially creative character of time. Indeed, Castoriadis maintains that the 'time of doing' is much closer to 'true temporality' than the 'instituted time of social representation', which ultimately 'denies temporality as otherness-alteration' (p. 212). It is indicative in this respect that Castoriadis uses the term 'other' primarily – if not exclusively – in relation to human creations, as when he writes, for example, that 'the *Iliad* and *The Castle* are not different – they are other' (Castoriadis, 1997a, p. 392).

In this conception of time we therefore once more encounter a fundamental attribute of the social-historical, namely its self-afflicted alienation, its self-concealment as an *instituting-creating* agency. This form of self-alienation, which in its extreme forms amounts to self-cancelation, is perhaps the most intriguing and most persisting of the enigmas generated by Castoriadis's conceptualization of the social and invites ever new attempts at rethinking the very nature of society and history in their belonging together.

References

Adams, S. (2011), *Castoriadis's Ontology: Being and Creation*, New York: Fordham University Press.

Castoriadis, C. (1987), *The Imaginary Institution of Society*, K. Blamey (trans.), Cambridge: Polity.

—. (1988), 'Εισαγωγή στον Μαξ Βέμπερ' (Introduction to Max Weber), in *Πρώτες Δοκιμές* (First Attempts), Athens: Ύψιλον, pp. 43–51.

—. (1997a), *Fait et à Faire: Les Carrefours du labyrinthe V*, Paris: Seuil.

—. (1997b), *World in Fragments*, D. A. Curtis (ed. and trans.), Stanford, CA: Stanford University Press.

—. (1999), *Figures du Pensable: Les Carrefours du labyrinthe VI*, Paris: Seuil.

Delcroix, I. (2006), 'Le social-historique, cet être-événement', in *Cahiers Castoriadis, Imaginare et création historique, no 2*, Bruxelles: Facultés Universtitaires Saint-Louis.

Habermas, J. (1987), *The Philosophical Discourse of Modernity: Twelve Lectures*, F. Lawrence (trans.), Cambridge: Polity.

Luhmann, N. (1995), *Social Systems*, J. Bedranz, Jr. with D. Baecker (trans.), Stanford, CA: Stanford University Press.

Mazlish, B. (1967/2006), 'Comte, Auguste', in D. M. Borchert (ed.), *Encyclopedia of Philosophy* (2nd edn), Farmington Hills: MacMillan Reference USA, pp. 408–413.

CHAPTER NINE

Institution

Johann P. Arnason

The concept of institution figures in the title of Castoriadis's main work, and a later text refers to the institution as 'one of the two factors in the hominization of man – the other being the radical imagination' (Castoriadis, 2007, p. 93). But this concept is not one of his original contributions to philosophical and social thought (as are the concepts of *magma*, social imaginary significations or autonomy); nor is it one of the Greek ideas which he reactivated and transformed (such as *physis*, *legein*, *teukhein* or *psyche*). Rather, it is an established sociological category which Castoriadis encountered and adapted to his emerging project. The concept of institution was, above all else, central to the Durkheimian branch of the sociological tradition. Beyond that context, it influenced other currents of French thought; and in the later phase of Merleau-Ponty's work, it became a theme for philosophical reflection. All these aspects were important for Castoriadis's approach.

As with most other aspects of his work, Castoriadis's critical assessment of Marxism is the appropriate point of entry to his thought on the institution. The specific theme that leads him in this direction is Marx's very inchoate theory of alienation. It is, on closer examination, bound up with tacit assumptions about institutions, and an alternative to its most troublesome implications can only be envisaged in more explicit institutional terms. This line of argument takes off from a widely shared concern of Western

Marxists in the early 1960s, but does so in a very distinctive way. Marx's youthful writings, especially the 1844 manuscripts and their account of alienation as a deformation of the human condition (Marx, 1970), were read as a corrective against Marxist-Leninist orthodoxy and a guide to more humanistic perspectives on history and society. This reception had to be grounded in a philosophical anthropology centred on self-realization through work. Castoriadis gave a different twist to Marx's idea of alienation; he contrasted it with revolutionary praxis understood as a creative and autonomous mode of action, and the alienated condition therefore appears, first and foremost, as a loss of autonomy. The encounter with limits and obstacles to autonomy is, to begin with, exemplified by the 'discourse of the other' that structures the unconscious; the institutional dimension is then introduced as both essential to and different from the formations discovered by psychoanalysis. On the level of collective anonymity, alienation 'therefore appears as instituted', and it is important that Castoriadis takes the term 'in its broadest sense, including in particular the structure of the real relations of production' (Castoriadis, 1987, p. 109). There is, in other words, a strong emphasis on the interrelations that constitute the social field, and are only in part identifiable with norms and rules. The point that they involve ways of distributing power remains unstated, and it was only at a much later stage that Castoriadis saw the need to define a concept of power that would match his distinctive interpretation of the social-historical.

The broadened and deepened concept of institution – understood as an aspect of the social-historical patterns imposed on the psyche and as a complex of relations irreducible to shared norms or intersubjective understandings – enables Castoriadis to extend the idea of alienation beyond its original Marxian framework (see *Social-Historical* and *Psyche*). It is no longer confined to class-divided societies, let alone to societies dominated by the capitalist mode of production. The phenomenon of alienation becomes a pervasive feature of human societies: in its capacity as 'instituted heteronomy', the institution 'possesses its own functions, its ends, and its reasons for existing' (p. 110; see *Heteronomy*). On the other hand, the institutional dimension also provides space for efforts to reverse these trends. With this redefinition of alienation as a problematic aspect of the relationship between society and its institutions, Castoriadis touches upon questions debated by other authors. In the sociological context, Marcel Mauss had already moved beyond Durkheim's first definition of social facts and singled out institutions, more precisely 'living institutions, as they emerge, function and transform themselves' as 'the properly social phenomena, the objects of sociology' (Mauss, 1969, p. 17). Institutions in this broad sense are patterns of action and thought, imposed on the individuals but also subject to changes in the course of historical events. Debates in the late 1950s and early 1960s, not least linked to the work of Georges Gurvitch, drew on this Maussian legacy and placed increasing emphasis on the active side of institutional life (for an argument in this vein that refers to Castoriadis under his pseudonym P. Cardan, see Lapassade, 1970). The distinction between *instituting* and *instituted* aspects of society, more or less clearly formulated, emerged as a theme for further variations. Castoriadis's particular approach to the issue was based on insights gained from his critique of Marx; the interplay of creativity and autonomy adds a more specific content to the duality of instituting and instituted society. Social imaginary significations are the main source of instituting potential, and they differ in terms of possible distance from instituted patterns. Autonomy, proposed by Castoriadis as the only defensible meaning of revolutionary action, involves a restructuring – more precisely a self-reflexive and self-questioning turn – of the relationship between instituting and instituted society.

On a more markedly philosophical level, Merleau-Ponty was at the same time developing the concept of institution into an alternative to the Kantian and phenomenological idea of constitution. This line of reflection, pursued most explicitly in lectures given at Collège de France in 1954–1955, was part of a broader effort to reorient phenomenological thought. The lecture notes were not published until much later (Merleau-Ponty, 2003), but although it is not clear how much Castoriadis knew about their contents, we can assume that he was aware of the main lines. Merleau-Ponty used the concept of institution to refer to the 'durable dimensions' (p. 124) that lend meaning to ongoing experiences and make it possible to integrate them into historical horizons. He linked this theme to Husserl's notion of a passive synthesis; and as Claude Lefort shows in his introduction to the lecture notes, time – in its capacity as a departure from the past and an opening to the future – becomes the most fundamental model of the institution. This is the point where both affinities and contrasts between Merleau-Ponty and Castoriadis become most visible. Instead of treating time as an institution, Castoriadis refers to the social-historical institution of time. Each configuration of the social-historical imposes its specific temporality – cyclical or linear, repetitive or creative, homogeneous or heterogeneous, to mention some basic points (more frequently mixed in varying ways than present in pure form). Each version of temporality also has particular connotations due to the central significations around which the world is structured in each case. This view draws on Merleau-Ponty's broadly conceived idea of the institution as a meaning-bestowing regularity, but re-anchors it in the social dimension. The phenomenological attempt to dissolve the constituting subject into an instituting field is thus redirected towards the social world.

Castoriadis describes the institution of temporality as the 'first one' that institutes society 'as being society and *this particular* society' (Castoriadis, 1987, p. 206), but this primacy of time is not maintained in the following discussion of the social-historical and its ramifications. The next chapter of *The Imaginary Institution* analyzes *legein and teukhein*, defined respectively as the ability to 'distinguish-choose-posit-assemble-speak' (p. 223) and as the operation of 'assembling-adjusting-fabricating-constructing' (p. 260); these interconnected aspects of social life appear as the most elementary institutions (see Legein *and* Teukhein). In more general terms, the distinction between primary and secondary or second-order institutions remains unclear. According to a brief reference at the end of the book, the *enterprise* is a 'second-order institution of capitalism' (p. 371), which would seem to imply that capitalism is a first-order institution, presumably in the sense that it imposes basic and central significations. A later text on 'primal institution of society and secondary institutions' (Castoriadis, 2007, pp. 91–101) tackles the problem indicated in the title only at the very end. Here the 'primal institution' is identified with 'the fact that society creates itself as society and creates itself afresh in each instance, by giving itself institutions quickened and sustained by social imaginary significations specific to that particular society' (p. 100), whereas second-order institutions are said to be of two kinds, exemplified on the one hand by language and the individual, which are transhistorical but exist only in specific forms, and on the other by the Greek *polis* and the capitalist business enterprise (p. 100). But this is no longer a definition of different types of institutions; it is a distinction – useful in its own right – between the instituting process as such and the concrete patterns through which it shapes the social-historical world. The question of institutional levels and hierarchies – including, for example, the problem of the religio-political nexus and its basic but changing role in the constitution of human societies – remains open.

This discussion would be incomplete without a mention of one particularly important development in Castoriadis's later writings. In an essay on 'Power, politics, autonomy', first published in 1988, he formulated a conception of power that is not to be found in earlier writings. It spells out implicit themes of *The Imaginary Institution of Society*, but with significant additions. It represents, first and foremost, an original synthesis of Weberian and Durkheimian approaches. Power is defined as 'the capacity for a personal or impersonal instance (*Instanz*) to bring someone to do (or to abstain from doing) that which, left to himself, s/he would not necessarily have done' (Castoriadis, 1991, p. 149). This is an obvious allusion to Weber's concept of power; the crucial difference is that an 'impersonal instance' is introduced at the most basic level, and this serves to justify a Durkheimian twist: the institution appears as the paradigm of impersonal power, more fundamental than any intersubjective relationship. The result is a twofold claim that goes beyond both Weber and Durkheim: institutions are to be analyzed as agencies of power (animated by significations), and power primarily as a matter of institutions (especially of the central instituting patterns that define a historical society). But there is yet another side to the argument. For a whole range of reasons which we need not recapitulate here, societies – including the individuals formed in and through them – are never wholly governed by the ground power of their institutional frameworks. Specific centres of explicit power, exercising control but also developing a logic of their own, are omnipresent in the history of human societies. In stateless societies such power is held by males, warriors or elders, while the reference to mythical ancestors serves to legitimize a more implicit ground power of custom. It follows that the political domain or sphere is a universal phenomenon, while the transformation of this sphere into a field of alternatives, linked to rival visions of power, is a rare historical breakthrough, first achieved in ancient Greece.

This outline of a theory of power was not taken further; it may, however, be seen as an indicator of possibilities inherent in Castoriadis's use of the concept of institution.

References

Castoriadis, C. (1987), *The Imaginary Institution of Society*, K. Blamey (trans.), Oxford: Polity; Cambridge, MA: MIT Press.
—. (1991), *Philosophy, Politics, Autonomy. Essays in Political Philosophy*, D. A. Curtis (ed.), New York and Oxford: Oxford University Press.
—. (2007), *Figures of the Thinkable*, H. Arnold (trans.), Stanford, CA: Stanford University Press.
Lapassade, G. (1970), *Groupes, organisations et institutions*, Paris: Gauthier-Villars.
Marx, K. (1970), *Economic and Philosophical Manuscripts*, London: Lawrence & Wishart.
Mauss, M. (1969), *Essais de sociologie*, Paris: Éditions de Minuit.
Merleau-Ponty, M. (2003), *L'institution. La passivité*, Paris: Belin.

CHAPTER TEN

Ensemblistic-Identitary Logic (Ensidic Logic)

Jeff Klooger

Critiques of reason are as old as its veneration. For the Enlightenment, reason was both the foundation and crowning glory of the authentically human. Nonetheless, Kant's critiques investigated the limits of reason as well as its power. Then, beginning with the Romantics, followed by Schopenhauer and Nietzsche, and continuing in the twentieth century with the Frankfurt School's critique of instrumental reason, phenomenology's subsumption of logic within lived experience, and Derrida's deconstruction of logocentrism, reason has been exposed as less and other than Western thought has generally proclaimed it to be. Castoriadis's critique of what he at first calls *ensemblistic-identitary* logic and later names *ensidic* logic for short – so named because it is the basis of the logical operations involved in the production and manipulation of ensembles or sets, operations which themselves presume the fully determinable identity of both ensembles and their components – may be read as part of this tradition. As such, its value may be assessed by how well it completes the three tasks necessary for such a critique: 1) to describe the nature and operation of reason, 2) to account for the effectiveness of reason and 3) to expose its limitations. If the critique is to be comprehensive and satisfactory, all three of these need to be achieved together, in a movement in which the responses to the second and third tasks mesh organically with the response to the first.

Key to Castoriadis's version of the critique of reason is the relationship between logic and ontology. Some recognition of this relationship is implicit in all such critiques, but Castoriadis makes it his explicit philosophical focus. The link between logic and ontology is important for Castoriadis because he comes to his critique of logic via a recognition of the limitations of traditional ontology. Setting out to elucidate the properties peculiar to society and history, Castoriadis discovers that traditional ontology prejudices the concept of 'being' in a way that excludes what is most essential to phenomena in these realms: creation and self-creation, and the comparative indeterminacy which is the essential precondition for these. Being is construed as determined; indeed, as determinacy. 'To be' means 'to be determined', and a thing exists precisely to the extent that it is determined in itself or can be determined by thought. Castoriadis contends that, despite passing realizations by the greatest philosophers that this definition of being is inadequate, the history of Western philosophy is dominated by the equation of 'being' and 'determinacy'. Having defined 'being' as 'determinacy', the tradition then proceeds to take as models of 'being' only those beings which best conform to this definition. Principally, this means purely physical and logical objects. Phenomena which elude the definition of being as determinacy, which resist being treated as determined or determinable, are either ignored or reduced to second-class status as mere appearances behind which true reality lies concealed. This is commonly the case with social-historical phenomena. Such phenomena are typically treated as though they existed in the same manner and sense as physical and logical objects as regards their identity, separateness and interactions. Alternatively, social-historical phenomena are simply ignored, or reduced to something more 'real', meaning something more amenable to being treated as a 'properly' determined being (Castoriadis, 1987, pp. 168–220; 1991, pp. 33–47).

The ubiquity and perniciousness of this equation of 'being' and 'determinacy' emerges for Castoriadis as he attempts to get beyond deterministic models of society and history. His critique of Marxism is prompted chiefly by his recognition of its deterministic conception of history, and he criticizes other explanatory models of society and history, specifically the functionalist and structuralist approaches, as being similarly deterministic (Castoriadis, 1987, pp. 168–220). What Castoriadis regards as most characteristic of the social-historical is its comparative indeterminacy – in fact, an interplay of indeterminacy and partial determinations, a forming which excludes both pure formlessness and the sort of fully determinate form which traditional ontology regards as essential to 'being'. This makes the social-historical alien to the schema of determinacy assumed by the traditional ontology. This comparative indeterminacy is both synchronic and diachronic. This means that social phenomena are indeterminate both in and across time. (The distinction is somewhat artificial from Castoriadis's perspective, which integrates the two into the notion of the social-historical, a form of being which exists only as unfolding in a perpetual movement of undetermined creation. Nevertheless, it is worth noting that the indeterminacy of the social-historical is not reducible to the fact that there is no determinacy across time, and that even if it were possible to extract a social phenomenon from the historical process, that phenomenon would still evade attempts to fully determine it.) This linkage of indeterminacy within and across time is mirrored in its opposite, the linkage of ontological determinacy and determinism. If beings understood as determined in themselves are to be conceived as related to one another, these relationships are bound to be conceived as deterministic. In Kant, for example, one finds that, once one moves from the nature of substance to the nature of succession and coexistence, the principle of determinacy implies the complete determination of all substances by all others with which they coexist, either within or across time (Kant, 1933). Indeed, as Castoriadis argues, the difference between succession and coexistence disappears when both amount to a universal determinacy. The determinacy of each implies the determinacy of all, and when it comes to temporality, that means determinism, the determination of each succeeding state by the preceding one, and underlying that, a determination of all things by universal laws or principles which make the sequence of succession inevitable because it is thoroughly predetermined (Castoriadis, 1987, pp. 168–220).

Obviously this constitutes a problem for the understanding of society and history. According to Castoriadis, if these are to be understood adequately, we must get beyond the ontological prejudice that equates 'being' with 'determinacy'. We must resist the temptation to model our understanding of being on beings of one or two types conformable to our preferred definition of being, and we must instead acknowledge the possibility that 'being' may not mean the same thing in every context, that a social institution or a psychical formation may 'be' in a different manner and sense than chairs and mathematical objects. Thus the move from ontological determinacy to comparative indeterminacy entails a move from a single and universal meaning of 'being' to a polysemic understanding of the term reflecting a recognition of real ontological differences in 'what is' and 'how' it is (pp. 167–169). This leads Castoriadis eventually to a model of the universe as ontologically stratified, with different modes of being corresponding to heterogeneous ontological realms (Castoriadis, 1984, pp. 145–226; 1997a, pp. 342–373; see the entries on *Magma* and *The Living Being*).

One cannot hope to escape the grip of the traditional ontology of determinacy merely by exposing it as flawed and partial, because this traditional ontology is more than a mere error. According to Castoriadis, it represents one (possible but not inevitable) intellectual development of a fundamental institutional dimension of the social-historical, a dimension which is ineradicable and omnipresent. It is a measure of Castoriadis's profundity as a philosopher that he does not dismiss the traditional ontology without attempting to trace it to its deepest roots and to understand it at its deepest level. He recognizes first, that if this ontology is to be transcended this can only be achieved on the basis of a deep understanding; and second, that the phenomenon of this ontology is worth understanding in and for itself, that it reveals important aspects of what it is to be human and, beyond that, important characteristics of what it is to 'be'. In this way Castoriadis recognizes that the third of the tasks of a critique of reason enumerated above cannot be separated from the first two.

For Castoriadis, the key to understanding the basis of the traditional ontology was the discovery that the logic which underlies this ontology, which presupposes it and is presupposed by it, is the logic of *sets* (Castoriadis, 1987, pp. 221–227). He argues that this logic is best encapsulated by the first or naive definition of the set presented by the mathematician Cantor. This definition has been superseded by more sophisticated versions which avoid some of the *aporias* the naive definition leads to, but according to

Castoriadis, the naive definition better represents the innate logic in question because the circularity it involves is essential to that logic in its native form. According to Cantor's definition, a set is 'a collection into a whole of definite and distinct objects of our intuition or of our thought. These objects are called the elements of the set' (Castoriadis, 1984, p. 208). In order to be an element of a set an object must be distinct or definite; it must be assumed to be such and treated accordingly. This encapsulates the ontology of determinacy explored previously. The logic further proposes that such elements may be collected together into wholes. In order for this to be possible, the objects must be separable from whatever may be their native or current context; in order to be separable they must be discrete and fully circumscribable – we must be able to determine precisely where one object ends and another begins. We must therefore be able to specify exactly what each object is in order to differentiate it completely from other objects. In order to separate objects and combine them into wholes, such objects must be fully determinable. The possibility of assembly into wholes presupposes not only separability of objects but the potential for combining objects on the basis of properties that are theoretically if not practically separable from other properties of these same objects. Thus objects are not only separable, they are internally analysable into discrete constituents.

The two sides of the definition – the possibility of assembly and disassembly, and determinability – presuppose and refer to one another. This is because, in Castoriadis's terms, this logic is '"an originary institution" – a true creation' (Castoriadis, 1987, p. 223). The logic is not a reflection of reality – though according to Castoriadis it does correspond to a certain dimension of reality (we will explore this shortly). Like all human representations and institutions, it is a non-determined creation which is imposed on and conditions our encounters with reality (see *Institution* and *Creation* ex nihilo). Castoriadis calls this logic which set-theoretical logic replicates and exemplifies *ensemblistic-identitary logic*. It is *ensemblistic* in that it involves schemata for the assembly of objects into wholes or ensembles; and it is *identitary* in that it posits the full and complete self-identity or determinability of objects as the basis for their assembly and disassembly (pp. 221–228).

This logic operates in the history of philosophy, underpinning the ontology of determinacy discussed already. It also operates in all theoretical constructions informed by this philosophical tradition: theories in the natural sciences, for which the logic is better, though not always perfectly suited (for reasons we will explore), as well as theories of society and history, for which the logic is quite ill-suited. But this logic is not a philosophical artefact. As stated earlier, it is, according to Castoriadis, an originary institution, and a fundamental one, whose operation is evident in all social institutions. All social institutions involve an ensidic dimension, a dimension which presupposes the ability to determine objects, and to separate and recombine elements. Castoriadis identifies two aspects of this ensidic dimension of the institution, which he calls *legein* and *teukhein* (pp. 221–272). *Legein* is distinguishing-choosing-positing-assembling-counting-speaking; it operates most conspicuously, though not exclusively, through language. *Teukhein* is assembling-adjusting-fabricating-constructing; it operates through all social doing. These fundamental dimensions of the institution, and of the activity of instituting, will be explored in more detail in the entry devoted to them (see *Institution* and Legein *and* Teukhein). The important thing to note here is that ensidic logic is seen by Castoriadis as embodied and operating through these (proto) institutional dimensions, that it is a social creation which emerges as these dimensions of the instituting and instituted life of society. No social life is possible without the ability to distinguish, choose, posit, assemble, count, construct and so on.

The ensidic dimension of the social institution is essential and ubiquitous, but it is not the whole of the social. The other dimension of the social is what Castoriadis identifies as the *imaginary* element. This is the dimension of meaning and meaning-creation. It requires the ensidic dimension and the schemata of ensidic logic in order to realize its creations and embody them in shareable forms. But these creations are never reducible to that logic, just as meaning is irreducible to the manner of its formation and presentation. Each society institutes itself and its world by bringing into being and utilizing the ensidic logic of *legein* and *teukhein* in its own way and to its own ends (pp. 221–272).

With his analysis of the emergence of ensidic logic as a social institution, Castoriadis fulfils the first of the three tasks of a critique of reason identified at the start of this entry. Only the second of these tasks remains to be addressed, and in addressing this task Castoriadis also deepens his understanding of the limits of ensidic logic, since the two go hand in hand: an explication of the effectiveness of a logic or form of reason and clarification of its limitations.

The ensidic logic which is only one dimension of the social institution, and which is ill-suited to the elucidation and explication of the social-historical as a whole, is nevertheless quite effective in describing and permitting the explanation of other types of phenomena, especially phenomena within the natural world. Why is this so? Ensidic logic fails in relation to the social-historical because in the social-historical the imaginary dimension is so important, and that dimension does not conform to the postulates and ontological assumptions of ensidic logic. Social-historical phenomena are not determined in the way that this logic and its associated ontology suppose; on the contrary, they exhibit a significant degree of indeterminacy. As discussed in other entries, this indeterminacy is so profound that it led Castoriadis to propose an alternative mode of organization to that of the set or ensemble as characteristic of human phenomena such as the human psyche and the social-historical: the mode of being he termed *magma* (Castoriadis, 1987, pp. 340–344; 1997b, pp. 290–318). It follows from this that the effectiveness of ensidic logic is dependent on the degree to which the objects to which it is applied approach the mode of being of an ensemble. Where they approach most nearly to ensembles or elements of ensembles, ensidic logic is most effective; where the mode of being of the objects is most *magmatic*, ensidic logic is least effective. To the degree that such logic is effective in relation to natural phenomena such phenomena must themselves possess a greater degree of ensidic organization (Castoriadis, 1984, pp. 145–226; 1997a, pp. 342–373).

There is an important point to be made here concerning Castoriadis's understanding of the relationship between logic and objects. Castoriadis insists that human institutions, and indeed all human representations, do not derive from a reality exterior to them. They are instead non-determined creations. However, if those creations are to permit the successful life activity of human beings, they must to some degree correspond to aspects of external reality. Castoriadis is a realist in this sense: he presupposes forms of organization intrinsic to reality which are independent of our construction of that reality. There may therefore be a correspondence – or non-correspondence – between our conceptual constructions and the innate characteristics of any aspect of reality. This 'correspondence' is not to be understood as similitude, but rather in terms of the effectiveness of our mental constructions for guiding practical encounters with reality and for permitting deduction of further facts and effective theories concerning the reality. It is the latter point that perhaps prevents one describing Castoriadis as a thoroughgoing pragmatist, though there is an element of pragmatism in his epistemological approach.

Associated with this question of the intrinsic organization of the object of knowledge is a shift in Castoriadis's use of the term 'ensidic'. What is at first a description of a form of logic becomes a description of an organizational characteristic of reality conformable to that logic in the sense that the reality can be understood and manipulated by the logic. Henceforth Castoriadis talks about strata of 'being' which exhibit ensidic characteristics to a greater or lesser degree, and which are to that degree more or less amenable to ensidic logic. The natural world, particularly that dimension of the natural world dealt with by classical physics, is the stratum most ensidic in its organization. The realm of quantum phenomena is less so, and the realm of the living being dealt with by biological science is only partially and imperfectly reducible to its ensidic characteristics. The human realms of the psyche and the social-historical are the least amenable to ensidic treatment since they exhibit the least degree of ensidic organization in themselves. It is crucial to note, however, that this is only ever a matter of degree. No realm of reality is ever completely devoid of ensidic characteristics; and no realm of reality is ever completely reducible to ensidic characteristics. The world as a whole is not, according to Castoriadis, an 'ensemble of ensembles', but a '*magma* of *magmas*' (Castoriadis, 1997b, pp. 290–318). Indeterminacy is everywhere present, and determinacy is nowhere perfect and complete. On the other hand, everything is to some degree determinable, everything exhibits in itself an aspect which makes it susceptible to an ensidic treatment. Everything is ensemblizable (or ensidizable), everything can be treated according to the logic of sets. What differs is the degree to which such a treatment ignores or distorts dimensions of the reality which exceed or deviate from the ensidic (Castoriadis, 1984, pp. 145–226; 1997a, pp. 342–373).

A core thesis for Castoriadis is thus that everything is a *magma*, that everything exhibits a degree of indeterminacy inconsistent with the nature of true ensembles. However, Castoriadis sometimes speaks as though true ensembles did exist or could be created (Castoriadis, 1997b, p. 298). The temptation to recognize the existence of true ensembles is greatest in relation to mathematical and other purely logical objects. Such objects are defined as completely determined or determinable, and if it is supposed that this definition determines their actual existence, one may imagine that they constitute true ensembles. Another of Castoriadis's theses, however, is the impossibility of complete and perfect partitioning of *magmas* (pp. 290–318). Logical and mathematical objects may be supposed to be true ensembles with nothing of the *magmatic* in them only as long as they remain unaffected by the indeterminacy they exclude as a matter of principle. But this indeterminacy haunts even mathematics and logic, particularly where the question of their foundations, and therefore the foundation of their core ensidic postulates, intrudes. The cost of preserving the effective ensidization of these objects is the deferral of an interrogation of their underlying assumptions. Where these are questioned, the appearance of their perfectly ensidic character begins to dissolve. They too are revealed as *magmas* rather than true ensembles, albeit the most ensidic *magmas* possible.

Finally, we should acknowledge that ensidic logic is not the only form of reason Castoriadis identifies and discusses. The other form is what might be termed *dialectical* or *dialogical* reason. This is the form of reason essential to the philosophical enterprise, the open-ended posing of questions and the giving of reasons for one's belief in the truth of any answers to those questions – Castoriadis often refers to the latter as the Greek formulation *logon didonai*, meaning 'to give an account to others of what you are doing' (Castoriadis, 1991, pp. 3–32; 1997a, pp. 342–373). This movement of questioning and argumentation is irreducible to any logic. On the contrary, logic itself is open to interrogation, even though that interrogation inevitably utilizes logic in order to pose its questions and propose answers. Though ubiquitous and unavoidable, ensidic logic must not be allowed to prejudge questions. Since one of the purposes of dialogical interrogation is to decide what should count as a valid reason, the answer to this question cannot be assumed to be given in logic itself. Castoriadis's critique of ensidic logic aims at exposing its limitations through a process of interrogation that is itself an example of dialogical reasoning, one which goes beyond ensidic logic not by throwing that logic aside but by using it as a tool in its own transcendence.

References

Castoriadis, C. (1984), *Crossroads in the Labyrinth*, K. Soper and M. H. Ryle (eds and trans.), Cambridge, MA: MIT Press.
—. (1987), *The Imaginary Institution of Society*, K. Blamey (trans.). Oxford: Polity; Cambridge, MA: MIT Press.
—. (1991), *Philosophy, Politics, Autonomy*, D. A. Curtis (ed.), New York and Oxford: Oxford University Press.
—. (1997a), *World in Fragments*, D. A. Curtis (ed.), Stanford, CA: Stanford University Press.
—. (1997b), *The Castoriadis Reader*, D. A. Curtis (ed.), Oxford and Cambridge, MA: Oxford University Press.
Kant, I. (1933), *Critique of Pure Reason*, N. Kemp Smith (trans.), London: MacMillan.

CHAPTER ELEVEN

Legein and *Teukhein*

Jeff Klooger

For Castoriadis, the social institution is the ontological form through and as which the social-historical creates itself. The institution is entirely unprecedented prior to the emergence of the social-historical. While the specific features of institutions are neither predetermined nor limited to a finite set of types, it is possible to identify elements that are universal because they are essential to the institution and instituting as such. These elements are those that permit the effective existence and operation of the institution/instituting, enabling the determination of thought and action that produces forms of social being. Castoriadis identifies two such elements, which he names *legein* and *teukhein*. *Legein* is distinguishing-choosing-positing-assembling-counting-speaking; *teukhein* is assembling-adjusting-fabricating-constructing. These two aspects of the institution and instituting are indissociable as well as universal. We never find *legein* in the absence of *teukhein*, or vice versa. To institute and to exist as an institution always involves both (Castoriadis, 1987, pp. 223–226).

Legein and *teukhein* institute *ensidic* logic; they are the fundamental dimensions of all institutions that posit this logic and establish operating schemata based upon it. *Identitary/ ensemblistic-identitary/ensidic* logic was discussed in the previous chapter. It is the logic that underlies set theory. As we saw in the previous chapter, the objects and sets posited by set theory and its logic partially capture aspects of the universe, especially in what Castoriadis terms the 'first natural stratum', though much less successfully in relation to the social-historical, which is essentially a *magma* rather than an order of sets (see *Magma*). Nevertheless, according to Castoriadis, society too must incorporate an ensidic dimension, a self-organization that is to some extent that of sets. Ensidic logic enables operations like separation, unification, assembly into a whole and decomposition into parts, iteration and ordering. In doing so it presupposes that 'what is' permits all of these operations, that the mode of being of the world is such that objects *can be* identified, defined, separated, assembled, etc. These operations are indispensable for the self-creation of society, for its self-determination as a construction of social institutions. For Castoriadis, *legein* and *teukhein*, as the primordial aspects of the institution/instituting, are the unrecognized basis of all more explicit and sophisticated formulations of ensidic logic, such as set theory (pp. 221–227).

Not only does society have to create itself in part in the manner of sets, but according to Castoriadis, society is the creator of sets per se, of the set as an *eidos* or form. Prior to the institution of *legein* and *teukhein* there are no real sets in the world. Only through society do proper sets emerge, because only society posits the set as a figure and model. Much hinges here on the qualification 'proper', sometimes substituted for 'real' or 'true'. Castoriadis admits that the ensidic representation of the world by society, as well as its ensidic self-constitution, leans on[1] a certain being-thus of the world, and especially of the first natural stratum, which incorporates the physical and biological dimensions of the universe. This region of the world is partly organized in an ensidic manner; or at least it is organized in a manner that makes it amenable to being grasped and manipulated in an ensidic fashion (p. 228). Castoriadis acknowledges in the self-constitution of the living being, as well as the organization of life as a whole, the creation of something approaching sets, something that functions, up to a point, in the manner of sets. One can see this in the partitions and systemic organization of living beings, as well as in the orderly and hierarchical relations between biological species and genera (p. 229). Castoriadis even describes this as indicating 'in a certain sense' the presence of *legein* and *teukhein* (p. 269). What the ensidic operations of the living being lack, however, are governing principles that are separable from their material realizations and that are subject to creative alteration. Without this, they remain limited to and are exhausted by the material reality of the body. In particular, they lack the operative schemata of the *signitive* relation and the relation of *finality* that respectively govern *legein* and *teukhein* as social institutions. (More about these later.) (p. 269)[2]

Ensidic logic never exhausts the being of society. It conditions the form of the institution but it does not determine the content, and so it does not determine which forms, which sets and objects, any given society will institute. These are created by the radical imaginary. Though the institution of society utilizes and embodies ensidic logic, society is never reduced to sets or a hierarchy of sets; it is always, on the contrary, a *magma* of *magmas* (p. 228). Social institutions, even those that most exemplify and materialize the ensidic, like language, only do so partially and when considered from one aspect. Considered as a whole, they are not ensidic. Their intrinsic indeterminacy as well as their fluidity means their correspondence with ensidic logic is only ever partial and approximate (see *Institution*).

There is considerable overlap between *legein* and *teukhein*. Both involve similar operating schemata with similar ontological presuppositions. There are some crucial differences between the two, which Castoriadis remarks upon, but for the most part he focuses on *legein* and extrapolates to *teukhein*. Arnason (1991) and Adams (2011, pp. 28–29, 56–58, 81–82) have rightly remarked that this emphasis on signification/representation is to the detriment of a fuller account of social doing, a problem Castoriadis began to explore in the first part of *The Imaginary Institution of Society* but did not pursue in any depth.

Unsurprisingly, much of Castoriadis's analysis of *legein* focuses on language as a central component of signification. Many of the characteristics he identifies within *legein* as language can be extrapolated to other forms of *legein*. Castoriadis distinguishes between two aspects of language: language as *langue*, which is language as full signification, and language as code. As *langue*, language is a *magma*; as code, language is an ensemble, it institutes itself as an ensemble. Language as *legein ensemblizes* the world – it represents and organizes the world as an order of sets and objects – and it can do so only because it is itself in part an ensidic code of sets, elements, definite relations of inclusion and exclusion, combination and differentiation and so on (Castoriadis, 1987, p. 238). Language is a code, first, in its abstract-material aspect, as a system of linguistic elements, of phonemes, morphemes and the like (pp. 240–241). But it is also partly a code in its signifying aspect, since significations themselves are organized as ensembles, involving a correspondence between sets of linguistic terms and sets of properties. As signification, however, language always exceeds and transgresses this ensidic dimension. All linguistic significations operate by referring in an open-ended fashion to other significations such that it is impossible to establish in a fixed and determinate manner the boundaries and the relations between them. This open-ended referral is the source of their signifying potency. On the other hand, if they are to operate at all it is just as necessary that it be possible to fix and limit their meanings to the extent that we are able to speak of 'this' meaning in contradistinction to 'that' – though 'this' meaning always bleeds into others. This balancing act between the *magmatic*-signifying dimension of language and its ensidic-code dimension is essential for the very being of language (pp. 242–244).

One of the principal creations of *legein* is the sign. Signs are identical figures. This means all particular instances of a sign are considered identical with respect to their existence and function as signs. Each x is identical to every other x in respect to its being x. In fact, according to Castoriadis, it is the creation of signs that brings into being strict or genuine identity. Identity is instituted, it is made to exist not because it is or can be, but because it *must* be in order for the sign to exist. Moreover, according to Castoriadis the creation of the identity of the sign, rather than being a reflection of the supposed identity of the object the sign is to represent, is instead the basis for the positing of the identity of the object. The object is identical to itself, is determinate and definable, because of its relationship with a sign that is itself posited as necessarily identical (pp. 244–245). In this way, the ensidic logic embodied in *legein* becomes the basis for an ensidic vision of the world.

All particular signs figure 'the' sign, the image/figure that transcends all concrete instances but which is the necessary basis for them all. Each social individual will bear an internal image of the sign, something 'sensuous without matter' (p. 246), a *phantasma*, as Castoriadis calls it, borrowing the term from Aristotle. This multiplicity of individual representations of the sign are bound together and owe their existence to the social sign, the social image, equally *phantasmatic*. This social image is what enables social individuals to recognize, use and make signs (pp. 246–247).

The sign is based on the *signitive* relation, which is another fundamental element of *legein*. *Quid pro quo* distils the essence of the signitive relation: *this* stands for *that*. This is the basis for all symbolism, including the symbolism generally essential to language. The signitive relation ties the sign and its object together through the bond of referral. This relation is entirely arbitrary, without basis in any congruity or association of the sign and its object – for this reason it differs from all instances of natural referral, such as mimicry. It is an entirely new and unique type of relation essential to *legein*, but which, as Castoriadis points out, cannot be given to itself by *legein*, since it is an imaginary creation that goes beyond ensidic logic (pp. 246–247). On the other hand, the signitive relation is crucial to the origin of ensidic logic, because it figures 'thisness' as self-reference. The identical object 'stands for' itself, and this self-reference is only possible on the basis of an already established signitive relation in which other-reference (the referral of the sign to an object that is other than itself) is made possible (p. 247).

Castoriadis analyses a number of operative schemata of *legein* and *teukhein* (mostly focusing on *legein*, as mentioned previously, and then extrapolating to *teukhein*). Some of these are implied in the aspects of *legein* already described in this chapter. Linguistic signs operate according to the qualifying or limiting schema of *with respect to* (pp. 250, 320–329), according to which all determinations, all ensidic divisions and unifications, are restricted in their validity and applicability, tied to specific contextual criteria. The other side of this is the obligatory co-belonging of the sign and its object, the ungrounded and ungroundable rule according to which 'this' sign must (*Sollen* – Castoriadis also uses the German word in this connection) designate 'this' object. The sign is, as Castoriadis describes it, a 'form-norm' (p. 252). Indeed, this *Sollen* aspect of the signitive relation is a primordial example of the normative, and therefore of the institution per se. As Adams remarks in this connection: 'It is the institution that makes for the possibility of rules, and rules are implied by and posited with the institution' (Adams, 2011, pp. 78–79).

The signitive relation also implies the schema of value in two forms, as *standing for* and as *serving for*. The sign stands for its object according to the rule of the signitive relation. Hence it can take the place of the object, carry the same value as it in certain contexts and for certain purposes. At the same time there is an exchangeability and equivalence whereby all instances of the sign can be exchanged for all others. The sign also serves a purpose, it has a use value.[3] Linguistic signs serve the purpose of constructing and conveying meanings by combination with other signs. How they do so depends on grammatical rules as well as broader social ones: what one is trying to achieve, how one is trying to influence or impact others and so on. In this way, all *legein* is at the same time *teukhein*, doing (Castoriadis, 1987, pp. 252–255).

The institution of value in *legein* is, according to Castoriadis, the origin of value per se, which brings into being the possibility of equivalence. (Here, too, the full meaning of 'value' and its calculation exceeds the ensidic dimension. Even logical equivalence inhabits an imaginary – in Castoriadis's sense – context that determines its criteria and field of operation. Castoriadis (1984, pp. 260–339) explored this in terms of Marx's and Aristotle's treatment of value.) This is tied to the institution of strict identity, according to which it becomes possible to ignore or put aside the indeterminacy and fluidity that creates differences between any two actual objects. The ensidic logic of *legein* and *teukhein* posits that social individuals and objects, insofar as they figure and bear the same imaginary significations, shall be considered equivalent *with respect to* relevant functions or roles (Castoriadis, 1987, p. 255).

By now it should be clear that it is impossible to think of any of these schemata and aspects of *legein* without implicating and assuming others. This reflects the circular nature of *legein* and *teukhein* as total creations. These fundamental institutions cannot be built up in piecemeal fashion. All of their essential elements presuppose the others in a manner that means the whole can only originate in one leap, by an act of creation that posits everything essential to them at once (pp. 248–249).

What is manifested here in this way is a decisive aspect of instituting as such and of original institution, which we could attempt to express – poorly – by saying that the institution 'presupposes itself', that it can exist only by acting as if it had already existed fully (and as if it had, indefinitely, to go on existing.) The social imaginary exists as a social-historical doing/representing; as such it institutes and is obliged to institute the 'instrumental condition' for its social-historical existence, in other words, *teukhein* and *legein*. This institution itself, however, the institution of the 'instrumental conditions' of doing and representing, is still itself a doing and a figure; the institution of *legein* and *teukhein* as such is still a *legein-teukhein*. (p. 249)

We could amplify this observation of Castoriadis's by saying that *acting as if* is itself a key characteristic of instituting, the institution coming into being through action that obeys rules and principles that only exist by virtue of action that observes and applies them.

As stated earlier, *teukhein* is assembling-adjusting-fabricating-constructing. It is *doing* in the sense of acting in and upon the world to produce change. We English speakers may be inclined to think of 'doing' as an action potentially without consequence or result. The French term *faire*, which unites the senses of 'acting' and 'making', makes the effective character of *teukhein* clearer. *Teukhein* is doing that which is productive.

The schemata Castoriadis identifies in *legein* are all found in *teukhein*, except for the signitive relation. Since *teukhein* is concerned with *doing* rather than *signifying*, this schema is absent. Instead of it, we find the schema of *finality*. In the relation of finality an inexistent possibility is posited as an end. From this schema a division of the world into the possible and the impossible is created, and this division constitutes 'the real' for each society. The real, Castoriadis argues, is not merely that which resists, but that which can be transformed – always only in specified ways and not others. This division of the world into possible and impossible is mirrored by *legein*'s division between obligatory and impossible *qua* excluded/not instituted.

Legein and *teukhein* are essential and core dimensions of all institutions, and they are themselves instituted, hence they are institutions. But they are not standalone institutions, they are only found as dimensions of full institutions that employ and embody them (pp. 256–257). This should be recalled when reading descriptions of *legein* and *teukhein* as 'proto-institutions'. Castoriadis himself describes them as such, as do many commentators. The 'firstness' of this 'proto' prefix does not signify that *legein* and *teukhein* existed or had to exist *before* other institutions, only that they had to exist *from the first*.

The primordial character of these institutions is emphasized by Castoriadis's assertion that what Kant analyses as the understanding is in fact a part of *legein*. In Castoriadis's view, Kant's analysis, like those of many before him, fails to recognize the instituted nature of even the most fundamental categories and schemata of human reason (p. 259).

Like all institutions, *legein* and *teukhein* are subject to historical development and alteration. This means that though the core schemata of *legein* and *teukhein* are essential to all instituting, the form these take, their 'tenor and consistency' (p. 270), changes historically and across societies. They are extensible and transformable, as Castoriadis puts it (p. 270). In this respect the main difference is that while *teukhein* in the guise of technique can progress and has done so in some societies, *legein* does not progress in that 'the totality of the possibilities of a language as *legein* are given straightaway as soon as language simply exists' (p. 270). This does not mean that no subsequent language can signify more, but that there are no advances in the nature of the sign and the code dimension of language.

One of the most significant historical developments involving *legein* and *teukhein* is that which abstracts them from their full institutional context. This Castoriadis sees as the basis of the logic-ontology of determinacy that has ruled much of Western philosophy, which abstracts *legein* from language and insists that 'being' must be determinate in itself rather than simply for the purposes of thinking and speaking it (pp. 257–258). Stripped of its imaginary flesh in this way, ensidic logic can be applied without limit. Or one can attempt to do so. Since the grasp of ensidic logic on the world, social and natural, is incomplete, there are always lacunae. This constitutes a problem for thought, but only if a logically and rationally complete grasp of reality becomes the criterion for all logic and rationality. Castoriadis argues that we in the Greco-Western tradition have installed this as our criterion, whereas other societies have not. For these other societies there is no problem of rational incompleteness, and they are able to represent and institute their world without being troubled by the sorts of lacunae that keep Western philosophers and scientists awake at night (p. 237). More serious than troubled sleep, of course, is how this approach hinders the perception and conception of non-ensidic aspects of the world, especially the social-historical. The counterpart of this development in relation to *teukhein* is the establishment of technique as the model for all social action, with technical feasibility, along with effectiveness and efficiency, becoming the sole criteria against which all social doing is measured. Technique in this form lends itself to fantasies of total mastery. According to Castoriadis, this accounts for much of the reality of modern capitalism (p. 265). As suggested in the previous entry, in this connection Castoriadis's analysis exhibits affinities with – and no doubt debts to – other critiques of modern rationality, such as Weber's theory of rationalization and the Frankfurt School's critiques of instrumental reason.

By implication, the future of *legein* and *teukhein* under conditions of social autonomy would involve putting them back in their rightful place, respecting their value and influence while acknowledging their limitations. Representing and doing inevitably involve the ensidic dimensions of *legein* and *teukhein*, but these need not fully determine what we think, say and do.

Notes

1   See the entry on *Anlehnung* for a more detailed explanation of the concept of 'leaning on'.

2   As Adams (2011) notes, there is a tension between Castoriadis's desire to mark the uniqueness of the social-historical and his awareness that features similar to those operative in the self-creation of the social-historical – like *legein* and *teukhein* – must be presupposed in the living being. Adams shows how this tension relates to a development of Castoriadis's thought involving an imperfectly clarified extension of concepts such as creation and self-creation from the social-historical realm to being more generally, or as she terms it, from *nomos* to *physis*.

3   As Adams remarks (2011, p. 76), there are echoes of Marx's distinction between exchange and use value here.

References

Adams, S. (2011), *Castoriadis's Ontology: Being and Creation*, New York: Fordham University Press.

Arnason, J. P. (1991), 'Praxis and action: mainstream theories and Marxian correctives', *Thesis Eleven*, 29, 63–81.

Castoriadis, C. (1984), *Crossroads in the Labyrinth*, K. Soper and M. H. Ryle (ed. and trans.), Brighton, UK: Harvester.

—. (1987), *The Imaginary Institution of Society*, K. Blamey (trans.), Oxford: Polity; Cambridge, MA: MIT Press.

CHAPTER TWELVE

Anlehnung (Leaning On)

Jeff Klooger

Castoriadis's concept of *Anlehnung* or 'leaning on' describes a type of relation in which creativity replaces deterministic causality. A phenomenon 'leans on' an extrinsic reality when that reality serves as foundation, resource and impetus for an indeterminate and variable creation rather than invariably and inevitably determining the phenomenon.

A key element of Castoriadis's philosophy is his rejection of determinism, beginning with historical determinism. For Castoriadis, deterministic explanations fail because the social-historical is essentially creative (Castoriadis, 1987, pp. 165–220; 1991, pp. 33–47, 124–142). 'Creation' is to be understood in the strongest sense. Something is a creation only if it cannot be determined on the basis of things external to it. Understood in sequential terms, this involves that which precedes the creation. It may also involve the context of the creation, though there is always an implicit sequential dimension to the relationship between the extrinsic and the intrinsic. Creation excludes the type of explanation that is usually employed in deterministic models tied to the traditional logic-ontology of determinacy. The only type of relationship between phenomena conceivable within this logic-ontology is a deterministic one, and this usually amounts to a relationship of causation.[1] If phenomenon A *causes* phenomenon B, this means that phenomenon A generates or produces phenomenon

B inevitably and uniformly according to universal laws which govern the relationship. If one knows the determinations of A, one also knows the determinations of B. Creation severs this relationship of determination. Once creation intervenes, one can no longer know or predict B on the basis of a knowledge of A. One can observe what emerges in the process of creation, one can describe it, but one cannot 'explain' it in the traditional sense, where this means showing the necessity of a phenomenon arising precisely as it does given preceding states and contexts. For example, the social-historical context, antecedents, events and forces that led to the Terror may be elucidated at length, which will enrich one's understanding of the Terror and its emergence out of the French Revolution. But to imagine that one can demonstrate the inevitability of the Terror as the outcome of these historical forces and events, or further, to imagine one could specify exhaustively what *had* to arise as the outcome of this or any such revolution, and therefore to 'explain' both the Terror in its specificity and the course of revolution generally, is to misunderstand the indeterminate, creative nature of the social-historical (Castoriadis, 1987, pp. 165–220).

Readers of Castoriadis receive this vision of creation with either a sense of liberation or shock. It is liberating in that it frees the researcher to study human phenomena without being compelled to reduce them to extra-social factors. Instead, one may devote one's energies to capturing the full complexity and vitality of social-historical phenomena as they are encountered. On the other hand, this conception of creation can seem like an excuse for our inability to provide satisfactory explanations of a conventional kind. What is most appalling is the notion of a gap between phenomena that is not governed by law of any kind. We have become accustomed to regard lawfulness as universal, and its absence from any corner of the world is shocking indeed. It may be supposed that where no law governs the passage from one phenomenon to another, there is and can be no relationship between the two. This misapprehension arises from the assumption that the only relationship possible is one of determination. If we free ourselves from this assumption, we find that other types of relationships are possible.

This is the role of Castoriadis's concept of *leaning on* or *Anlehnung*. The term originates in Freud's analysis of the origin of psychological drives (Freud, 1984).[2] According to Freud, psychological drives are not directly determined by somatic drives;

rather, they lean on the latter. This means that in order for the psychological drive to be formed, work needs to be done by the psyche, work that utilizes the being-thus of the somatic drives. For Castoriadis, this work is the work of creation. Freud does not have a concept of creation as radical as Castoriadis's, but the creativity of the psyche more loosely understood is implied in his usage of *Anlehnung*, and this is what Castoriadis takes up in his reinterpretation of the concept (Castoriadis, 1987, pp. 229–237).

Castoriadis expands this concept from its original psychoanalytical context to incorporate all human phenomena, and particularly social-historical phenomena. *Leaning on* becomes a catch-all term for the type of relationship that obtains between extrinsic phenomena and those that result from creation, which includes both the human psyche and the social-historical as instances of self-creation. Castoriadis utilizes the concept of leaning on particularly in connection with the relationship between social-historical phenomena and those in what he calls the *first natural stratum*. The latter comprises the natural world up to and including the human body considered as an organism. Relations between beings within this ontological level tend to be more ensidic in nature (though never entirely or perfectly ensidic), following fixed patterns related to functionality. According to Castoriadis, this natural stratum does not determine social-historical phenomena. Rather, the social-historical leans on nature, taking up and utilizing in a creative, non-deterministic manner that which is given (pp. 229–237). One example of this is sexual identity. Maleness and femaleness, considered in purely biological terms, are everywhere the same, but masculinity and femininity vary from society to society. To say that masculinity and femininity lean on maleness and femaleness is to say that the characteristics of the male and female human organism never in and of themselves determine how sexual identity is constructed in any society. Rather, these somatic characteristics serve as the basis for an ongoing creation which results in gender as it operates in the social world (pp. 229–237).

Castoriadis acknowledges the obligatory character of the relationship of leaning on in some instances (pp. 229–237). There are some elements of the first natural stratum that the social-historical *must* respond to because if it failed to do so human beings could not survive. What the concept of *leaning on* stipulates is that this response, albeit obligatory, is non-determined. Thus, sustenance, and therefore the identification and obtaining of food, is a universal problem for humans as for all organisms. But the definition and meaning of food, the division into edible and inedible and the significance of each and the relationship between these definitions and divisions and other social institutions and significations, depend on a creativity that can never be predicted or explained in a deterministic manner.

According to Castoriadis, leaning on is not always obligatory. There are biological phenomena that the psyche and the social-historical ignore. There is also a creative spontaneity that cannot be subsumed under the category of leaning on, that is not related in any way to its context, that responds to nothing. Some social imaginary significations are pure creations in this sense. Castoriadis terms these 'central significations' as opposed to 'second order significations', which as a rule lean on something extrinsic to themselves (pp. 340–373). He cites the concept of God as a prime example (pp. 229–237). This contention continues to be the subject of discussion, with scholars such as Arnason (1989) and Adams (2007, 2011a, b) arguing that even concepts such as God serve an interpretative function, responding to elements of the human experience of the world. The question of the obligatory nature of the relationship with context is also an issue in relation to the problem of historical creation, with Arnason (2001, 2003) and Adams (2005) both arguing that Castoriadis's account of social-historical creations such as the Greek *polis* does not sufficiently acknowledge the importance of contextual conditions and precedents. These critics are certainly not arguing for a return to a deterministic approach to the evolution of social forms, but their criticisms could be interpreted as suggesting that leaning on is more universal and obligatory than Castoriadis acknowledged.

Castoriadis first introduces the concept of leaning on in connection with the relationships betweenthe psyche and the soma, on the one hand, andthe social-historical and the first natural stratum, on the other. But the concept applies wherever creation operates in the relationships between phenomena: primarily, wherever the *for-itself* occurs. For Castoriadis, the for-itself, a category which includes all forms of self from the organism – and even below the level of the whole organism, at that of the single cell – to the human psyche and the social-historical, is always self-creating. It creates itself by creating its own aims, its own representational world and its own mode of being (Castoriadis, 1997a, pp. 137–171). All instances of self-creation are non-determined, but all lean on what exists externally; and, as we have already seen, some instances of leaning on will be obligatory (Castoriadis, 1987, pp. 229–237). The general pattern of leaning on, as Castoriadis conceives it, is that it involves relationships between different levels of being. Castoriadis regards the universe as ontologically stratified, with different strata corresponding to different modes of being with their own laws and their own types of law – that is, not only different laws, but other meanings of 'law' and 'lawfulness'. The laws of one stratum do not rule beyond that stratum, and thus do not determine the phenomena within other strata. So, purely physical laws do not determine biological phenomena, biological laws do not determine psychical phenomena, and psychical laws do not determine social-historical phenomena. Instead, relationships flowing from lower to higher strata are to be understood as instances of leaning on, with creation intervening between and at the same time bridging the strata. It is important to understand this dual character of leaning on: it separates and it joins, it precludes the determination of phenomena within one stratum by the laws of another, and at the same time it links phenomena in one stratum to those within others (Castoriadis, 1984, pp. 145–226; 1997a, pp. 342–373).

The question of the applicability of the concept of leaning on where there is no self and therefore no creative agency was never adequately addressed by Castoriadis. As Ciaramelli (1997) and Adams (2011b) show, Castoriadis posits a creative dimension of 'being' in general – *a vis formandi*, as he sometimes calls it in his later work (Castoriadis, 1997a, pp. 172–195; 1997b, pp. 319–348). Does this mean that non-living being is creative in the same sense as living being? If the passage from older to newer strata is inevitably creative, then the passage from quantum to classical physical strata must be regarded as an instance of creativity, and the unfolding of physical processes in the moments after the Big Bang involves creation. But does this creation differ in nature from the creativity of the *for-itself* at its various ontological levels?

Castoriadis employs the concept of leaning on chiefly in connection with the relationship between ontological strata. The foregoing account suggests there may be justification for extending the concept to encompass relationships between phenomena within a single stratum in the case of the human realms of psyche and social-historical. Leaning on concerns the relationship between phenomena governed by one set of laws and one form of lawfulness, and phenomena governed by others. The human realms of the psyche and social-historical are peculiar not only in that they inaugurate in themselves new laws and forms of lawfulness, but because each also involves continuing creation. The psyche creates its own internal plurality of instances, each with its idiosyncratic mode of operation; and the social-historical to a considerably greater degree involves the continual, open-ended creation of forms of sociopolitical being: there is not one type of social institution, one type of society, there are many, and new types continually emerge. These realms are not singular creations but continuing processes of creation, and as such, the relationship between one created form and those which succeed it can be thought of in terms of leaning on. Thus the institutions of capitalism may be thought of as leaning on the economic and political – and also religious, as the analyses of Weber, Durkheim, Mauss and others suggest – institutions of preceding societies.

This suggestion goes somewhat beyond Castoriadis's most typical usage of the concept of leaning on. But it is in the nature of the concept to invite and require interpretation and development. The concept is a stop-gap one. It points to a type of relation we are forced to posit, but about which we know hardly anything. It remains to be determined precisely what is and is not an instance of leaning on, and also precisely what any instance of leaning on involves. Excluding determinism only answers the question of what leaning on is not. The fact that leaning on involves instances of creativity which by their very nature cannot be subsumed under universally applicable models does not mean there may not be common features and patterns. At the same time leaning on may mean very different things in different contexts. What happens when phenomena in the biological stratum lean on the physical is not the same as what happens when social-historical phenomena lean on the psyche. We need to ask what it means in each case for an element of a lower stratum to be leaned on by the organism, by the psyche and by the social-historical. How is the creative activity of each stratum connected to the being-thus of preceding ontological forms? If such questions are already being asked in some manner by biologists, psychologists, anthropologists and sociologists, Castoriadis's conceptual innovations allow them to be asked anew, freed from the chimera of reductive causal explanation.

Notes

1 Today we think of causation as equivalent to efficient causation, and this is how it is mostly meant here. As we know, Aristotle distinguished four varieties of causation, including material, formal and final causes (Aristotle, 1996, II 3, pp. 38–42; 1960, V 2, pp. 88–90). Efficient causation has tended to supplant the other three in modern times with the development of the empirical sciences. It is worth noting that these neglected alternatives can be equally deterministic. For example, one can imagine a course of events being thoroughly determined in a teleological manner by the end or final cause.

2 The standard English translation of Freud gives *Anlehnung* as *anaclasis*. The latter is derived from a grammatical term – enclitic – for relationships between particles which cannot stand alone but must be appended to others in a sentence (Freud, 1984, p. 81, n. 1.). This relationship of dependence is certainly a type of *Anlehnung*, though a rather specific and technical one, whereas the German word expresses the idea more directly. Readers should note that the term *anaclasis* has found its way into some of Castoriadis's own writings as well as English translations of his work.

References

Adams, S. (2005), 'Interpreting creation: Castoriadis and the birth of autonomy', *Thesis Eleven*, 83, 25–41.

—. (2007), 'Castoriadis and the permanent riddle of the world: Changing configurations of worldliness and world alienation', *Thesis Eleven*, 90, 44–60.

—. (2011a), 'Arnason and Castoriadis's unfinished dialogue: Articulating the world', *European Journal of Social Theory*, 14, 1, 71–88.

—. (2011b), *Castoriadis's Ontology: Being and Creation*, New York: Fordham University Press.

Aristotle (1960), *Metaphysics*, R. Hope (trans.), Ann Arbor: University of Michigan Press.

—. (1996), *Physics*, R. Waterfield (trans.), New York: Oxford University Press.

Arnason, J. P. (1989), 'Culture and imaginary significations', *Thesis Eleven*, 22, 25–45.

—. (2001), 'Autonomy and axiality: Comparative perspectives on the Greek breakthrough', in J. P. Arnason and P. Murphy (eds), *Agon, Logos, Polis: The Greek Achievement and its Aftermath*, Stuttgart: Steiner.

—. (2003), *Civilizations in Dispute: Historical Questions and Theoretical Traditions*, Leiden and Boston: Brill.

Castoriadis, C. (1984), *Crossroads in the Labyrinth*, K. Soper and M. H. Ryle (eds and trans.), Cambridge, MA: MIT Press.

—. (1987), *The Imaginary Institution of Society*, K. Blamey (trans.), Oxford: Polity; Cambridge, MA: MIT Press.

—. (1991), *Philosophy, Politics, Autonomy*, D. A. Curtis (ed.), New York and Oxford: Oxford University Press.

—. (1997a), *World in Fragments*, D. A. Curtis (ed.), Stanford, CA: Stanford University Press.

—. (1997b), *The Castoriadis Reader*, D. A. Curtis (ed.), Oxford and Cambridge, MA: Oxford University Press, pp. 338–348.

Ciaramelli, F. (1997), 'The self-presupposition of the origin: Homage to Cornelius Castoriadis', D. A. Curtis (trans.), *Thesis Eleven*, 49, 45–67.

Freud, S. (1984), 'On narcissism: An introduction', in J. Strachey (ed. and trans.) and A. Richards (ed.), *On Metapsychology: The Theory of Psychoanalysis, The Pelican Freud Library Vol. 11*, Harmondsworth: Penguin, pp. 59–97.

CHAPTER THIRTEEN

The Living Being

Suzi Adams

Cornelius Castoriadis displayed an enduring interest in the question of the natural world. He approached this problematic in two ways: as a *philosophy of nature* and as a *political ecology* (see, for example, Castoriadis, 1997; Castoriadis and Cohn-Bendit, 1981). These two levels of analysis were intertwined, and each was undertaken as an aspect of his project of autonomy. Castoriadis's philosophy of nature exemplified the philosophical aspect of autonomy as the interrogation of instituted society and its world; his political ecology elaborated the political aspects of autonomy in the strong and explicit sense of politics (*la politique*; see *Autonomy*). For present purposes, the elucidation of his philosophy of nature – or *Naturphilosophie* – is the most relevant.

Castoriadis included a discussion of the living being in his most systematic work, *The Imaginary Institution of Society* (1987), but it was not yet a question in its own right. At that time – in the 1970s – Castoriadis was primarily interested in elucidating the connections between political autonomy and his ontology of the social-historical as radically creative (see Howard, 1988). The main discussion of the living being in *The Imaginary Institution of Society* is found in the chapter on *legein* and *teukhein* in the context of *Anlehnung* (see also Legein *and* Teukhein and Anlehnung). Castoriadis elaborated the living being as more or less *discontinuous* from human modes of being (see the *Social-*

Historical and *Psyche*); the characterization of the living being as self-*organizing* acted as a counterfoil to the human capacity for self-*creation*. At that point, Castoriadis generally relegated the living being to discussions of the *first natural stratum*. This is the 'ensemblizable dimension' of the world and the domain of 'natural facts' (Castoriadis, 1987, pp. 226–227 ff.), which includes both biological and physical strata of nature (see *Ensemblistic-Identitary Logic*). Castoriadis uses the term *living being* more specifically to refer to organic nature in both its vegetable and animal modes. He contrasts it to non-living – physical – nature, on the one hand, and to human modes of being, on the other. The human psyche can be said to form an anomaly in his thought, however, in that it is regarded as *more than nature* but *not yet fully human*.

Castoriadis characterizes living beings in *The Imaginary Institution of Society* as 'identitary automata' (p. 232). The living being is understood to be its own end, and, as such, as beings *for-themselves* (e.g. Castoriadis, 1997, p. 145). Critiquing cybernetic models, Castoriadis argues that information is not presented fully formed in its objectivity to the living being, rather the living being selects what for it is pertinent. Living beings 'possess an initial transforming filter by means of which part of the events deemed "objective" are transformed into events *for* the living being or as *information* for it' (Castoriadis, 1987, p. 232). They possess a 'series of mechanisms' that elaborate what for them is relevant information that endows them with 'weights, values, univocal "interpretations", and promoting, in turn, the activation of response mechanisms' (p. 232). Yet even though Castoriadis elucidates the living being as 'self-operating' or 'self-organizing', it still remains in the realm of machines, and thus of ensemblistic-identitarian logic and deterministic ontology. Living beings exist by 'ensemblizing parts of the world, distinguishing therein elements possessing stable properties, and usable as instances of classes, and so on' (p. 232).

Towards the end of the 1970s, Castoriadis started to rethink the problematic of nature, both in relation to questions of autonomy and ontological creation. Although it cannot be said that his theorization of the natural world ever comprised the main focus of his intellectual agenda, its elucidation gained momentum in his thought during the 1980s, and continued into the 1990s. The primary shift in his theorization of nature appears in his rethinking of the 'creativity' of nature; he no longer reduced it to its 'organizing' capacity as an ensemblistic-identitarian stratum. This rethinking took part in the context of an emerging field of broader intellectual debates on *complexity* and *auto-poiesis* that gained traction in the early 1980s. He sharpens his articulation of autonomy – especially the question of *biological autonomy* – in an enduring dialogue with Chilean biologist Francisco Varela, spanning around 20 years, from Castoriadis's review of Varela's *Principles of Biological Autonomy* (Varela, 1979; Castoriadis, 1980) to their dialogue hosted by Radio *France Culture* in the mid-1990s (see Varela, 1979; and Castoriadis, 1997a; 2011).

Drawing on Aristotle and Husserl, Castoriadis's elucidation of an ontology of the social-historical at the time of *The Imaginary Institution of Society* in the 1970s took the form of a *regional* ontology. For him, being formed itself as an irregular stratification and heterogenous regionality, and, unlike other regions of being, the social-historical was characterized by ontological self-creation in a radical sense (see *Social-Historical* and *Creation* ex nihilo). In the 1980s – and in light of his rethinking of the ontological implications of creation in relation to nature – he expanded this regional ontology of *anthropos* into a *poly-regional ontology* of modes of being *for-itself*, where each level of the *for-itself* is characterized by varieties of self-creation.[1]

Castoriadis identifies six interacting modes of being for-itself. They are: the living being, the psyche, the social-individual (i.e. the socially fabricated individual as the product of the social-historical's transformation and (partial) socialization of the psyche; see *Psyche*), society, the autonomous subject and autonomous society (Castoriadis, 1997, pp. 142 ff.). The first four levels are the 'merely real'; the final two levels are not given per se, but are *to be made*: they are the respective instances of subjectivity capable of deliberative activity and reflection (see *Autonomy*). Here it is important to note that the varieties of *selfhood* or *self* that is a basic characteristic of each level of the *for-itself* is not synonymous with Castoriadis's understanding of the *subject* in the strong and explicit sense by which he refers to the human breakthrough to autonomy (see also Smith, 2010).

All levels of the *for-itself* have three characteristics in common: calculation, the finality of self-preservation and the creation of a world of one's own (*Eigenwelt*; Castoriadis, 1997, p. 143). The living being proper is elucidated as the 'archetypal' *for-itself*. Taking Fichte's notion of *Anstoß*, Castoriadis articulates the 'shock' of the living being's encounter with the 'external' world – with the X – but argues, in criticism of biological approaches that took the living being as a cybernetic system, that the X is not to be understood as presenting 'information' to the living being: 'Nature contains no "information" waiting to be gathered' (p. 145). Instead the 'shock' sets into motion the living being's forming capacities: 'This X becomes something only by *being formed* (in-formed) by the *for-itself* that forms it' (p. 145; emphases in original). The living being *leans on* (see Anlehnung) the 'being-thus' of what is, which supports the creation of its world, but as with his earlier elucidations of *Anlehnung* in the human domain (see Castoriadis, 1987), it is characterized by creation and not determinacy. Information is not given but *created* by the particular level of the self in question.

Central to Castoriadis's elucidation of the living being during the 1980s is the emphasis on its creation of a *proper world for itself* (*Eigenwelt*). Castoriadis's identifies three elements of the living being's creation of its own world (*Eigenwelt*). They are: representation, affect and intention. These rearticulate the three dimensions of the *for-itself* as identified by the ancient Greeks – the *logico-noetic*, the *thymic* and the *oreactic* (Castoriadis, 1997, p. 146). World creation includes a presentation of *in-formation* – of its *meaning* – to the self. This involves a setting into images and a bringing into relation that draws on 'in an abuse of language' the aesthetic/sensorial and noetic/logical dimensions. The setting into images follows certain 'rules' and exhibits a certain regularity – what is important to note here is that these are ordered in line with the self-finality of the living being. The *presentation-representation* of these images and relations – these meanings – are given a negative or positive value that guides the intention ('desire') of the living being either towards it or away from it, in avoidance (of the X). Finally, world formation is selective: As Castoriadis points out, 'A tree's goal of preserving itself does not lead to the same sort of selections within the environment that a mammal's goal of sexually reproducing itself does' (p. 147).

The *world* of the *for-itself* is not reducible to its *environment*. Castoriadis now emphasizes that the living being *creates* – rather than simply organizes or constructs – its own world. The 'world' – as opposed to 'environment' – is that which 'emerges though and with this creation' as an horizon of proto-meaning (p. 148). The appearance of world (and concomitantly, of meaning – they go hand-in-hand) forms the basis of what Castoriadis calls the 'subjective instance' that characterizes the living being. In putting non-living nature into meaning, the living being represents an ontological rupture with the physical strata of being. Finally, the world of the living being is created in *closure* – as an enclosed sphere (p. 168) – rather than openness, and as an *interiority* (causal explanation only takes us so far in elucidating the living being) (p. 149). This is connected to universality and participation in other interlaced levels, such as eco-systems: Not only does the eucalyptus tree only exist as one of many possible eucalypts, it is also integrated into the level of the forest, which relies on organic matter and animals – from worms to birds – and so on.

From a philosophical perspective, Castoriadis rethought the ontological creativity of the various levels and strata of nature – in particular, of the living being – through an engagement with the Aristotelian notion of *physis* (see especially pp. 331–341). Castoriadis's engagement with ancient Greek philosophy is to be situated within the context of modern rediscovery and reconfiguration of ancient sources. In this particular case, Castoriadis's rethinking of the creativity of nature (*physis*) is to be understood as part of the intermittent, modern intellectual tradition of *natura naturans/natura naturata* (i.e. *productive nature* and *produced nature*). This philosophical problematic was prominent as a critique of Enlightenment conceptions of nature in early German Romanticism; of the new, modern positing of a radical discontinuity between human modes of being and nature and of the over-reliance on paradigms of rationality to the exclusion of creativity and the imagination (for more detailed discussion of Castoriadis's philosophy of nature, see Adams, 2011).

Castoriadis's rethinking of the idea of nature in the 1980s emphasized its ontological creativity, which was absent in his earlier work in the 1970s. In this context, his most important philosophical interlocutor was Aristotle. Here, two of Aristotle's understandings of *physis* were particularly important for him (Castoriadis, 1997, pp. 331–341). The first was the idea of nature as teleological; the second was the idea that nature is characterized by internal (self-)

movement. (Movement is understood in the *qualitative* sense of change, not the *quantitative* sense of locomotion that is more familiar to moderns.) In a heterodox interpretation, Castoriadis radicalizes both these aspects. First, Aristotle's understanding of *alloiosis* – as qualitative change – is reconfigured to signify not only creation but *ontological* creation. For Castoriadis this specifically means the self-creation of the living being's world (*Eigenwelt*) of (proto)meaning. Second, the *teleological* conception of nature is rethought as *teleonomic*. Here Castoriadis characterizes the purposiveness of the *physis*, in general, and of the living being, in particular, as '*pushing-toward-giving-itself-a-form*' (p. 333; see *Creation* ex nihilo). For Castoriadis, the proper world (*Eigenwelt*) is the most important form (*eidos*) to be created. In this vein, he writes: 'Beings [*les étants*] have in themselves principle and origin of creation of forms, being [*l'être*] itself is defined by *alloiosis* in the strong sense of the word – self-alteration, self-creation' (p. 336).

Castoriadis's elucidation of the living being and its capacity for creation provides a greater context of commonality with *anthropos*. However, when it came to the question of autonomy, Castoriadis retained a sharp break between the living being and human modes of being. Unlike Varela, Castoriadis rejects the notion of *biological autonomy* and prefers the term 'self-constitution' for the living being (Castoriadis, 1997, pp. 336–341; 2011, pp. 58–73). For him, the project of autonomy remains a human capacity. It involves deliberative action, unlimited interrogation of the instituted world and the explicit creation of forms – as politics (*la politique*) and philosophy (*la philosophie*) in the strong and explicit sense – that goes beyond the self-constitution of the living being.

For Castoriadis, the human capacity for autonomy rests on the order of *nomos* – human convention – rather than *physis* (nature or natural law; see *Autonomy*). The *physis* and *nomos* debate can be understood as the contestation between conceptions of – and tensions between – natural and human *world orders*, and the corresponding debates about the scope of natural law and norms versus the vagaries of human convention. Although Castoriadis radicalized the Aristotelian notion of *physis*, he does so not by reducing *anthropos* to nature, but through a reconfiguration of the *physis* and *nomos* problematic, whereby he rediscovers the creative aspects of *physis* but retains *nomos* as a human specific order.

Note

1 Castoriadis's poly-regional ontology was further nested in a trans-regional ontology of *à-être* as 'always-becoming-being' that included non-living strata of nature as well. It is important to note, though, that he did not reduce human modes of being to natural modes of being. He always maintained the distinction between *physis* and *nomos*, although the configuration between them shifted over time in his thought. For further discussion, see Adams, 2011.

References

Adams, S. (2011), *Castoriadis' Ontology: Being and Creation*, New York: Fordham University Press.

Castoriadis, C. (1980), 'Francisco Varela: *Principles of Biological Autonomy*', *Le débat*, 1, 126–7.

—. (1987), *The Imaginary Institution of Society*, K. Blamey (trans.), Cambridge, UK: Polity Press.

—. (1997), *World in Fragments: Writings on Politics, Society, Psychoanalysis, and the Imagination*, D. A. Curtis (ed. and trans.), Stanford, CA: Stanford University Press.

—. (2011), *Postscript on Insignificance: Dialogues with Cornelius Castoriadis*, G. Rockhill (ed. and trans.) and J. V. Garner (trans.), London: Continuum.

Castoriadis, C. and Cohn-Bendit, D. (1981), *De l'écologie à l'autonomie*, Paris: Seuil.

Howard, D. (1988), *The Marxian Legacy*, Minneapolis, MN: University of Minnesota Press.

Smith, K. E. (2010), *Meaning, Subjectivity, Society: Making Sense of Modernity*, Leiden: Brill.

Varela, F. (1979), *Principles of Biological Autonomy*, New York: Elsevier.

CHAPTER FOURTEEN

Paideia

Ingerid S. Straume

Paideia is a Greek term that holds a special place in the thought of Castoriadis. Its root is *pais*, the Greek word for child (*paideuo:* I am raising a child, *paideusis:* child rearing). In his three-volume work called *Paideia: The Ideals of Greek Culture*, Werner Jaeger notes that in the early fifth-century BCE *paideia* was used for child-rearing, but later took on a 'higher' meaning (Jaeger, 1965, p. 5). In the Greek city states, and Athens in particular, *paideia*, education and self-improvement were common concerns for the *polis* as a whole. The Athenians' engagement with *paideia* is historically unique, but understandable, since the government and well-being of the city depended on each and every one acting responsibly. As citizens, the Athenians saw themselves not only as participating in the government of the *polis*, they *were* the *polis*, as attested by the fact that the same term was used for Athens and the Athenians (Αθῆναι, *Athenai*). In the words of the historian Thucydides, 'the *polis* is the men' (cited in Castoriadis, 1991, p. 109).

Paideia is a comprehensive concept that can designate the *contents*, *processes* or *goals* of education, and often all at the same time. Werner Jaeger sees in *paideia* the unification of 'culture', 'civilization', 'tradition', 'literature' and 'education'. According to Jaeger, classical Greek culture was the first to be oriented towards 'ideals' – an orientation that was developed in Athens in particular (Jaeger, 1965, p. xvii). The Athenians valued their own education, and, as a collective, reflected upon themselves in terms of their *paideia*. When Pericles held his funeral oration for the Athenians who fell in the Peloponnesian war, he called attention to the *paideia* of the *polis*, and only in extension, to the virtue of the fallen soldiers. Due to the central role of *paideia*, Pericles could call Athens the '*paideusis* – the education and educator – of Greece' (Castoriadis, 1991, p. 123). Likewise, the downfall of Athens was explained by Jaeger, as well as by Aristotle and Plato, as a crisis of *paideia*.

The proper meaning and contents of *paideia* was a much-debated theme among philosophers and sophists at the time of Socrates and Plato. Jaeger even goes so far as to claim that *all* of Plato's dialogues were in essence about *paideia* or 'the problem of education' (Jaeger, 1986, p. 123). Some of the central questions were: what is the nature of knowledge; and how can it be taught? What is a good education? And above all, especially for Plato, what is virtue, and can it be taught? The philosophical disputes between Socrates and the sophists around their respective views on the *paideia* of Athens tragically culminated in the sentencing of Socrates on the very same question. For the young Plato, this represented a very tough lesson; for how could a city that valued *paideia*, deliberately cause the death of one of its wisest men?

Castoriadis shares Jaeger's openly hellenocentric understanding of the role of *paideia* in Greek culture, but with a different emphasis. While Jaeger takes most interest in literature and poetry, and holds the Greek imaginary as the *telos* – ideal and germ – of Western culture, Castoriadis discusses *paideia* in the political context of Greek democracy (see *Democracy*). The concept is not treated in a systematic way anywhere in Castoriadis's oeuvre,[1] but plays a key role in the three following essays: 'The Greek *polis* and the creation of democracy' (Castoriadis, 1991, pp. 81–123), 'Power, politics, autonomy' (in 1991 pp. 143–174) and 'Democracy as procedure and democracy as regime' (Castoriadis, 1997c). Written in the years 1979 to 1996 – the period when Castoriadis gave his seminars on the Greek imaginary at the *École des hautes études en sciences sociales* – they reflect his extensive studies of ancient Greece, which in the essays are brought to bear on contemporary discussions. In all three texts, *paideia* is seen as the key to understanding the nature of political democracy, with clear references to the Athenian *polis*. However, Castoriadis also uses the term in a less demanding sense, as socialization and education in general. In the following, we will first look briefly at this latter use of the term and then turn to its more comprehensive meaning: that which Castoriadis calls 'true *paideia*' or '*paideia* in the deepest sense'. After some elaboration and discussion of the latter, I round off by situating *paideia* in relation to the more contemporary concepts of education and *Bildung*.

In 'Power, politics, autonomy', Castoriadis defines *paideia* thus: '. . . there is a "part" of almost all institutions that aims at the nurturing, the rearing, the education of the newcomers – what the Greeks called *paideia:* family, age groups, rites, schools, customs, laws, etc.' (Castoriadis, 1991, p. 149). In another context, he states that: '*Paideia* (upbringing, training, education) is development; it consists of bringing the newborn little monster to the fit state of a human being' (p. 182). In this *descriptive* sense, every society has a *paideia* upon which its social reproduction depends. The quotes mention institutions of primary socialization (family, age groups) and secondary socialization (school, rites), which both consist of conscious/explicit as well as non-conscious/implicit dimensions. For example, schooling is an explicit institution for secondary socialization, whereas norms are (for the most part) implicit institutions of primary socialization. *Paideia*, thus conceived, is simply another term for the socialization process whereby the psyche is transformed from its monadic state to form *the social individual* (see *Psyche*).

Castoriadis further describes 'socialization' as 'the social fabrication (nurturing, rearing) of the individual' (p. 42). The term 'individual' is used in a strictly sociological sense. This fabrication process, which at first sounds rather mechanical, takes place when the psyche invests in socially meaningful ways of behaviour, motives and objects (Castoriadis often uses the psychoanalytic term *cathexis:* concentration of psychic energy on some particular object). This investment in society's significations is what Castoriadis calls *sublimation*: the process through which the psyche abandons its initial, primitive state and accepts the socially instituted imaginary significations as its own, thus becoming socialized.[2] The process can therefore be analysed from two perspectives: From the viewpoint of psyche, there is *sublimation*, and from the viewpoint of society, there is *socialization* (Castoriadis, 1991). The psyche, in return for its internalization of the social institution, is provided with socially instituted meaning, which it cannot produce from itself, yet *needs* in order to exist as a human being. Moreover, society also 'needs' sublimation: Through the psyche's acceptance of the institution of the society as a whole, society's *'effective validity'* is ensured (p. 149). According to Castoriadis, a society's reproduction and existence depends entirely upon the socialization whereby individuals become 'embodiments' of its principles of organization, power structures, practices and norms – relations which, on another level, are embodiments of the imaginary significations that configure what counts and does not count as parts of that society's reality (an extensive discussion of sublimation is found in Castoriadis, 1987, pp. 316–320).

Every society has *paideia* in this general sense – without it, societies would not be able to reproduce themselves as de facto legitimate and meaningful. In modern societies, the most important institution in this respect is probably what Castoriadis calls 'schooling' (1991, p. 144). Most of the time, however, Castoriadis does not refer to *paideia* in this sociological, descriptive sense. What interests him more is what he calls a 'true' *paideia*, or *paideia* 'in the strongest and most profound meaning of the term' (Castoriadis, 1997c, p. 15).

In terms of *paideia*, we have seen that sublimation and socialization are two sides of the same coin. However, when discussing *paideia* Castoriadis usually has more substantial concerns in mind. As we know from the entry on *Autonomy*, some significations have a special status for Castoriadis, viz. the significations that characterize *the project of autonomy*, such as the quest for truth, investment in the value of knowledge, validity de jure and, above all, freedom (see, for example, Castoriadis 1997b, pp. 361–417). A *paideia* fostering these ideas is what Castoriadis calls a *true paideia*, and thus has a central connection to Castoriadis's understanding of autonomy. In 'Democracy as procedure and democracy as regime', he holds forth *paideia* as the criterion for whether a democracy is 'effective' (i.e. realized), or merely nominal:

> Let us even suppose that a democracy, as complete, perfect, etc. as one might wish, might fall upon us from the heavens: this sort of democracy will not be able to endure for more than a few years if it does not engender individuals that correspond to it, ones that, first and foremost, are capable of making it function

and reproducing it. There can be no democratic society without democratic *paideia*. (Castoriadis, 1997c, p. 10)

There are several ways in which a democratic *paideia* is essential for democracy. On a general level, there is the relation of institutional *embodiment* just described, where society institutes – creates – itself by 'the creation of the human individual in which the institution of society is massively embedded' (Castoriadis, 1991, p. 84). On the functional level, '[a]n autonomous society, as a self-instituting and self-governing collectivity, presupposes the development of the capacity of all its members to participate in its reflective and deliberative activities' (Castoriadis, 1997a, p. 132). This requires an effort on the part of the social institution: '. . . for individuals to be capable of making democratic procedures function in accordance with their "spirit", a large part of the labor of society and of its institutions must be directed toward engendering individuals that correspond to this definition [. . .]' (Castoriadis, 1997c, p. 10), such as 'schooling'.

In order for democracy to work, the citizens must make use of the public space that was created with democracy (Castoriadis, 1991, p. 113). This implies that a true *paideia* is not merely education, it is also an *ethos*. Through their *paideia*, the people (or the *polis*) are able to evaluate experts in various fields, according to Castoriadis. For:

> The proper judge of the expert is not another expert, but the *user*: the warrior and not the blacksmith for the sword, the horseman and not the saddler for the saddle. And evidently, for all public affairs, the user, and thus the best judge, is the *polis*. (p. 109)

Castoriadis dryly points out that, judging by the results – the building of the Acro*polis* and the tragedy contests – the judgement of Athens appears to have been quite sound.

Another principle at stake is that a democratic *paideia* justifies the principle of equality (in ancient Greece, *isophephia*). Castoriadis expresses the latter dimension in the following:

> Majority rule can be justified only if one grants equal value, in the domain of the contingent and the probable, to the *doxai* of

free individuals. But if this equality of value among opinions is not to remain a 'counterfactual principle', some sort of pseudotranscendental gadget, then the permanent labor of the institution of society must be to render individuals such that one might *reasonably* postulate that their opinions all have the same weight in the political domain. Once again, the question of *paideia* proves ineliminable. (Castoriadis, 1997c, p. 11; emphasis added)

A premise in the above passage is that the principle of political equality can and should be justified through actual qualifications such as skills and judgement. The same idea can be found in educational reforms of modern nations, where the right to vote came hand in hand with the expansion of the school system (see, for example, John Dewey's *Democracy and Education* from 1916).

In Athenian democracy, the citizens acquired relevant experience and skills through their participation in the city's various bodies of governance (see *Democracy*). A democratic *paideia*, for Castoriadis, is not a question of political expertise or a specialized knowledge (*episteme*), but a matter of 'judgment, caution and verisimilitude' (Castoriadis, 2007, p. 127). It is perhaps telling that when magistrates were selected for office (by lot), they were faced with questions regarding their character and behaviour, and not with regard to their knowledge, intelligence, experience or skill, that is, expertise (Samons, 2007, p. 8). Through the exercise of political, military and administrative duties and collective governance of the city, the Athenians became 'capable of governing and of being governed' (Aristotle, *Politics*, 1277a26–27).

Castoriadis sees democracy as a *regime* embodying certain values that must be practiced, lived for, achieved by its members, and not a set of procedures that can be transplanted from one setting to another. Without democratic individuals, democracy would just be a word. Against this background, it is clear that a democratic *paideia* is something substantial. But what kind of *paideia* is a true *paideia*? What are its qualities? The tasks of a democratic *paideia* are complex, and its nature would vary from one instituted type of democracy to another. Even though an exhaustive list of qualities or virtues cannot be made, Castoriadis does name a few in various connections. First of all, to justify the principle of equality mentioned above, cognitive skills, or what Castoriadis calls 'effective judgmental ability', is necessary (Castoriadis, 2007, p. 125). Democratic individuals need to sublimate the value of knowledge, an investment that Castoriadis sees as a 'quest for truth' (Castoriadis, 1997b). More specifically *political* virtues are frankness or courage in speaking the truth (*parrhesia*) and a specific kind of shame (*aidos*) that is connected to self-limitation (Castoriadis, 1991, p. 113). All of these can be assembled under the general principle of *responsibility*: a sense of responsibility for the social institution; a commitment to politics as such (Castoriadis, 2007).

To characterize the ethos of a democratic *paideia*, Castoriadis frequently invokes Greek terms, as we have seen. This is not done simply for the sake of decoration; there is also the problem that modern languages fail to offer the corresponding terms – an indication that these significations are not as effective in contemporary democracies. Castoriadis's definition of a true *paideia* gains much of its substance from his notion of democracy. Since 'true' democracy, as conceptualized by Castoriadis, is directly linked to the project of autonomy (Castoriadis, 1997c, p. 16), a true *paideia* means an investment in the significations that correspond to this project. In other words, true *paideia* is the *conscious social reproduction* that aims towards the autonomy of individuals and of the collective. In 'Democracy as procedure', Castoriadis portrays *paideia* 'in the strongest and most profound meaning of the term' as 'aiding individuals to become autonomous' (p. 15). This brings us closer to an understanding of what a true *paideia* would be vis-à-vis – with an abuse of terms – an 'untrue' *paideia*. True *paideia* can never signify mere social reproduction, whatever its contents, where norms are simply transferred and values inculcated. It seems fair to summarize 'true' *paideia* as practices that lead individuals toward autonomy, while 'non-true' *paideia* (a term Castoriadis does not use) is heteronomous. Following the logic of the project of autonomy, a true *paideia* is self-reflexive, thus putting its own contents into question. Again, we approach the Greek meaning of the term, recalling that the Greeks never ceased to discuss what a true *paideia* would mean.

Castoriadis's notion of *paideia* has a double character: it contains an emphatic meaning that reveals itself when viewed in light of the project of autonomy. If we draw together Castoriadis's views on what it means to become autonomous, putting *paideia* at the centre, we can say that a true *paideia* – which means investment in the value of *paideia* itself – is only possible in a society that has instituted the signification of autonomy. By drawing in Castoriadis's discussion of *paideia* and education in 'Psychoanalysis and politics' (Castoriadis, 1997a, pp. 125–136), we can say that true *paideia* for Castoriadis refers to a kind of socialization that is able to establish 'another relationship' between the 'instituted' and the 'instituting' society, the conscious and the unconscious, namely a reflective or questioning relationship that reaches beyond – or rather, forms a break with – mere internalization of the social institution. From this rupture, two new types of beings emerge: 'the subject' at the individual level, and 'democracy' or 'autonomous society' at the social level (Castoriadis, 1997a). I will return to these points in the final section.

Let me round off this section with some conceptual considerations. It seems clear that a true *paideia* is something that cannot exist in a heteronomous society. However, as a conceptual distinction, true versus non-true *paideia* is clearly unsatisfactory, especially when considering the statement that '. . . there is a "part" of almost all institutions that aims at the nurturing, the rearing, the education of the newcomers – what the Greeks called *paideia*' (Castoriadis, 1991, p. 149). Castoriadis, who did not devote as much thought to the question of education as he would have liked to (Castoriadis, 1997b, pp. 80–81), could easily have worked out a more sophisticated distinction between a *paideia* as mere socialization vis-à-vis the kind of *paideia* that aims at individual and collective autonomy. However, to do so, a fundamental rethinking of the autonomy–heteronomy distinction might also be necessary.

One question that remains concerns the relationship between the classical term *paideia* and its German counterpart *Bildung*, as well as the more contemporary terms education and pedagogy. Castoriadis discusses *paideia* mostly in the context of politics, while invoking education and pedagogy in various other contexts, with some conceptual overlap. His most systematic discussion of education/pedagogy is found in 'Psychoanalysis and politics' where he discusses the aim of psychoanalysis with parallels to the aim of (true) politics and (true) pedagogy/education. Here, education and pedagogy are treated in much the same way as true *paideia*, but on the level of the individual subject rather than the *polis*. Compared to the wider scope of *paideia* (the *polis*), education and pedagogy relate to a more limited setting, where the practices of teaching and learning are made explicit. The aim of the educational process is crystallized in Castoriadis's concept of 'the subject'. Once again, he does not talk about *any* kind of education – such as the more restricted (heteronomous) notion of schooling – but education in an ideal sense, as 'true' or 'non-mutilating' education. According to Castoriadis, 'individuals capable of self-reflective activity' are only possible with a 'non-mutilating education, a true *paideia*' (Castoriadis, 1997a, p. 133). A common denominator for psychoanalysis, politics and pedagogy is their inherent connection with the project of autonomy:

> In terms of the project of autonomy, we have defined the aims of psychoanalysis and pedagogy as, first, the instauration of another type of relation between the reflective subject (of will and thought) and his Unconscious – that is, his radical imagination – and, second, the freeing of his capacity to make and do things, to form an open project for his life and to work with that project. (p. 132)

The *subject* is a reflexive subject, capable of putting its very conditions into question (Castoriadis, 1997a). It is further characterized by 'the *will* or the capacity for deliberate action, in the strong sense of this term' (Castoriadis, 1997a, p. 143). A non-mutilating education aims at freeing the radical imaginary of the emerging subject, and enhancing the capacity for reflection, deliberate action and self-limitation.

The strong, normative ideals contained in the emphatic conceptions of *paideia* and education are apparent at both the collective and individual levels of autonomy. However, we need not see these as 'regulative ideals' or utopias. Instead, in Castoriadis's thought they function as critical, dynamic concepts much the same way as they did at the time of Plato: notions that serve to critique and redefine themselves when applied in a practical context. They represent what Castoriadis calls genuine questions: questions that must remain open (Castoriadis, 1991).

The German historian Reinhart Koselleck has crafted a conceptual historical analysis for the term *Bildung* that can be used to elucidate Castoriadis's notion of *paideia*. Koselleck points out that the concept of *Bildung* contains a 'productive tension' that allows it, through various historical phases, to be 'stabilized over and over again through critical self-use' (Koselleck, 2002, p. 170). In other words, the notion of *Bildung* has been used as a lever to destabilize instituted significations and norms, and posit the fundamental questions anew: Can this rightly be called *Bildung*? If not, then what is *Bildung*, what kind of *Bildung* do we want to defend? On what grounds? Are these the norms we ought to have? and so forth. Readers of Castoriadis will easily recognize this kind of questioning from, for example, 'The Greek *polis* and the creation of democracy'. Castoriadis did not use the term *Bildung*, which he saw as too attached to German idealism to be of any use. However, as a concept whose contents are never fixed once and for all, but taken up for reflection, critique and reconsideration in political and scholarly debates, there are clear parallels between Koselleck's *Bildung* and Castoriadis's notion of *paideia*. In addition, the notion of a *true paideia* signifies an investment in the notion of *paideia* itself: *paideia* as an ideal, as Jaeger would have put it. In this respect, Castoriadis's use of the term in the 1980s and 1990s certainly draws him very close to ancient Greek attitude towards – and valuation of – *paideia*.

Notes

1 Neither democracy nor *paideia* are indexed in *The Imaginary Institution of Society*.
2 Castoriadis's usage of the term sublimation lacks the normative meaning attributed by Freud, for whom sublimation was a mature type of defence mechanism.

References

Aristotle (1992), *The Politics*, T. A. Sinclair (trans.), revised by T. J. Saunders, London: Penguin.
Castoriadis, C. (1987), *The Imaginary Institution of Society*, K. Blamey (trans.), Cambridge: Polity.
—. (1991), *Philosophy, Politics, Autonomy. Essays in Political Philosophy*, New York: Oxford University Press.
—. (1997a), *World in Fragments*, D. A. Curtis (ed. and trans.), Oxford: Blackwell.

—. (1997b), *The Castoriadis Reader*, D. A. Curtis (ed. and trans.), Oxford: Blackwell, pp. 361–417.

—. (1997c), 'Democracy as procedure and democracy as regime', *Constellations*, 4, 1, 1–18.

—. (2007), 'What democracy?' in H. Arnold (trans.), *Figures of the Thinkable*, Stanford, CA: Stanford University Press, pp. 118–150.

Dewey, J. (1997 [1916]), *Democracy and Education. An Introduction to the Philosophy of Education*, New York: Simon and Schuster.

Jaeger, W. (1965), *Paideia: The Ideals of Greek Culture. Vol. I, Archaic Greece and the Mind of Athens*, New York: Oxford University Press.

—. (1986), *Paideia: The Ideals of Greek Culture. Vol. II, In Search of the Divine Centre*, New York: Oxford University Press.

Koselleck, R. (2002), 'On the anthropological and semantic structure of *Bildung*', in *The Practice of Conceptual History*, Stanford, CA: Stanford University Press.

Samons, L. J. (2007), 'Introduction: Athenian history and society in the age of Pericles', in *The Cambridge Companion to The Age of Pericles*, Cambridge: Cambridge University Press.

CHAPTER FIFTEEN

Capitalism

Jeremy C. A. Smith

Cornelius Castoriadis advanced an insightful revolutionary theory of capitalism's mobilization of creativity. At the same time, he critically elucidated the threats that capitalism itself posed to the very existence of that creativity. In his own words, capitalism is 'profoundly irrational and full of contradictions' (Castoriadis, 1988b, p. 93); a new condition of life that 'is *in fact* the central objective of human existence' (Castoriadis, 1991, p. 184); and a system producing bureaucratic corporate institutions 'now looting the planet, guided only by the short-sighted prospect of immediate profits' (Castoriadis, 2007, p. 70).

Castoriadis's censorious tones are hardly unique, but his deep critique of the most fundamental dimensions of modern capitalism is original. In this entry, I elucidate some of the shifts in emphasis in Castoriadis's understanding of capitalism from his early critique of bureaucratization through to his demolition of the incoherence of political economy and finally to the exploration of the effects of the capitalist imaginary on the modern human condition (see also *Heteronomy, Autonomy, Socialism* and *Modernity*). The chapter concludes with Castoriadis's salient connections between the challenges presented by an unlimited tendency to growth and the potentiality of ecology for a new culture of self-limitation.

Castoriadis's conception of capitalism evolved through his critical assessment of Marxism (Howard, 1988, pp. 320–333). His critique of Marxism centred on problems particular to the theoretical corpus of the workers movement. Early in his life Castoriadis also oriented to inter-related problems of capitalism neglected by the Stalinist Left: alienation and the bureaucratic organization of work, time, the social construction of needs, the character of technology and the nature of 'value'. Along with his comrades in *Socialisme ou Barbarie*, Castoriadis's deliberations on Marxism led him to the conclusion that Marxism and revolutionary change had become incompatible. Castoriadis elected for the latter. Considering capitalism in light of this departure from the chief pole of anti-capitalist critique, Castoriadis focused on those precise aspects of the social institution that he thought Marxism had misunderstood: alienation, time, needs, technology and value.

The first problem to stimulate critical assessment was that of alienation.[1] Castoriadis steadfastly argued that the fundamental tendency of capitalism was its self-contradicting drive to conquer the creativity of workers on which the edifice of production depended. One of the central permanent crises of capitalism is the 'drive to eliminate the human element in productive labor and, in the long run to eliminate man altogether from the productive process'. This is the 'deepest tendency of capitalism' (Castoriadis, 1988b, p. 104). Yet, this tendency engenders a permanent crisis because the complete reification of people is unachievable. The organization of production compels its 'directors' to control and direct the creativity and the organic self-organization of workers, while at the same time depending on that creativity and self-reliance for its continuation (pp. 168–188). While management pursues the maximization of results and concomitant minimization of costs, the workforce is oriented to the greatest reward possible for what it regards as a just amount of work (pp. 158–159, 186–188). Taylorism and Fordism are great historical manifestations of this very contradiction (159–166). Daily resistance stems from this asymmetrical arrangement:

> Long before one can speak of revolution or political consciousness, people refuse in their everyday working lives to be treated like objects. The capitalist organization of society is thereby compelled not only to structure itself in the absence of those most directly concerned but also to take shape against them. The net result is not only waste but perpetual conflict. (p. 93)

Castoriadis reconstructs Marx's vision of the enmity of classes by placing the struggle for *control* of production 'its nature, its content, its methods, the very instruments and purpose' at its centre (p. 94). The class struggle is thus amplified beyond an economistic focus on the contest over surplus value to the control of production and, implicitly, to the nature of work itself. The contradiction lies in the fact that independence in decision making is needed for the entire complex and creative process of production to work. Production of goods and services cannot occur without the practical resolution of daily problems of organization, which often requires workers to go beyond the rules of rational organization set down by managerial elites. Thus, Castoriadis argues, capitalism is unimaginable without independent human creativity, even while, at every moment, capitalism's tendency is to the conquest of creativity.

In 'Modern capitalism and revolution' Castoriadis commences analysis of modern capitalism's self-modernization (pp. 226–343). At length, he sets out how capitalism has stabilized the most erratic effects of its internal contradictions. He observes that wages are increasing steadily, unemployment has become negligible, the public sector has grown in weight and contributes to stabilization, the accumulation of capital is subject to fewer and less dramatic fluctuations and trade unions and social democratic parties are entwined in the state's regulation of markets. Over this short period, it looks as though the laws of capitalism disclosed by Marxist political economy (the impoverishment of the proletariat, the tendency of the rate of profit to fall, the impulse to expand the reserve army of labour) are no longer at work. With the benefit of hindsight, some of his predictions look overly categorical to say the least. For example, few would suggest in the wake of the Global Financial Crisis that the scale of destabilization that occurred in the Great Depression could not re-occur (even though one concerns finance, the other relations of production).

Of course, Castoriadis's main argument goes deeper. What is new in 'Modern capitalism and revolution' is his updated view of the impact of class struggle on strategies to lessen the oscillations of accumulation:

> The proletariat's struggle has forced the ruling class to modify its politics, its ideology, its real way of organizing society. Capitalism has been objectively modified by this century-old

struggle. But it also has been modified on a subjective level in the sense that its leaders and ideologists have accumulated, often against their will, a historical *experience* of managing modern society. (p. 269)

According to Castoriadis, historical experience has led capitalism's leaders to constant bureaucratization in the spheres of production, in states, and in unions and political parties (p. 271). By fragmenting authority, specialist bureaucratization erodes the ethics of responsibility in public administration and private management and thus bridles creativity. This process perpetuates the problem of motivation for everyone in modern society.

Castoriadis observes that the deeply contradictory process of bureaucratization even reaches into the organization of cities, the enjoyment of community life and the arts. These are the very spheres one might imagine would most resist bureaucratization (pp. 278– 281). And resistant they are; indeed Castoriadis's argument is that resistance to rationalization is everywhere. This is the reason why the complete assimilation of complex, multidimensional modern societies by capitalism is not possible, even though this is the principal impulse of capitalism. The very measures that the ruling classes and bureaucracies put in place perpetually provoke opposition and conflict, and are thus ultimately self-defeating.

By the mid-1970s, Castoriadis's thought had advanced from this critique of bureaucratization to building up a case against the labour theory of value. His starting point was a key insight that Aristotle opens up: the relationship of equality and 'value' (Castoriadis, 1984, pp. 260–339). Marx revives Aristotle's insight in a contemporary context. Marx's conception of capitalism as commodity production led him to try and unlock the secret of value, that '"equal something" which is the basis of the quantitative proportions found in the exchange of objects' (p. 262). For Marx, abstract labour is the common substance which can balance the difference (and thereby equalize the value) of different things making exchange possible.

According to Castoriadis the labour theory of value burdened Marx's political economy with the metaphysics of labour, leaving political economy's central myth of the market untouched. In other words, it took Marx back to the very myth whose historical institution needs to be challenged. Consideration of the so-called labour market shows how. The commodification of human work is always necessarily and uniquely incomplete in a way that commodification of objects is not. Markets for goods work quite differently from the labour 'market'. Just as workers tend to defy, work around and supplant the rules of the factory and the office, workers allegedly do not readily obey laws of the posited labour market. In fact there is ample evidence brought to bear in current-day debates about migration and the 'mobility' of labour that workers often cannot obey the 'laws' of the labour market in the manner theoreticians suppose.

So if value in capitalist societies does not inhere in abstract labour, whence does it come? Castoriadis starts to address this question by working back, through the medium of Aristotle, from exchange value to 'proto-value'; that is, the untraceable origins of value itself which are instituted in a hermeneutic circle of meaning. This leads Castoriadis towards a theorization of value that is very different from explanations given in the tradition of political economy. Castoriadis denounces the idea of value as a sort of thing, an underlying substrata that must be disclosed. Instead, it is the core meanings that institute value. At the level of meaning, capitalist societies presuppose a commensurability of exchange, which is a commensurability of people who are agents of every facet of that exchange (and in complex societies there are a great many). This is a social law (*nomos*) so basic to life that it seems 'natural' and an objective 'law' of the economy. The worth of people, their skill and their labour is instituted by society on the basis of 'geometrical proportionality' or an equalization of different and unequal instances of labour *that is adequate* for the maintenance of reciprocity.

Castoriadis's exposition of an imaginary theory of value stands in an underdeveloped state in one notable sense. His sociology of bureaucracy, reification and the factory rests on analysis of the class conflicts which are perpetuated in capitalist organizations. Class conflict does not figure in his thinking on proto-value. Alternatively 'value' can be understood as a homogenizing force imposed by capital on the heterogeneous activity of labour in the course of the war of classes.[2] Rather than value inhering in labour (as Marx argued in *Capital* and Castoriadis critiques in the essay on value), value can be theorized as itself the product of lived social relations.

The meanings described above are theorized by Castoriadis as the 'social imaginary significations' of capitalism. He writes expansively on the nature of the latter in *The Imaginary Institution of Society* (a more general exposition of this concept is given by Arnason in this volume; see *Social Imaginary Significations*). When it comes to capitalism social imaginary significations frame value, utility, fairness and the calculable. The different dimensions of capitalism depend on social imaginary significations. From the accumulation of capital, the Taylorist, Fordist and Post-Fordist organization of production and the commodification of goods and services to the moulding of the capitalist class and the creation of markets, all presume the 'concatenation of significations' that makes capitalism operative and makes meaningful the very creativity of capitalism stressed above. In this way capitalism is animated by a larger totality of meaning beyond any ensemble of causes.

Three sets of imaginary significations correspond to the elements of capitalism mentioned above. First, capitalism generates its own temporality instituting chronometric time with an exact and finely divided calibration of hours, minutes and seconds. Without time 'organized' in this manner trade, production and disciplined labour would not be possible. Capitalism generates temporality consubstantially at a second level also. Time is an 'infinite' continuity of 'indefinite progress, unlimited growth, accumulation, rationalization, time of the conquest of nature, of the always closer approximation of a total, exact knowledge, of the phantasy of omnipotence' (Castoriadis, 1987, p. 207). Capitalism's own rate of self-transformation is notionally limitless and operates as an organizing principle of everyday economic life. The fact that Castoriadis's comments on this set of social imaginary significations are brief makes them no less significant.

Second, social imaginary significations of the 'economy' and 'commodities' assume unprecedented importance in modernity (pp. 362–365). The centrality of the economic dislocates the totality of prior social imaginary significations and thereby reorganizes and reorients the 'activities and values' of the world (p. 363). But 'the economy' does not refer to some sphere separable from the entirety of society. Just as it has no referent, so also does the signifier 'commodity' refer to nothing outside of itself. 'Commodity' denotes a host of objects and activities but none in particular. Even so, commodities are the regular focus of activity of billions of peoples and are thereby 'more real than reality itself' as Castoriadis frequently asserts about imaginary significations.

Third, Castoriadis's premises for consideration of the creation of commodities and consumption is that needs are entirely particular to the capitalist culture of this epoch (pp. 25–28). No 'inalterable human nature' exists that can determine an eternal set of needs and provide a fund of economic motivations to learn and train, go to work, obey, produce and reproduce (p. 27). Consumption does not do the latter. Rather it acts to 'preserve a semblance of meaning only if new needs or new methods of satisfying them are constantly being created' (Castoriadis, 1988b, p. 277).

Castoriadis progressively emphasizes in his later work another social imaginary signification of modern capitalism: 'the thrust towards the unlimited extension of "rational mastery"' (Castoriadis, 2007, p. 54). Capitalism is the first social formation to legitimate itself on the grounds of instrumental reason. In a universe of meaning instituted with capitalism 'development' is synonymous with the unending expansion of human powers over nature (pp. 182–187). Development is the rational unfolding of 'new attitudes, values and normal, a new social definition of reality and of being, of what counts and what does not count' (p. 184). In a mathematical self-understanding of the world, advocates of development seek the optimal models of measurable outputs and inputs. The mania for measurement of the 'factors of production' results in the 'equally impossible' task of real assessment of costs. Economists and accountants set about estimation of the costs internal to a firm and calculation of the Gross Domestic Product (GDP) of a national society (excluding necessarily much of the informal economy and the unpaid labour of households). 'Externalities' (the consumption of nature) are inestimable and yet this may well prove to have the greatest real cost of all.

Particular points in this critique were not unusual in the 1970s. The originality of Castoriadis's perspective lay in his connection of infinite growth to a longer social-historical institution of rationality, science, economics and mathematics. From his perspective, science and political economy could not be neutral in any meaningful sense. He thus endeavoured to repudiate arguments that the evident excesses of capitalism in poverty, social inequality and environmental degradation resulted from the irrational and the application of science, or that technology could be harnessed under different conditions to moderate or overcome the contradictions of capitalism.

How does rationality so pervade political economy? Castoriadis strives to answer this by picking apart the logic of economics. Measuring the course of infinite expansion has led academic economists to model ideal markets that, theoretically at least, exist in equilibrium. Using differential calculus to represent a vast number of economic movements, activities and transactions, economists attempt to condense the complexity and dynamism of capitalism into a mathematical form. The result is a pseudo-science which is closed to critique of its categories and is thus self-assured that its models furnish a basis for prediction. Castoriadis's view goes to the heart of political economy by honing in on its methodology. Echoing his critique of Marx's labour theory of value, Castoriadis submits that the pseudo-science of economics fails to grasp the heterogeneity of elements in the living world that cannot be homogenized in mathematical form. The real world is composed of roughly approximate regularities which will not dutifully obey the demands of economic models for precision. A number of complicating factors intercede to make a mess of the world of markets to which economic theory endeavours to give a rational form. Technological innovation, the actions of unions and oligopolies, and the unpredictable fluctuations of stock and currency markets all intervene to render economics problematic.

Notwithstanding the virulence of Castoriadis's attack on economics – the 'theoretical ideology' of capitalism (p. 56) – he does not dismiss economics in its entirety. In fact, his 22-year employment as a professional economist with the Organization for Economic Cooperation and Development (OECD) equipped him well to dissemble Ricardian market theory and Hayekian economics on their own grounds, as well as from the radical vantage-point of his theorization of the social imaginary (pp. 66–70). Moreover, he eloquently describes the historical amnesia of contemporary economics concerning its own history. Eighteenth-century thinkers had keen regard for the specificity of capitalism and how it disrupted existing world orders (pp. 50–52). That awareness has faded with the ascendancy of neo-liberal orthodoxy (Castoriadis, 2010). The centrality of economics to the operation of governments, corporations and the international financial institutions testifies to the potency of the 'theoretical ideology' of capitalism. But

Castoriadis's point is that economics uncritically echoes the social imaginary signification of the expansion of rational mastery. This is a key point that goes back to his critique of the quantitative thinking inherent in the institution of capitalism.

In a modern kind of conquest, capitalism is compelled to impose itself constantly on different dimensions of social life. In past societies, conquest meant annexation of other lands. Capitalist conquest is more internal, harnessing human creativity to schemes of maximization of output and minimization of cost. Although it is always incomplete, this kind of conquest is powerfully productive. The drive to maximization of output itself is evidence of hubris, a condition of trying to live without limits. In the late twentieth century, industrialism and megacities have become visible incarnations of this social imaginary signification.

Castoriadis's essays on ecology highlight such problems of capitalism's conquest of human and non-human worlds. The mastery of nature, the mobilization of the full range of human powers and the optimal use of resources are premises so fundamental to the utilitarian conceptual apparatus of capitalism that they do not get questioned. Castoriadis is emphatic that five centuries of capitalist expansion have been indistinguishably bound to widespread hubris:

> What we realize now is the huge margin of uncertainty as to the facts and prospects for the future of the environment on Earth . . . My personal opinion is that the darkest prospects are the most probable. But the true question is elsewhere: it's the complete disappearance of cautiousness, of *phronesis*. Since no-one can say conclusively that the greenhouse effect will or will not cause the level of the oceans to rise . . . the only proper attitude is that of the *diligens pater familias*, the conscientious father who says to himself since the stakes are so huge, even if the probabilities are unknown, I'll proceed extremely cautiously, and not as if the problem does not exist. (p. 198)

Science in itself gives no guide to the limits humanity should impose for itself; that is, no guide to prudence. Can ecology provide a politics capable of this? In his writings on ecology (starting with an exchange with Daniel Cohn-Bendit), Castoriadis's perception was that the rising green movement had great potential reviving the question of autonomy as a comprehensive alternative to the capitalist imaginary (Castoriadis, 1981; Adams, 2011). However, green politics is itself not a singular vehicle for such a dramatic transformation. The problems indirectly and explicitly posed by ecology do, however, situate human life in the world in more complete ways. The ecological horizon repeatedly reminds us of the overwhelming ontological boundaries of existence:

> Human beings are anchored in something other than themselves; the fact that they are not 'natural' beings does not mean that they hang in thin air . . . ecology isn't a love of nature; it's the need for self-limitation (which is true freedom) of human beings with respect to the planet on which they happen to exist by chance, and which they are now destroying. (Castoriadis, 2010, p. 203)

According to Castoriadis, we need to end up at the point of radical reorientation: necessary self-limitation to which the range of existing programs of ecological politics (from Greens parties to more far-reaching visions of eco-socialism and anarchism) ought to orient. In the last decade of his life, he argued for restraint not merely to the excesses of capitalism as such, but to hubris, the collective desire for mastery that gives rise to excess itself (Castoriadis, 2011).

To Castoriadis's mind, capitalism is much more than an economy or a sub-system of society. Capitalism is an entire social form that involves what is framed as important in the world, how value and rationality are conceived, how people are raised and how what is elsewhere known as 'trust' operates. Capitalism is not only the organized production, trade and consumption of goods and services. It is the instituting apparatus of imaginary significations which envelops economic agency and which supports the belief that everything can be subject to calculation and control. Furthermore, the significations that are instituted involve a kind of promise of calculation and control. Capitalist relations continue because capitalism has partly met its own promise of general prosperity, employment and the provision of order in the rich countries of the world. At the end of the twentieth century, the prospect of expansion of industrialism to greater parts of the globe presented an unsustainable prospect. At this time, Castoriadis echoed the exhortation often made by environmentalists for limits to growth and then he went much further. His work on capitalism urges our attention to excess and hubris as signs of the irrationalities governing economic agency while calling for the comprehensive re-imagination of conceptions of needs and nature. Castoriadis's reproblematization of capitalism puts into question the promise of the continuing outgrowth of human powers and satisfaction of an expanding range of needs. Of greatest significance is his perception of the retreat of prudence from the core of social life. His critique forcefully argues for a re-emergence of self-limitation in response to the predicaments of the contemporary human condition, particularly those of our ecological worlds.

Notes

1 See the shift in his thinking from Castoriadis (1988a, pp. 76–106, 290–309) to Castoriadis (1987, pp. 15–16, 132–135, 140–142).

2 John Rundell outlines such a view in his sympathetic mobilization of Castoriadis's insights to retrieve the critical power of Marx's subsumption model (Rundell, 1987, pp. 194–198):

References

Adams, S. (2011), *Castoriadis's Ontology: Being and Creation*, New York: Fordham University Press.

Castoriadis, C. (1981), 'From Ecology to Autonomy', *Thesis Eleven*, 3, 1, 8–22.

—. (1984), *Crossroads in the Labyrinth*, K. Soper and M. H. Ryle (ed. and trans.), Cambridge, MA: MIT Press.

—. (1987), *The Imaginary Institution of Society*, K. Blamey (trans.), Cambridge, MA: Polity.

—. (1988a), *Political and Social Writings Volume 1, 1946–1955: From the Critique of Bureaucracy to the Positive Content of Socialism*, Minneapolis, MN: University of Minnesota Press.

—. (1988b), *Political and Social Writings Volume 2, 1955–1960: From the Workers' Struggle Against Bureaucracy to Revolution in the Age of Modern Capitalism*, Minneapolis, MN: University of Minnesota Press.

—. (1991), *Philosophy, Politics, Autonomy*, D. A. Curtis (ed.), New York: Oxford University Press, pp. 175–218.

—. (2007), *Figures of the Thinkable*, Stanford, CA: Stanford University Press.

—. (2010), *A Society Adrift. Interviews and Debates 1974–1997*, H. Arnold (trans.), New York: Fordham University Press.

—. (2011), *Postscript on Insignificance Dialogues with Cornelius Castoriadis*, London: Continuum International Publishing Group.

Howard, D. (1988), *The Marxian Legacy*, Minneapolis, MN: University of Minnesota Press.

Rundell, J. (1987), *Origins of Modernity: The Origins of Modern Social Theory From Kant to Hegel to Marx*, Cambridge, MA: Polity.

CHAPTER SIXTEEN

Socialism

Anders Ramsay

Socialism is central both as a term and as a concept in Castoriadis's writings in the 1940s and 1950s. Socialism as a goal is emphasized by the name of the radical left-wing collective and journal *Socialisme ou Barbarie*, which was officially founded by Castoriadis, Lefort and others in 1949. The name, which poses the seemingly somehow schematic alternative, either we will choose socialism, *or* we are faced with the barbarism of ever-advancing capitalism, dates back to a tradition in the labour movement, which ultimately can be traced to the early writings of Karl Marx and Friedrich Engels, such as *The Communist Manifesto*. In the case of *Socialisme ou Barbarie* it did not, however, connect to any rigorous theoretical conceptions (Gabler, 2009, p. 42). In 1915, Rosa Luxemburg used the expression with a more concrete reference to the prevailing situation where the victory of socialism was conceived as the only alternative to a triumphing imperialism and the end to all civilization (p. 42). Castoriadis transfers the catchword to the situation after the Second World War, where socialism was considered the only alternative to a new war between Russia and the United States, the victory of either side implying the acceleration of 'the drift of this society toward barbarism' (Castoriadis, 1949, p. 87). Barbarism to Castoriadis 'is not a historical stage suddenly appearing after the capitalist system has reached its point of impasse. It already makes its appearance in decaying capitalism too' (Castoriadis, 1948,

p. 67). Barbarism in both its forms, 'capitalist and bureaucratic' (Castoriadis, 1949, p. 102), can only be challenged by the proletariat (see *Capitalism*).

The term 'socialism' also appears in the title of a series of comprehensive articles in the journal, written by Castoriadis in the middle and later half of the 1950s (Castoriadis, 1955; 1957; 1958), and in a more widely circulated article and pamphlet from the beginning of the 1960s, where Castoriadis complains that little discussion is taking place about socialism – even among socialists (Castoriadis, 1961a, b). Socialism is also in the title of one of the collections of articles from *Socialisme ou Barbarie* that Castoriadis published at the end of the 1970s (Castoriadis, 1979a). Finally, in the introductory essay of that volume, the terms socialism and communism are abandoned for 'autonomous society' or just 'autonomy' (Castoriadis, 1979b, p. 314; see *Autonomy*).

Although this change of terminology can be said to mark a reorientation for Castoriadis (and which was actually evident in his thought for a couple of decades), there is nonetheless a consistent concept of socialism, which he basically worked out in the 1950s that runs through Castoriadis's whole work until his death in 1997. This concept of socialism is based on a new theory of the Union of Soviet Socialist Republics (USSR) and of modern capitalism. For Castoriadis, socialism is not a goal, rather it is a transitional period between capitalism and communism (Castoriadis, 1957, p. 149), where a break is taking place with capitalism, exploitation is abolished, and autonomy is established. Socialism, Castoriadis stresses, is first and foremost autonomy, defined as 'people's conscious direction of their own lives' (p. 92). Socialism is widely elaborated in his writings against the background of his theory of capitalism, in contrast to communism, of which he says very little. What seems to be schematic in the catch-phrase 'socialism or barbarism' is misleading. Socialism is not an unavoidable result of historical evolution (as in traditional Marxism), neither does it follow from a programme that is derived from what is supposed to be the correct theory (which is the Trotskyist notion; Gabler, 2009, p. 68). Rather, it is based in the contradictions of concrete, everyday experiences of society and working life in capitalism.

From the start of *Socialisme ou Barbarie* – as both collective and journal– socialism is widely discussed, against the particular background of the situation that was set by the Cold War. After the

Second World War, any position which neither identified with the Stalinism of the east nor with reformist Western social democracy, was facing the question of presenting a credible concept of socialism. Castoriadis took this seriously, as did few other thinkers on the left in those days.

The quest for a solution may be said to have been twofold: First, it was necessary to theoretically determine and analyse what kind of social formation the USSR was. The second task was to elaborate a positive concept of what socialism really would imply. These tasks may be said to have been carried out in two steps. First, Castoriadis and his comrades investigated and determined the nature of the USSR. This was done in the context of the discussion within the Trotskyist Fourth International, where *Socialisme ou Barbarie* was formed as the Chaulieu-Montal-tendency in the French section, Parti Communiste Internationaliste (PCI), in 1946. (Chaulieu was Castoriadis's alias; Montal was the alias of his then friend Claude Lefort.) This discussion provides an important background to *Socialisme ou Barbarie*'s and Castoriadis's conception of socialism and critique of the USSR. Trotsky had, in *The Revolution Betrayed* (Castoriadis, 1973, p. 8) labelled the USSR a degenerated workers' state. According to this theory, the working class had successfully carried through the revolution and seized power over the means of production. A new bureaucratic *caste* (*not* a class), consisting of, among others, bureaucrats, administrators, technicians and directors, had seized power in the party and in the state apparatus. Since the means of production, however, were not privatized, relations of production were not capitalist and the workers's state was kept intact, albeit under a bureaucratic rule. Therefore, Trotsky concluded, the USSR should be defended against any attack that could imply a capitalist restoration.

After the war, Trotsky's analysis became a vivid topic of discussion within the movement. The more orthodox leadership stuck to Trotsky's analysis and the political consequences derived from it, such as the defence of the USSR. Several opposing groups in the Trotskyist movement questioned it and some of those would, for example, label the mode of production in the USSR as state capitalist (Castoriadis, 1946, pp. 38–39). The Chaulieu-Montal-tendency did not settle for this. In a sense they still connected to Trotsky's insight concerning the role of bureaucracy, but the group (i.e. Castoriadis) drafted their own theory of the USSR as bureaucratic capitalism. In the first issue of the journal they criticized not only the pretence of the Soviet Union to have realized anything like actual socialism but also the Trotskyist analysis that the USSR was far beyond such degeneration. A new bureaucratic class 'consisting of the bureaucrats in the political and economic apparatus, of technicians and intellectuals, of leaders of the "Communist" party and of the trade unions, and the top military and police personnel' (Castoriadis, 1949, p. 85), with its own interest in keeping up exploitation had emerged after the Russian revolution. On Castoriadis's account, the USSR was a whole new historical formation and a new kind of class society: that is, bureaucratic capitalism (Castoriadis, 1946, pp. 40–41).

This theory left no room for any strategy of defence of the USSR or any ambivalence concerning the character of the system:

> 'Socialism', we are told, has been achieved in countries numbering four hundred million inhabitants, yet that type of 'socialism' appears inseparable from concentration camps, from the most intense social exploitation, from the most atrocious dictatorship, and from the most widespread brutish stupidity. (Castoriadis, 1949, p. 76)

The importance of the concept of bureaucracy to Castoriadis is, however, more comprehensive than just the name of the new ruling class in the USSR. As a more general phenomenon, bureaucracy is significant for a new phase in capitalism; it is 'a new social stratum tending to replace the bourgeoisie in the epoch of declining capitalism' (p. 78). As such the concept of bureaucracy also explains the non-socialist character of Western reformist social democracy, where capitalism has transformed – mutated – into new forms of exploitation, or what Castoriadis later called 'modern capitalism' (Castoriadis, 1960–1961, p. 226) (see *Capitalism*). In the new phase, private ownership of the means of production is no longer characteristic of capitalism. Instead, reforms that are high on the agenda of the labour movement, such as nationalization and planning, are in the interest of the bureaucracy and the maintenance of capitalism (Castoriadis, 1949, p. 79).

The experience of the Russian revolution and the rise of bureaucratic capitalism are decisive for Castoriadis, since it leads to the reformulation of both the concepts of capitalism and socialism. Bureaucratic capitalism and modern capitalism actually have several traits in common. A managing bureaucratic class with its roots in the movement against capitalism rules in both systems. In the first case, bureaucracy rose out of the Bolshevik party and the post-revolutionary rule, when trade union leaders, specialists and technicians took over management of production (p. 97). In the second case, a new stratum of political and trade union bureaucrats rose out of the petty bourgeois intelligentsia and of labour-aristocracy, which had separated itself from the exploited class in their strivings to satisfy their own interests and aspirations (p. 90). Consequently, a new conflict arises which is common to bureaucratic and modern capitalism. In traditional, liberal capitalism the main contradiction was between property owners and the unpropertied. In both systems the workers are obliged to execute the tasks prescribed by the bureaucracy. Thus, a new opposition, between executants and directors, tended to replace the old (p. 97). Castoriadis's analysis of capitalism, just like his idea of socialism, here turns to the factory floor, rather than to the economy and the market. The everyday, direct experiences of the workers are more important than historical necessities or theoretical abstractions. To this end, he could build directly on the testimonies of factory work by American and French workers that were published in *Socialisme ou Barbarie*.

Castoriadis argued that, in order to achieve socialism, a total break with this organization of production is necessary. This leads to the necessary second step, the elaboration of a positive concept of the content of socialism. In the Marxist tradition and in the Marxist labour movement, there has been a reluctance to prescribe concrete receipts for the future. Marx himself did not have any practical examples to refer to before the Paris Commune. But Castoriadis's vision of socialism is not an unfounded utopia. The most important experience in the history of the labour movement is that of self-organized, directly elected workers' councils: in Russia in 1905 and 1917–1918; in Germany in 1918 and in Spain in 1936. Castoriadis refers repeatedly to these; they are 'historic creations of the working class' (Castoriadis, 1957, p. 95). And while writing 'On the content of socialism' he witnessed another example of self organized workers' councils, this time within the USSR's direct sphere of influence; that is, the 1956 revolt in Hungary, which for *Socialisme ou Barbarie* was seen as the living confirmation of their own theories. In this context, Castoriadis also recognized the work of the Dutch veteran of council communism, Anton Pannekoek, as a forerunner to his own attempt to elucidate the content of socialism (p. 97).

Workers' councils are the concrete form of the essential content of socialism, workers' management of production, also called collective management or self-management (a term Castoriadis later uses with some reserve) (Castoriadis, 1979b, p. 320). Workers' management of production is the negation of the bureaucratic pattern of organization, where not only production, but also people's lives as a whole are organized from the outside and as a result, experienced as something alien. However, this kind of organization is riddled with crisis, since people cannot be organized against their own interests. Paradoxically, capitalism has to base itself on people's capacity for self-organization, but this capacity for self-organization is simultaneously suppressed by the official organization (Castoriadis, 1957, p. 93). In contrast, socialism no longer represses this capacity but takes full advantage of it: Socialism is '. . . namely, the elimination of all externally imposed norms, methods, and patterns of organisation and the total liberation of the creative and self-organizing capacities of the masses' (pp. 94–95).

For Castoriadis, self-organization and workers' self-management are not just the goals, but also the *means* for the establishment of socialism. The whole transition of society, work, economy, state and politics must be permeated with striving for – and the establishment of – autonomy. Socialism cannot be attained by force, despotism or other non-autonomous means. Again, the historical example of the Russian Revolution serves as a negative backdrop for Castoriadis. Although Lenin first proclaimed 'All power to the Soviets' (i.e. the workers' councils) autonomy could not be established under party rule. The party had little confidence in the workers' ability of self-management. 'All power to the Soviets' became in reality 'All power to the Bolshevik party' (Castoriadis, 1949, p. 95). It is necessary to avoid reproducing what Castoriadis sees as the common trait of bureaucratic and modern capitalism, the division into directors and executants. This means self-organization in all of society, just not in production: 'Socialist society implies people's self-organization of every aspect of their social activities. The instauration of socialism therefore entails the immediate abolition of the fundamental division into a class of directors and a class of executants' (Castoriadis, 1957, p. 95).

In 'On the content of socialism II', Castoriadis provides his most penetrating text on the subject of socialism. It is a detailed and sometimes very technical account of the workings of socialist society, its institutions, the transformation of work and technology, the management of the factory, the principles and the management of the economy and the management of society as a whole by workers councils, including state and politics (Castoriadis, 1957). The content of socialism, that is, workers' self-management, is dependent on institutions that are understandable and controllable by the workers. Only then can institutions be a meaningful part of people's lives. Disinterest and lack of engagement in politics is one of the features of modern society, which is opaque and dependent on institutions in which the citizens do not take any interest, and which they do not understand. According to the principles of collective management, society must be organized in such a way that it becomes transparent to its members (p. 97). Councils are composed of revocable delegates, directly elected at the place of work. They 'unite the functions of deliberation, decision and execution' (p. 95). A system of delegates does not mean that power is handed over to a new class of professional politicians. They are rather 'an expression of the power of the people' (p. 101). A council system can be described as a base and a summit, where the summit does not, as in modern society, become a concentration of power and information. For people in the base to take active part in the process of management and express their opinion, they must have adequate knowledge and information. Between the summit of the councils, the central council government and the base, a two-way flow of communication must be set up, where the summit collects and transfers information, and the base makes decisions for the summit to carry out.

Socialism is the self-organization of the autonomy of the working class, but this autonomy cannot, however, be purely political, as this might still imply slavery in production and 'Sundays of political freedom' (p. 101). Workers' self-management has to be workers' management of *production*, which means workers determining the production process directly on the floor. No separate managerial apparatus may exist, as there is a risk that power would fall into the hands of those experts and administrators who are set to manage production. Workers' management of production also implies other crucial points: a change of work and a new relation to work (p. 102), as well a transformation of technology, which according to Castoriadis is the most important task confronting socialist society (Castoriadis, 1961b, pp. 244–245).

In Castoriadis's view, the most important aspect of the new relation to work is the institution of complete equality of wages. This is perhaps the most fundamental change, just like its corollary of the abolition of production norms, bonuses, etc., Castoriadis supports this claim by reference to workers' actual demands, when they are given the possibility to express themselves, against hierarchies and wage differentials. Wage differentials cannot be justified, other than by exploitation. Equality in wages is a presupposition for the whole new mentality that is necessary in socialism. Unequal wages cause competition and division among individuals that will disappear with wage equality (Castoriadis, 1957, pp. 126–127).

Castoriadis argues that technology in capitalism cannot be understood as a neutral device for the development of the productive forces. It cannot be neutrally adapted for the purpose of satisfying the needs of the consumers. It is not socially neutral. The intention of capitalist technology is to subordinate and dominate the producers and to eliminate the human element in production. The machines have a disciplinary function in relation to the hostility and indifference of the workers towards the production process. It imposes its rhythm on the work process. Work must also be measured, defined and quantified from the outside and labour power must be interchangeable. To all these ends, capitalist technology is adapted. This is a problem that must be tackled in socialism. Technology must be subordinated to human needs, which means the needs of humans as producers. As Castoriadis argues, 'the hallmark of socialism is *the transformation it will bring about in the nature and content of work*, through the *conscious and deliberate transformation of an inherited technology*' (p. 103).

Castoriadis does not return to the discussion on socialism until his introductory article from 1979 on 'Socialism and autonomous society'. Here, on the one hand, he comes to the conclusion that 'massive realities cannot be combated through etymological and semantic distinctions'. Socialism signifies to a majority either what was then known as the really existing socialism of the USSR, or

Western social democracy, '"political" cogs of the established order in Western countries'. Therefore, 'it is obvious that henceforth the terms "socialism" and "communism" are to be abandoned' (Castoriadis, 1979b, p. 314). Anyone familiar with the writings of Castoriadis that have been referred to above may of course wonder if this was not the case already in 1949 or 1957, and why it was actually possible for Castoriadis to continue to use outdated terminology for so long. The obvious answer is of course that Castoriadis had left the days of activism in a small left-wing group behind and had now gone on to psychoanalysis and more academic work. Actually, this change had been apparent in his thought for some time. Already, in what is considered his main work, *The Imaginary Institution of Society* (1987; first published in 1975), which he wrote in the period after the great split of 1963 that led to the dissolution of *Socialisme ou Barbarie*, socialism is barely mentioned and the discussion of the topic is marginal. Castoriadis now, in 1979, finally adopts the term autonomous society. His work becomes more centred on freedom and democracy and he looks more towards the ancient Greek *polis* than the factory floor for his intellectual sources.

On the other hand, it does not mean that Castoriadis *substantially* abandoned the concept of socialism that he so meticulously worked out in the 1950s. Neither does it mean that he became less of a revolutionary (a question he often had to answer in interviews during the last decades of his life; see Castoriadis, 2010). Nor are there any problems reconciling the new orientation with the previous work. He explicitly refers back to the implications of what he now prefers to call 'collective management', such as equality in wages and transformation of technology (Castoriadis, 1979b, pp. 320–321), which he still considers as central to the vision he now prefers labelling autonomous society.

References

Castoriadis, C. (1961a), 'Socialism and capitalism', *International Socialism*, 4, Spring 1961 www.marxists.org/history/etol/newspape/isj/1961/no004/cardan.htm
—. (1979 [1961b]), 'Ce que signifie le socialisme', *Le contenu du socialisme*, Paris: UGE, pp. 223–260.

—. (1979a), *Le contenu du socialisme*, Paris: UGE.

—. (1993 [1979b]), 'Socialism and autonomous society', in D. A. Curtis (ed. and trans.), *Political and Social Writings, Volume 3: 1961–1979. Recommencing the Revolution: From Socialism to the Autonomous Society*, Minneapolis, MN: University of Minnesota Press, pp. 314–331.

—. (1987), *The Imaginary Institution of Society*, K. Blamey (trans.), Cambridge: Polity.

—. (1988 [1946]), 'On the regime and against the defence of the USSR', in D. A. Curtis (ed. and trans.), *Political and Social Writings, Volume 1: 1946–1955. From the Critique of Bureaucracy to the Positive Content of Socialism*, Minneapolis, MN: University of Minnesota Press, pp. 37–43.

—. (1988 [1948]), 'The concentration of the forces of production', in D. A. Curtis (ed. and trans.), *Political and Social Writings, Volume 1: 1946–1955. From the Critique of Bureaucracy to the Positive Content of Socialism*, Minneapolis, MN: University of Minnesota Press, pp. 67–75.

—. (1988 [1949]), 'Socialism or barbarism', in D. A. Curtis (ed. and trans.), *Political and Social Writings, Volume 1: 1946–1955. From the Critique of Bureaucracy to the Positive Content of Socialism*, Minneapolis, MN: University of Minnesota Press, pp. 76–106.

—. (1988 [1955]), 'On the content of socialism I', in D. A. Curtis (ed. and trans.), *Political and Social Writings, Volume 1: 1946–1955. From the Critique of Bureaucracy to the Positive Content of Socialism*, Minneapolis, MN: University of Minnesota Press, pp. 290–309.

—. (1988 [1957]), 'On the content of socialism II', in D. A. Curtis (ed. and trans.), *Political and Social Writings, Volume 2: 1955–1960. From the Workers' Struggle against Bureaucracy to Revolution in the Age of Modern Capitalism*, Minneapolis, MN: University of Minnesota Press, pp. 90–154.

—. (1988 [1958]), 'On the content of socialism III', in D. A. Curtis (ed. and trans.), *Political and Social Writings, Volume 2: 1955–1960. From the Workers' Struggle against Bureaucracy to Revolution in the Age of Modern Capitalism*, Minneapolis, MN: University of Minnesota Press, pp. 155–192.

—. (1988 [1960–1961]), 'Modern capitalism and revolution', in D. A. Curtis (ed. and trans.), *Political and Social Writings, Volume 2: 1955–1960. From the Workers' Struggle against Bureaucracy to Revolution in the Age of Modern Capitalism*, Minneapolis, MN: University of Minnesota Press, pp. 226–343.

—. (1988 [1973]), 'General introduction', in D. A. Curtis (ed. and trans.), *Political and Social Writings, Volume 1: 1946–1955. From the Critique of Bureaucracy to the Positive Content of Socialism*, Minneapolis, MN: University of Minnesota Press, pp. 3–36.

—. (2010), *A Society Adrift: Interviews and Debates, 1974–1997*, H. Arnold (trans.), New York: Fordham University Press.

Gabler, A. (2009), *Antizipierte Autonomie: zur Theorie und Praxis der Gruppe Socialisme ou Barbarie (1949–1967)*, Hannover: Offizin.

CHAPTER SEVENTEEN

Modernity

Karl E. Smith

For Castoriadis, the term modernity is highly problematic; it has been oversimplified and misconstrued in philosophical thought. Part of the problem here is that the term modernity refers to radical transformations in both philosophical thought and in social-political institutions (see Wagner, 2001, pp. 1–2). As we shall see, Castoriadis argues that too much contemporary theorizing focuses exclusively on the former, while ignoring the latter.

Focusing on the *imaginary* dimensions of social-historical change, Castoriadis traces the emergence of modernity to the twelfth century in various European city-states, marked by the rising demand for political *autonomy*, that is, self-governance by a *polis*.[1] This demand was accompanied by changing intellectual and artistic attitudes which congealed into an opposition to tradition and authority and opened the way to a widespread acceptance of innovation. The breakdown of traditional authority had implications not only in the political realm but also in material practices, especially in science, technology and the economy. The ripening of this new social imaginary in the early eighteenth century marks the transition from the early-modern period into what Castoriadis refers to as 'classical modernity' (Castoriadis, 1997a, p. 37). During this period, democracy takes root and spreads concomitantly with the rise of industrial capitalism. But contrary to liberal philosophy, which views capitalism and democracy as natural bedfellows,

Castoriadis sees these two social institutions as diametrically opposed, founded in opposing social imaginaries of autonomy and *rational-mastery*. Whereas democracy is a product of the project of autonomy, grounded in a principle of *self-limitation*, capitalism is a product of a project of (pseudo-)rational-(pseudo-)mastery – or rather, of a quest for *unlimited* accumulation (of wealth, knowledge, power, control). Castoriadis sees the global spread of capitalism in the late nineteenth century as leading into an 'age of generalized conformity' in the early twentieth century, where the burst of creativity which characterized classical modernity has been exhausted, replaced by imitation; the quest for individual and social autonomy has given way to 'privatization, depoliticization and individualism' (p. 39).

Castoriadis begins his most systematic discussion of modernity by addressing Hegel's idea of a self-reflexive society (p. 35), which he sees as overly simplistic and misdirected. Castoriadis argues that not only is it a mistake to see Hegel's unification of rationality and Absolute Spirit as anything more than an erroneous illusion, but that if Hegel had been correct, this declared 'end of history' would be antithetical to modernity (p. 35). For Castoriadis, the modern era is characterized by continuous transformation brought about through unleashing the creative potential of *anthropos*. As such, it must be seen as a period of dynamic historical change, in contrast to the stasis implied in Hegel's notion of the end of history.

He is similarly dismissive of Foucault's claim that modernity 'begins with Kant', who was, for Foucault, the first philosopher to show 'an interest in the actual historical present' (p. 34). Besides the fact that we can find numerous ancient philosophers (Castoriadis cites Pericles and Plato for a start) who engaged in their historical present, like Hegel, this approach reduces modernity to a philosophical problem, or a philosophical moment, with no regard for broader social and cultural developments.

Rather than a necessary or inevitable trajectory (or any sort of functionalist, revolutionary or theological evolution) Castoriadis understands the forms that characterize an historical epoch – a social-historical formation – to be contingent (p. 102), and argues that the modern period is best characterized by the conflict between, the 'mutual contamination and entanglement' of, two irreducible and incompatible 'projects' (drives, tendencies, motivations): the project of autonomy (see *Autonomy*) and the project of 'rational-mastery' (p. 37). As the project of autonomy is discussed in detail in its own chapter in this volume (as well as other chapters; see, for example, *Heteronomy*), I will only briefly outline it here, before elaborating on the project of rational-mastery, and then outlining some of the key aspects of the tension between them.

It is important to note that one of the significant obstacles to fully appreciating the complexity of the social-historical formation that we call modernity has to do with what Castoriadis refers to as the infelicity of the word itself. Etymologically, 'modern' refers to 'the now', the present in a historical and temporal sense. It is in this vein that Hegel sees self-reflection as the defining characteristic of the era, claiming that the European society of the Enlightenment was the first society to refer to itself as 'the present' (Castoriadis, 1997a, pp. 34–35; Habermas, 1990, p. 43). This refers to a conscious break with the past; a rejection of custom, tradition and religious superstition in favour of the newly developing rational sciences. In this sense, it refers to those societies that developed in Western Europe after what Polanyi (1944/1985) calls 'The Great Transformation', characterized by the three revolutions: industrial, scientific and democratic. It is on this basis that authors such as Habermas and Foucault (Castoriadis, 1997a, pp. 34–35) refer to modernity as the society developing out of Western Europe since about 1800. In which case, we are not referring simply to a fleeting (ever-changing) temporal moment, but to a cultural or civilizational constellation that, at least initially, could be associated with a particular place.

Castoriadis observes, however, that the society created in the great transformation was a culmination (or rather, an accumulation which will never culminate) of other social tendencies, trends and practices which had appeared in certain parts of this region and had congealed into an opposition to tradition and authority, opening the way to a widespread acceptance of innovation. He notes that as early as the twelfth century we can find outbreaks of political autonomy in some European city-states, manifest in the rising demand for self-government, most notably in 'the self-constitution of the protobourgeoisie' (p. 36). These demands, he argues, 'were accompanied by new psychical, mental, intellectual and artistic attitudes that prepared the ground' for the transformations which would develop over the next five to six centuries. Most important of these attitudinal shifts was that the authority of tradition was no longer seen as sacred in its own right – it could now be questioned. Such questioning led to an equally important shift in the valuation of innovation, which had been disparaged throughout the Middle Ages (pp. 36–37).

The Enlightenment and the democratic revolutions mark the beginning of the 'classical' (or 'critical') modern epoch, which Castoriadis argues came to an end just over a century later with 'the two world wars of the twentieth century' (p. 37). During this period (ca. 1800–1950), he maintains, all existing social institutions were called into question, and for the first time ever 'philosophy definitively broke with theology' (p. 37), clearing space for the tremendous growth in rational science witnessed during the nineteenth century. But this period also saw the consolidation and exponential expansion of a new socio-economic phenomenon: capitalism.

Two things must be noted before proceeding further. First, in many respects capitalism is a direct continuation of an age-old impulse towards unlimited accumulation (of land, territory, wealth, slaves, etc.); but it is also a radical transformation of this impulse, for it adopts scientific rationality in an unrelenting quest to totally transform the means of accumulation, the conditions under which accumulation occurs, and thus the very 'stuff' that is to be accumulated. Whereas the kings and armies of old had sought material possessions and territorial conquests towards the accumulation of further material wealth, in the age of capitalism all such possessions are the consequences of, or instruments for, the unlimited expansion of rational-mastery. Second, the imaginary signification of the unlimited accumulation of rational-mastery becomes the guiding light for both capitalist economic enterprises and for the entire edifice of modern 'techno-science' (p. 109). In this guise of techno-science, the quest for the unlimited expansion of rational-mastery established the bureaucratic-hierarchical organization as the predominant form of social organization in Western capitalist society, thus imposing supposedly 'external' (rationalized) limits upon the quest for self-institution and self-limitation.

Autonomy (*auto-nomos*) literally means 'setting one's own norms' (or rules, laws, and customs, etc.); that is, self-limitation. The opposite of autonomy is heteronomy, which in the simplest terms means rule by the other; someone else makes our rules, laws, etc. (see *Heteronomy*). For Castoriadis, almost all societies in human history have been heteronomous, enforcing and abiding by rules, laws and practices given by an other – by the ancestors, tradition, God or the gods or some other extra-social source. In such societies, social individuals do not question, debate and decide the law for themselves, but follow the norms established for them by an other. However, while such individuals are undoubtedly socialized to be heteronomous subjects, Castoriadis argues that, in fact, every society institutes its own rules and practices – for the social-historical is nothing other than the continuous creation and reproduction of *nomos*. Yet almost every society has denied this fact, creating a world of social imaginary significations in which the law is given by an other. The motivation for this self-deception is to posit an extra-social authority for the norms, to establish them as unquestionable, unchallengeable by the collective and its members.

The only two exceptions to the institution of heteronomous society in human history, Castoriadis argues, are ancient Athens (ca. 800–500 BCE (p. 88)) and the modern West (p. 86). Both of these societies can be characterized by a rupture in 'the closure of signification' (p. 86) and in inherited tradition (practices, beliefs, norms, etc.); ruptures which entail the clear and lucid understanding that society makes its own norms, laws, rules, etc. From this perspective, the project of autonomy seeks to institute the type of society that socializes autonomous subjects, social individuals who clearly understand that they are responsible for negotiating and deciding upon the *nomoi* by which they will live.

The historical manifestation of autonomy in ancient Greece is most evident in the birth of philosophy and the creation of democracy, both of which are founded on calling the existing order into question (the 'unlimited interrogation' of norms, laws, practices, etc. (p. 87)), and taking responsibility for maintaining and/or changing that order as the *polis* deemed most appropriate. In the modern European context, the partial thrusts towards autonomy which began in the twelfth century (pp. 36–37), can be seen in the Protestant Reformation,[2] which ostensibly removed a hierarchical intermediary from the relations between the individual and God, and in the English Revolution, which made the king's power subordinate to the people's assembly (the parliament). Each of these events radically transformed relationships between social individuals and social institutions. The effects of these changes spread and intermingled with others, informing and being informed by the nascent scientific ideas of Copernicus and Galileo, which later blossomed into the scientific revolution of the eighteenth century. One way to characterize the scientific revolution is to say that it symbolizes the normalization or mainstreaming of a belief that there is a correct method for interrogating the laws of nature, which ought to displace society's reliance on revelation and tradition. Similarly, the democratic revolutions that occurred in the United States and France at the end of the eighteenth century established that sovereignty lies with the people, rather than with a divinely ordained monarch, and that the people are entitled to hold their government to account (i.e. call it into question).

An overarching objective in Castoriadis's work is to bring this tendency towards autonomy into clearer focus, in order to more lucidly realize it. As a political project, this entails not only recognizing the *right* of the people to question the government, but recognizing and accepting the *responsibility* to actively participate in governance (politics), which entails calling the existing order into question. Here it is necessary to understand that all social institutions are, in fact, what Maurice Merleau-Ponty called *instituting-institutions* (Merleau-Ponty, 1963, pp. 107–108). That is, they have been instituted by social actors, and they institute the social actors within their domain. Importantly, once instituted, they also become self-instituting, with an ineliminable tendency to becoming autonomous (or alienated) from the social actors who instituted them. The circularity here continues, for in the vast majority of instances of social institutions, the instituting actors aspire to institutional closure. That is, having created a social institution, there is a strong desire that it should survive and prosper in an unadulterated form. These are what Castoriadis calls 'closed' institutions; and these closed institutions are characteristic of heteronomous societies.

By definition, then, it is necessary for autonomous societies to create open institutions; institutions that can be called into question; institutions that can be transformed, reformulated or replaced as a result of interrogation; institutions that do not become alienated from social actors, but remain subject to the lucid deliberations of the collective. But while this is the aspiration of the autonomous society – a necessity for the continuation and enlargement of the project of autonomy – it is in the nature of institutions to tend towards closure. Castoriadis's understanding of history, and his critique of teleology, indicate that 'open' institutions are far from 'normal' and are hardly inevitable – yet they are *possible*; indeed, it is possible (it has happened) for a society to institute itself in such a way that the rupture of closure is accepted as a norm; a society in which there are no fixed barriers or obstacles to questioning the validity, efficacy, justice, etc. of existing institutions.

On the one hand, this is precisely the type of society that emerged from the European Enlightenment – societies in which, in principle, there is no social institution that is beyond questioning; societies in which traditional authority is not too sacred to question; societies in which, as a matter of course, political authority must always be questioned. But, on the other hand, techno-science has assumed the guise of an authority – has posited an illusion of certainty (quite contrary to its own methodologies and practices) – which is beyond traditional or political authority. So, whereas during the classical modern era societies stopped looking towards (or accepting) the extra-social authority of God or the gods, the ancestors, spirit beings or tradition, the political autonomy that was achieved during the classical modern era was whittled away or undermined by the increasing tendency to ground social norms in the (supposedly) extra-social authorities of scientific reason (including sometimes history, sometimes nature and often reason).

Of course, leading scientists are well aware that science cannot answer questions of what we should do, or how we should live. Nor can it answer questions of what we should produce, or what we should produce it for. However, one of the fiercest public battles of recent decades in the United States, and to a lesser extent elsewhere, is that between science and religion; and one of the key issues under debate is who should decide what scientists can and cannot do, especially in fields concerning human biology (stem cell research, the human genome project, etc.). In an autonomous society, these questions *ought to be* debated in public, and *ought to be* decided by the *polis*. But the debate that we are witnessing is not about whether such research is for the public good or not, but rather about whether it transgresses God's law. Indeed, as Richard Dawkins (2006, p. 61) (and many others) has noted, we are living through a period of incredible paradox, when the supposedly most technologically advanced nation on the planet – the society that first and most clearly instituted a secular society, the society that most lucidly quarantined religion from politics – has recently become the most fundamentally religious society in the world, as religious conservatives do everything in their power to undermine the democratic foundations of the nation by radically reinterpreting its constitution and its founding fathers as explicitly and unambiguously Christian (see Neuhaus, 2009, pp. 23–24). Yet this is only one, and not the most widespread one, of the ways in which the twenty-first-century heirs of the Enlightenment are, in Castoriadis's terms, retreating into what he calls *conformism* (Castoriadis, 1997a, p. 39).

Despite the tumultuous social movements of the 1960s, Castoriadis maintains, 'the project of autonomy seems totally eclipsed' (p. 39). Indeed, all of the diverse civil rights movements aimed at expanding the franchise in one way or another, addressing various bigotries and biases that had excluded one group or another from full political participation; but none of them (with the exception of the ecological movement) 'proposed a new vision of society' or any new ways of facing 'the overall political problems as such' (p. 39). What we see, instead, alongside this ever-increasing enfranchisement is a correspondingly growing disenfranchisement of privatization, depoliticization and individualism. In other words, various social movements succeeded in breaking down barriers to inclusion even while the field into which they sought to be included was transformed beyond recognition. In short, what we find in this era mistakenly called *postmodern* is a society that has lost any vision of itself as a society; a society whose members do not count themselves as active participants in the society, but rather as individuals who want society to leave them alone. At the level of everyday life, then, we find a newly disenfranchised generation:

> Leaving a weakened family, frequenting – or not frequenting – a school lived as a chore, the young individual finds herself confronted by a society in which all 'values' and 'norms' are pretty much replaced by one's 'standard of living', one's general welfare, comfort, and consumerism. No religion, no 'political' ideas, no social solidarity with a local or work community or with 'schoolmates'. If she is not marginalized (drugs, delinquency, unstable 'personality'), there remains the road to privatization,

which she may enrich by indulging in one or several crazes. We are living the society of *lobbies* and *hobbies*. (Castoriadis, 1997b, p. 260)

At the same time as the *polis* is increasingly retreating into a privatized comfort zone, governments around the globe are increasingly constrained from enacting this or that legislation by fears of how 'the market' will respond; self-constitution has given way to the discourses of the other. Since the 1950s, the International Monetary Fund (IMF) and World Bank have imposed 'structural adjustment programs' as 'conditionalities' on national development loans (Ofori, 2009). From the beginning these conditionalities compromised national sovereignty, but this compromise became far more pervasive towards the end of the twentieth century, in response to a string of financial crises such as the Asian Economic Crisis of 1997, the collapse of the Argentinian and other South American economies around 2000 (Palast, 2001) and finally reaching the European Union in the wake of the Global Financial Crisis of 2008. At the time of writing, similar 'austerity measures' are being imposed upon Greece by the European Central Bank (Evans-Pritchard, 2012). The 'governments' of Italy, Spain and Portugal are desperately trying to avoid imposition of any further austerity measures – but the only way to avoid such an imposition is to voluntarily adopt the bankers' austerity measures. What we see, then, is an even more draconian retreat from autonomy, moving ever closer to the centre of what was once autonomous modern society. The Greeks today are confronting the realization that it does not matter whether they elect a government of the left, the centre or the right; whoever 'governs' is governing on behalf of the European Central Bank, rather than the electorate (Alogoskoufis, 2012, pp. 29 ff.; Featherstone, 2011; *The Economist*, 2012).

Thus, whereas in the early 1990s Castoriadis observed that, contrary to the triumphalism of the Western political and capitalist intelligentsia, the collapse of the Soviet Union was not a victory of capitalism over communism, but rather an internal collapse of an ineffective regime (Castoriadis, 1997b, p. 253), today we seem to be witnessing the collapse of democratic politics – and this time it actually *is* a victory of capitalism. That is, the capitalists appear to be on the brink of bringing an end to democracy as we have known it,[3] imposing a new heterodoxy of government by bankers. At the same time, however, this is anything but a victory of industrial capitalism; rather, what we are seeing is the outcome of two decades of what we might call 'casino capitalism' (p. 256), as debt-fuelled speculation in the money markets takes precedence over any form of rational investment or management strategies.

In short, during the long developmental years from which modernity emerged, the project of autonomy succeeded in displacing entrenched tradition and authority, coming to a rich and profound head in the eighteenth century with the great transformation which inaugurated the period of classical modernity. The next 150 years or so can be characterized by the conflict between autonomy (democracy) and rational-mastery (bureaucracy, science and capitalism) as various social and political movements struggled to contain 'the irrationalities of capitalist "rationalization"' (Castoriadis, 1997a, p. 39). Since the middle of the twentieth century, however, the irrationalities of rationalization have achieved the upper-hand, as citizens and governments alike find themselves increasingly fettered to the demands and dictates of the 'market'.

As we have seen, Castoriadis's polarized characterization of modernity offers strong insights into both the strengths and weaknesses of modern societies. However, we must recognize that there are also various ways in which this polarized view distorts or diffracts our vision of important aspects of modern societies – most notably its tendency towards economic and political determinism. That is, Castoriadis's polarization focuses almost exclusively on economic and political factors, which implies that these fields and their respective institutions are determinative of all other aspects of society.

In contrast to this polarized view, Arnason suggests that we should understand modernity 'as a loosely structured constellation' which is constituted by 'horizons of meaning' or 'cultural orientations' which are 'embodied in institutions but not reducible to them' (Arnason, 2000, pp. 64–65). Arnason's more nuanced understanding of modernity recognizes that there are numerous other spheres of social life – culture, identity, religion, to name but a few – which cannot be reduced to either economy or politics. Among other things, this perspective opens the way to recognizing that the tension between autonomy and rational-mastery appears in life-fields other than politics and economics, and that the project of autonomy can be pursued – and obstructed – from multiple perspectives. In concrete terms, consider the myriad ways in which contemporary politicians who embrace the neoliberal agenda of small government and non-interference restrict their *laissez-faire* liberalism to the economic realm while increasingly extending the reach of government control into the personal lives of individuals, for example: the same-sex marriage debate, reproductive rights, religion in public schools and a myriad of health related issues such as vaccinations, alcohol consumption, tobacco control, etc. In each of these cases, individual and social autonomy are undermined by heteronomizing tendencies. Hence, while Castoriadis's analysis of modernity provides powerful insights into the constitution of the contemporary world, further analysis of these other life fields is required for us to develop a fuller understanding of modernity.

Notes

1 For an account of the rise of self-governing republics in twelfth-century Europe, see Black, 2003.

2 Note, however, that Castoriadis never explicitly acknowledges this particular breakthrough, in part, perhaps, because despite the rupture to the existing order, the intentions of its initiators were simply to institute a new heteronomy; but also because he was loath to acknowledge that there could be any correlation between autonomy and any action that was religiously motivated. Nevertheless, we must recognize the Protestant Reformation as an important development in the emergence of modernity, although only as an oblique and partial step towards autonomy (see Adams, 2011).

3 I say 'as we have known it' for Castoriadis maintains that 'representative' democracy is not 'really' democracy, but rather some sort of mystification which amounts to a form of oligarchy which goes through the motions of consulting the populace (as an electorate) on a periodic basis (Castoriadis, 1997a, pp. 89 f.).

References

Adams, S. (2011), *Castoriadis's Ontology: Being and Creation*, New York: Fordham University Press.

Alogoskoufis, G. (2012), 'Greece's sovereign debt crisis: Retrospect and prospect', GreeSE Paper No. 54, Hellenic Observatory Papers on Greece and Southeast Europe, London School of Economics and Political Science. http://eprints.lse.ac.uk/42848/1/GreeSE%20No54. pdf, accessed 13 November 2012.

Arnason, J. P. (2000), 'Communism and modernity', *Daedulus*, 129, 1, Proceedings of the American Academy of Arts and Sciences.

Black, A. (2003), *Guild and State: European Political Thought from the Twelfth Century to the Present*, New Brunswick: Transaction.

Castoriadis, C. (1997a), *World in Fragments*, D. A. Curtis (ed. and trans.), Stanford, CA: Stanford University Press.

—. (1997b), *Castoriadis Reader*, D. A. Curtis (ed. and trans.), Oxford: Blackwell.

Dawkins, R. (2006), *The God Delusion*, London: Black Swan.

Economist, The (2012), 'Polarised prospects', *The Economist*, 10 May. www.economist.com/blogs/graphicdetail/2012/05/european-economy-guide, accessed 13 November 2012.

Evans-Pritchard, A. (2012), 'Debt crisis: Europe's democracies must not subcontract their destiny to the Bundesbank', *The Telegraph*, 13 November. www.telegraph.co.uk/finance/comment/9322861/Debt-crisis-Europes-democracies-must-not-subcontract-their-destiny-to-the-Bundesbank.html, accessed 13 November 2012.

Featherstone, K. (2011), 'The Greek sovereign debt crisis and EMU: A failing state in a skewed regime', *Journal of Common Market Studies*, 49, 2, 193–217.

Habermas, J. (1990), *The Philosophical Discourse of Modernity*, Cambridge: MIT Press.

Merleau-Ponty, M. (1963), *In Praise of Philosophy and Other Essays*, J. Wild and J. Edie (trans.), Evanston, IL: Northwestern University Press.

Neuhaus, R. N. (2009), 'Secularizations,' *First Things*, 190, 23–28.

Ofori, E. (2009), 'Structural adjustments and their effects: Is there a way out for Africa?' *MPRA*, 12 September. http://mpra.ub.uni-muenchen. de/17334/1/MPRA_paper_17334.pdf, accessed 13 November 2012.

Palast, G. (2001), 'IMF's four steps to damnation', *The Observer*, 29 April. www.guardian.co.uk/business/2001/apr/29/business.mbas, accessed 13 November 2012.

Polanyi, K. (1985 [1944]), *The Great Transformation*, Boston: Beacon.

Wagner, P. (2001), *Theorizing Modernity: Inescapability and Attainability in Social Theory*, London: Sage.

CHAPTER EIGHTEEN

Democracy

Ingerid S. Straume

What is democracy? This question has been met with various answers, some normative and theoretical; others historical and descriptive. Castoriadis's answer is a combination of the two: drawing deeply on the historical case of Athens, his notion of a true democracy is most of all connected to an idea, or an impulse: the project of autonomy (see *Autonomy*).

Theorists of democracy have argued that the *polis* democracy created in the sixth- and fifth-centuries BCE and modern liberal democracies have rather little in common (e.g. Habermas, 1994; Held, 1996). Castoriadis also sees significant differences between the two instances; but instead of viewing the former as a more primitive, undifferentiated form, he finds in the case of Greece – and Athenian democracy in particular – a critical corrective to contemporary democracies. While stressing that the Athenian democracy is not a model that can be transposed to modern, largely specialized, societies, he strongly believes in its relevance and potential to inspire us today. For Castoriadis, ancient and modern democracies are rooted in the same impulse, as two instances of the project of autonomy. However, the latter has become so far estranged from this common source that the ancient form can be used as a reminder, and an inspiration for reviving and recreating modern democracy.

Judged in the light of Athens's institutional arrangements, which were very complicated and elaborate, Castoriadis largely dismisses modern-style representative democracies as 'liberal oligarchies' (see, for example, 'What democracy?' Castoriadis, 2007). The decisive criterion for Castoriadis is whether or not people effectively govern themselves (*demos kratein*). In liberal oligarchies, people are only allowed to give their vote in matters over which they have very little influence, while the political agenda is decided in fora that are inaccessible to the public. Strongly dismissive of oligarchy, hierarchy, bureaucracy, the principle of representation and the conflation of capitalism and democracy, Castoriadis invokes many of the principles and qualities of Greek democracy to urge modern polities in a more autonomous – self-reflexive and politicized – direction.

Castoriadis's most extensive and explicit discussions of democracy are found in three essays written during the 1980s and 1990s: 'The Greek *polis* and the creation of democracy' (Castoriadis, 1991),[1] 'What democracy?' (2007) and 'Democracy as procedure and democracy as regime' (1997c). Questions about democracy were also central in debates and interviews during the 1980s and 1990s (see Castoriadis, 2010). And even though democracy was not a theme in *The Imaginary Institution of Society* (Castoriadis, 1987), it would be a mistake to think that it was absent until the 1980s; rather, Castoriadis's discussion of democracy is an elaboration on the project of autonomy that furthers his longstanding interest in self-management (*autogestion*) from the *Socialisme ou Barbarie* years (see the entry on *Socialism*). It is therefore a continuing political concern that is elucidated through his studies of the historical case of Athens, documented in his seminars published as *Ce qui fait la Grèce* (Castoriadis, 2008; 2009; 2011a).

In the following, Castoriadis's concept of democracy will be discussed from three perspectives. First, his essays on democracy are presented and situated in a political and theoretical context. We then take a closer look at what Castoriadis calls a true democracy, as exemplified by Athenian democracy. Finally there will be a brief discussion of the prospects for democracy today.

In the three aforementioned essays on democracy, Castoriadis positions himself within scholarly debates about the nature of politics and democracy that were dominant in Western political philosophy during the 1980s and 1990s. The contested question was: what makes democracy 'democratic'? Is it the distribution of and checks on relations of power? Or is it a form of communicative decision making? The most important controversy of the 1980s and 1990s was set between *political liberalism* and *communitarianism*, following John Rawls's influential work *A Theory of Justice* (from 1971) and Alistair MacIntyre's *After Virtue* (1981) respectively. A third party was of course Jürgen Habermas and his theory of *deliberative* or *procedural* democracy. The discussion that concerns us here is whether democracy should be limited to questions of rights, procedures, principles etc., or whether it also involves certain communal values – in short, the relationship between form and substance. In the essays 'What democracy?' (2007) and 'Democracy as procedure and democracy as regime' (1997c) Castoriadis strongly opposes the idea that democracy – and politics in general – can be reduced to principles and procedures without any (specific) substance. In the first essay, he names the political liberal theorists John Rawls and Robert Nozick as his opponents, while the second addresses the proceduralism of Jürgen Habermas alongside political liberalism.[2] The political context is important.

In North America, the discussion was fuelled by several political struggles connected to multiculturalism and the claims of indigenous groups to control natural resources. In Europe, there was the rapid crumbling of the Eastern European 'communist' states on the one hand and increasing multiculturalism and mobility on the other. As uncurbed capitalism raided the former Eastern bloc, politicians, economists and political philosophers with anti-socialist leanings used the opportunity to declare the general defeat of socialist thought, and with it, all philosophical notions of collectivity. Based on what they saw as historical evidence – conflating, in effect, capitalism and democracy – slogans against collectivity in all forms inspired right-wing politicians and think tanks all over the West, culminating as it were in Francis Fukuyama's infamous statement (first in an article from 1989) that 'history' had now come to its 'end' (Fukuyama, 2006).

The mainstreaming of political theory in the 1980s and 1990s was not well-received by Castoriadis, who expressed little esteem for contemporary political thinkers. A great part of his writings on democracy is devoted to drawing basic distinctions and addressing what he saw as false oppositions, such as the juxtaposition of individual versus collective freedom and the (typically liberal) problem of freedom versus equality which occupied Isaiah Berlin and John Rawls. He spends considerable effort, in several texts, explaining why autonomy is always individual and collective at the same time, thus refuting the characteristically liberal assumption that individual and collective concerns must be 'balanced' or 'weighted' (Rawls, 1971; 1993). Concerning the question of equality versus freedom, Castoriadis sees these as interrelated phenomena, created in ancient Greece. With the initial rupture of heteronomy – that is, as democracy was created – it became clear that equality and freedom are interdependent since, in a democracy, 'the autonomy (the effective freedom) of all is and has to be a fundamental concern of each. [. . .] In its effective realization, my own freedom is a function of the effective freedom of others . . .' (Castoriadis, 1997c, p. 6). Since it is impossible to exercise one's freedom in a community of unequals, inequality and hierarchy are simply incompatible with freedom as autonomy.

Concerning the need for distinctions, Castoriadis saw it as essential to distinguish between the institutional arrangements of *democracy* and *capitalism*. In his earlier work on Western and Eastern state systems, Castoriadis sought to address the conflation of capitalism and democracy through his analysis of 'bureaucratic capitalism', which he saw as the Western counterpart of the 'capitalist bureaucracy' of the Union of Soviet Socialist Republics (USSR) (Castoriadis, 1988; see also entry on *Capitalism*). In later works, he addressed the problem in terms of social imaginary significations. In this framework, the *central* distinction resides in the idea that the two significations of modernity, rational-mastery and autonomy, co-exist in a state of *tension*, where capitalism is the embodiment of rational-mastery (or pseudo-rational pseudo-mastery) whereas autonomy is the central signification of democracy (see also *Heteronomy*). Accordingly, in 'What democracy?' Castoriadis takes great care in separating the capitalist imaginary of rational-*mastery* from the imaginary of *freedom* relating to autonomy and democracy. The problem with contemporary political liberalism, as he sees it, is that the capitalist imaginary *replaces* democracy and autonomy (Castoriadis, 2007, p. 137).[3] Through their ahistorical approach and by ignoring the importance of substance, Castoriadis sees his opponents as mistakenly analysing the existing state of affairs (liberal oligarchy) as a set of philosophical norms: 'Both Nozick and Rawls, blinded by their historical provincialism, view as axiomatic what is more or less self-evident in their own country, today' (p. 135). The historically contingent state of advanced capitalism is thus mistakenly represented as the crown of a long, democratic, progressive development. This kind of thinking is not only lacking, but serves as an ideological background for the establishment of (deeply undemocratic) corporate capitalism under the guise of freedom and democracy.

Communitarian thinkers have criticized various aspects of political liberalism, such as its atomism and value pluralism. In 'Democracy as procedure', Castoriadis posits himself against the liberal and proceduralist side(s) of the contemporary debates, refusing to theorize the individual as something other than a product of society and rejecting democratic proceduralism. Does this make him a communitarian? In a certain sense, yes, since he clearly states that democracy is a regime, with certain, substantive values, and by stressing that politics is unthinkable without its anthropological basis, that is, a certain democratic *paideia* (see *Paideia*). Nevertheless, in other, important respects the communitarian category fails to describe the position of Castoriadis. The quest for autonomy that saturates all his political writings clearly has universalist pretensions – universalist in the sense that once 'autonomy' has been invented it becomes indispensable as a 'yardstick' for society's self-evaluation. In a different discussion with Habermas ('Done and to be done', Castoriadis, 1997b, pp. 384 ff.), Castoriadis questions the validity of different types of social norms while arguing that autonomy is a condition for this questioning. He is also clear that modernity holds an aspiration to universality – incorporated in modern democracies as universal franchise and rights – that is a genuine expression of the project autonomy in its modern version (Castoriadis, 1997a, pp. 84–107). It is precisely this capacity for universalization that enables us moderns to recognize the political *relevance* of Greece, that is, to see it as an inspiration without converting it into a model.

On these grounds, Castoriadis is no communitarian, but more of an enlightenment thinker – as are (especially the classical) liberals and proceduralists. In fact, the position of Castoriadis transgresses the communitarian/liberal divide, first by arguing that many liberal values are also substantial and second by demonstrating that there are certain values and significations that hold a special position in the Graeco-Western world, significations that serve as the very conditions for there being such a controversy, such as the valuation of political and philosophical *questioning*, commitment to the question of *justice* and the demand for providing reasons and *justifications* (Castoriadis, 1997b). In a truly communitarian *cum* heteronomous framework, this kind of debate would be meaningless.

As far as theories of democracy are concerned, Castoriadis's notion of a 'true democracy' does not fit the established categories, for example, republican, liberal or procedural democracy (Habermas, 1994). His thought certainly reflects ideas of radical, participatory and direct democracy, communitarianism and republicanism, but to read him through these categories would mean to risk obscuring the main point of seeing democracy as the regime of autonomy (Castoriadis, 1997c, p. 16). What seems clear is that Castoriadis's conception of democracy is more *politicized* than most contemporary theories of democracy. His conception of a 'true' democracy rests upon the central distinction between 'the political sphere in the general and neutral sense' (*le politique*) and 'politics' (*la politique*) (1997c, p. 1; see also Castoriadis, 1991, pp. 156 ff.). 'The political' (*le politique*) pertains to 'the power-related dimension within society, how it is exerted and access thereto' (Castoriadis, 2010, p. 216). This dimension is instituted in all known societies. 'Politics' has a broader range, 'bearing on the institution as a whole, including of course the power-related dimension' (pp. 216–217). More precisely, politics is the explicit activity of putting the social institution into question (Castoriadis, 1991, p. 159). This distinction is usually conflated in political theory, with a few exceptions (notably in the works of Hannah Arendt, 1958; 1963; Chantal Mouffe, 2005a, b and Jacques Rancière, 2006, with varying terminology and analyses). However, the distinction between 'the political' and 'politics' is helpful in order to problematize political theories that seek to posit existing institutions as (philosophical) norms, as Castoriadis accuses Rawls and Nozick of doing. It serves as a criterion for identifying depoliticization and bureaucratization of the political field, thus creating an opening for radical questioning as well as political creativity.

The crucial point for Castoriadis is that, whereas *all* known societies have instituted 'the political' in general – 'the explicit, implicit, sometimes almost ungraspable dimension that deals with power', such as governmental and judicial power – *only a few societies have instituted 'politics'* (Castoriadis, 1997c, p. 1). 'Politics', as 'the explicit putting into question' of a society's institutions, is an invention, a social-historical creation that can be traced to Greece in the sixth-century BCE. This 'putting into question' emerged together with the invention of the public sphere and other institutional arrangements that dealt with self-limitation, law-making, the exercise of power and the overall (re-)institution of society. The continuous political process of 'explicit, conscious self-institution of society' was thus embodied in institutions that enabled people to 'effectively control' their community (Castoriadis, 2010, p. 122).

In various contexts, Castoriadis noted the connection between autonomy as a central signification, and democracy as the corresponding regime, but he did not elaborate it in any depth. As we have seen, the connection sometimes follows from the argument that the freedom of each depends on the freedom of all, and on effective participation (pp. 5–6). In the following passage it is also associated with *justice* as an inherent value in the movement toward autonomy:

> [T]his self-institution is a movement that does not stop . . . [I]t does not aim at a 'perfect society' (a perfectly meaningless expression) but, rather, at a society that is as free and as just as possible. It is this movement that I call the project of an autonomous society and that, if it is to succeed, has to establish a democratic society. (Castoriadis, 1997c, pp. 4–5)

In order to gain some insight into what this might imply, we now turn to what Castoriadis considers the most emblematic case: the Athenian democracy.

Even though there were other democratic *poleis*, the term 'Greek democracy' often means Athenian democracy, since this was the best developed democracy and the one for which there are most historical sources. In Castoriadis's treatment, Greece (or Athens) is neither a specimen among others, nor a model, but what he calls a *germ* to 'ourselves', that is, to Western or European societies (Castoriadis, 1991, p. 84). This means that when he uses the Greek example to criticize modern societies – liberal oligarchies – he uses standards that are historically familiar and intrinsic to these societies: or 'upstream' to ourselves, as he would call it (Castoriadis, 1997b, p. 394). We can accept the criticism as relevant insofar as the project of autonomy is *our* project.

Polis democracy is not, in Castoriadis's analysis, mainly characterized by its procedures for decision-making or its egalitarian distribution of power – some of these arrangements were already in place, such as voting; rather the social transformation was much deeper, representing a 'rupture' with heteronomous social reproduction and thought. Something entirely new emerged with the signification of autonomy, and democratic *politics* was part of this. Castoriadis frequently makes a strong point of the fact that the birth of democracy in ancient Greece coincided with the creation of *philosophy* and *politics*. Both practices represent a rupture with the traditional state of heteronomy by probing and questioning the nature and limits of the social institution and the world itself:

> Just as in Greek political activity the existing institution of society is called into question and altered for the first time, similarly Greece is the first society where we find the explicit questioning of the instituted collective representation of the world – that is, where we find philosophy. (Castoriadis, 1991, p. 102)

The notion of politics as self-government was radical by acknowledging that there is no special knowledge or science (*episteme*) in political matters, and that the laws have no metaphysical or ontological foundations. There are no guarantees, nor any external limits in the political domain – all that can be hoped for in deliberation and judgement is that everyone acts responsibly and cares for the common weal. 'The Greek *polis* and the creation of democracy' analyses the birth of democracy in light of the Greek attitude to the human being and the world as ultimately meaningless (pp. 102–103). Castoriadis sees politics, philosophy and tragedy as so many expressions of the human condition in the face of ontological chaos, what he calls 'the abyss'. The quest for autonomy arises from this condition of ontological hopelessness, and mortality and responsibility are understood as two sides of the same coin. In the political domain, which is what concerns us here, the lack of ontological foundations leads to the need for self-limitation in the social domain. Accordingly, says Castoriadis: 'In a democracy, people *can* do anything – and must know that they *ought not* to do just anything' (p. 115). Castoriadis understands democracy as a *tragic* regime, whose only 'foundation' is the realization of the fact that no foundations can exist. With this insight comes increased responsibility for 'that which depends on us' (i.e. the domain of *nomos*), but along with responsibility, there is also *hubris*. According to Castoriadis, '[t]ransgressing the law is not *hubris*, it is a definite and limited misdemeanor. *Hubris* exists where self-limitation is the only "norm," where "limits" are transgressed which were nowhere defined' (p. 115). Even though there are no extra-social foundations for democracy as such, Athenian democracy rested on numerous instituted principles that were aimed at self-limitation. Such arrangements are strikingly lacking in contemporary Western societies, according to Castoriadis (2010; 2011b). I will mention a few.

The main difference between Athenian and modern democracies is probably that the citizens of Athens had not only opportunities to speak and to vote – that is, a right to participation – but more importantly, a duty to serve in the public administration of the city.[4] One example is the Council of 500 (the *boulē*), where a large majority of the citizens served. In the fourth century 'over a third of all citizens over eighteen, and about two thirds of all citizens over forty, became councillors, some of them twice' (Hansen, 1991, p. 249). The council assisted the people's Assembly (*ecclesia*). Among its most important political functions was the preparation of the Assembly's agenda. For, in contrast to the party system, there were no privileged or expert groups to decide which 'programmes' the citizens could choose between on voting day. Service in the council lasted one year, and in addition came various administrative committees, military service and service in popular courts. Such public service was an important learning process that increased the political competence and commitment of the citizens.

In various contexts, Castoriadis would invoke a sense of responsibility for 'that which depends on us'. An important concern in his later years was the emerging environmental crisis (see, for example, 'What democracy?' Castoriadis, 2007). More generally, he commented, in several interviews and debates in the 1980s and 1990s, on the general lack of involvement and passion for political affairs in Western societies. He saw his own time as drawn by insignificance, indifference and cynicism (Castoriadis, 2011b). Such political apathy would be very difficult in Athens:

For example, when the city was in civil strife, there were sanctions against citizens who did not want to take sides (Castoriadis, 1991, p. 107). Since Solon, the principle of public *accountability* was instituted throughout the administrative and political apparatus (Balot, 2013). The possibility for recall was also instituted, as a safeguard against hidden agendas and false promises.

The use of lot and rotation meant that a large part of the citizenry were trained in the administration of public affairs, experiencing themselves as directly responsible for the well-being of the city. This ethos of care for the common weal was underscored by public rituals, such as the tragedies, which Castoriadis centrally connected with the emergence of democracy itself (see *Tragedy*), and the Greeks' fondness for poetry and art which has been seen to represent a general interest in *paideia* (Jaeger, 1986). But there were also sharper issues at stake, manifested in the duty to speak one's mind in publicly contested matters. Not only did citizens have the right to speak (*isegoria*), they were also 'under moral obligation to speak their minds (*parrhesia*)' (Castoriadis, 1991, p. 107). In matters where the majority may be wrong, or under poor influence, the Athenians even had institutions meant to bring forth the truth – or the common good – through commitment to a higher, collective *ethos* (see Castoriadis's discussion of 'unlawful laws', pp. 116–117).

Before concluding the case of Athenian democracy, it should of course also be added that the great involvement of all (per definition, male) citizens had great costs, and also that the city was engaged in several wars and, in periods, acted as an imperial power. That is, democratic Athens was in a state of expansion that could not last, and at the same time, was incredibly efficient, as described by Josiah Ober in several works (e.g. Ober, 1996).

A fair question to ask Castoriadis is whether his democratic ideals, inspired by a direct democracy that developed in a fairly homogenous community, can be applied in a contemporary context where the social units are much larger, culturally more heterogeneous and with a high degree of specialization. Although he was careful to stress that the Greeks were a 'germ' to ourselves, not a 'model', the challenge still remains as long as he refers to Greek institutions to criticize those of today. He is, for example, very clear that the principle of representation is 'alien to democracy' (Castoriadis, 1991, p. 108). When faced with such questions, Castoriadis did not attempt to outline what a real democracy would look like today. Even though this could be said to make it easy for himself, it is still in accordance with the project of autonomy, since a real democracy today would have to be created as a unique form by the people in question (see, for example, Castoriadis, 1997a, p. 104).

Since democracy is neither a theory, nor a set of procedures of principles, it cannot be transposed, pre-planned, exported or implemented. The open question today, however, is whether people in contemporary societies are able to recognize the original impulse of autonomy. In one of his interviews, Castoriadis was asked how the passion for political affairs could come into being: how it could be encouraged. Castoriadis's simple response was:

> I don't know. But I know that it has existed in the course of history. There have been times, and whole eras, in which people cared passionately about community affairs. They went into the streets; they made demands; they imposed a number of things. (Castoriadis, 2010, p. 6)

When faced with concrete political problems, on the other hand, Castoriadis would not hesitate to offer his analyses. In his advice to the students in mid May 1968, Castoriadis urged the students to 'define' and organize themselves, the failure of which would mean to render power to the established institutions, capitalist bureaucracy ('The anticipated revolution', Castoriadis, 1993, pp. 132 ff.). During his lifetime, Castoriadis always sought to identify and encourage initiatives of autonomy. It would therefore be a mistake to think that direct democracy *à la* Athens is the only acceptable political system for Castoriadis. The central idea is the project of autonomy, which can give itself an endless variety of forms, some of which will be entirely new.

In his later phase of life, Castoriadis was not too optimistic about the future of politics (Castoriadis, 2010; 2011b). We can only speculate about whether he would have changed from pessimism to optimism in light of recent political events such as reforms in the Arab world, starting in 2011. However, in my view, we need not speculate for long. The global trend, despite shifting events, is a social order that is apolitical, oligarchic and environmentally unsustainable. For example, the European Union, governed by what Castoriadis would certainly have seen as an oligarchy, has met the current financial crisis (starting in 2008) by cutting back on public welfare in order to 'save' financial institutions, and replacing politicians with economic administrators. Elected politicians, on their side, frequently switch careers to become corporate consultants, using their first-hand knowledge of political systems to circumvent democratic processes. At the time of writing, the crises caused by an increasingly aggressive finance-driven capitalism are used as levers for anti-political and semi-authoritarian reforms. Hence there is little reason to believe that Castoriadis would have been optimistic on behalf of contemporary Western democracies, at least in the short-term. However, he also says that 'as long as there continue to be people who reflect, who put into question the social system or their own system of thought, there is a creativity to history that no one can forget' (Castoriadis, 1997a, p. 104).

Notes

1 The chapter is also published in a shortened version in Castoriadis, 1997b.

2 Even though Habermas and Rawls had substantial disagreements and debated each other, they found themselves on the same side in the debate between liberalism (or, with a term that better describes the position of Habermas: universalism) and communitarianism (or particularism).

3 Even though Castoriadis dismisses contemporary liberal scholars, he acknowledges the original thought of early liberals such as Mill, Constant and Tocqueville (Castoriadis, 2010).

4 The public apparatus of Athens is too complicated to be accounted for here (but see Hansen, 1991 or, for a brief introduction, Raaflaub, 2007).

References

Arendt, H. (1958), *The Human Condition*, Chicago: Chicago University Press.
—. (1963), *On Revolution*, London: Penguin.
Balot, R. (2013), 'Democracy and political philosophy: Influences, tensions, rapprochements', in J. P. Arnason, K. A. Raaflaub and

P. Wagner (eds), *The Greek Polis and the Invention of Democracy: A Politico-cultural Transformation and Its Interpretations*, Chichester, West Sussex; Malden, MA: Wiley Blackwell, pp. 181–204.

Castoriadis, C. (1987), *The Imaginary Institution of Society*, K. Blamey (trans.), Cambridge: Polity.

—. (1988), *Political and Social Writings Vol 1, 1946–1955: From the Critique of Bureaucracy to the Positive Content of Socialism*, D. A. Curtis (ed. and trans.), Minneapolis: University of Minnesota Press.

—. (1991), *Philosophy, Politics, Autonomy. Essays in Political Philosophy*, New York: Oxford University Press.

—. (1993 [1968]), 'The anticipated revolution', in *Political and Social Writings Vol. 3*, D. A. Curtis (ed. and trans.), London: University of Minnesota Press, pp. 124–156.

—. (1997a), *World in Fragments*, D. A. Curtis (ed. and trans.), Stanford, CA: Stanford University Press.

—. (1997b), 'Done and to be done', in *Castoriadis Reader*, D. A. Curtis (trans.), Oxford: Blackwell, pp. 361–417.

—. (1997c), 'Democracy as procedure and democracy as regime', *Constellations*, 4, 1, 1–18.

—. (2004), *Ce qui fait la Grèce, I: D'Homère à Heraclite*, Paris: Seuil.

—. (2007), 'What democracy?' in H. Arnold (trans.), *Figures of the Thinkable*, Stanford, CA: Stanford University Press, pp. 118–150.

—. (2008), *Ce qui fait la Grèce, II: La cite et les lois*, Paris: Seuil.

—. (2010), *A Society Adrift, Debates and Interviews 1974–1997*, H. Arnold (trans.), New York: Fordham.

—. (2011a), *Ce qui fait la Grèce, III: Thucydide, la force et le droit*, Paris: Seuil.

—. (2011b), *Postscript on Insignificance*, G. Rockhill and J. Garner (trans.), G. Rockhill (ed.), London: Continuum.

Fukuyama, F. (2006), *The End of History and the Last Man* (with a new afterword), New York: Free Press.

Habermas, J. (1994), 'Three normative models of democracy', *Constellations*, 1, 1, 1–10.

Hansen, M. H. H. (1991), *The Athenian Democracy in the Age of Demosthenes: Structures, Principles and Ideology*, J. A. Crook (trans.), Oxford: Blackwell.

Held, D. (1996), *Models of Democracy*, 2nd edn, Cambridge: Polity.

Jaeger, W. (1986), *Paideia: The Ideals of Greek Culture. Vol. II, In Search of the Divine Centre*, New York: Oxford University Press.

MacIntyre, A. (1981), *After Virtue: A Study in Moral Theory*, London: Duckworth.

Mouffe, C. (2005a), *The Return of the Political*, London: Verso.

—. (2005b), *On the Political*, London: Verso.

Ober, J. (1996), *The Athenian Revolution: Essays on Ancient Greek Democracy and Political Theory*, Princeton, NJ: Princeton University Press.

Raaflaub, K. A. (2007), 'Introduction', in K. A. Raaflaub, J. R. Ober and W. Wallace, *Origins of Democracy in Ancient Greece*, Berkeley, CA: University of California Press, pp. 1–21.

Rancière, J. (2006), *Hatred of Democracy*, S. Corcoran (trans.), London: Verso.

Rawls, J. (1971), *A Theory of Justice*, Cambridge, MA: Belknap, Harvard University Press.

—. (1993), *Political Liberalism*, New York: Columbia University Press.

CHAPTER NINETEEN

Tragedy

Sophie Klimis

Ancient Greek tragedy came to play a central part in Castoriadis's understanding of what he has called the 'Greek creation', that is to say the simultaneous invention of democracy (a project of political autonomy) and of philosophy understood as a process of unending interrogation (Castoriadis, 2004, pp. 56–59; see the entries on *Autonomy* and *Democracy*).[1] This importance is due to the fact that, according to Castoriadis, ancient Greek tragedy should not be understood as a literary genre nor as a mere religious ritual, but as an instance of the political institution of the Athenian *polis* (Castoriadis, 1997, p. 284; 2004, p. 37; 2008, p. 139). Indeed, there is no 'Greek' tragedy according to Castoriadis but only *Athenian* tragedy, as it is closely linked to the democratic project of self-institution (Castoriadis, 1997, p. 284; 2004, pp. 36–37; 2008, pp. 137, 224; see *Institution*).

Athenian tragedy is understood as a self-limiting institution for the autonomous community of the Athenians, exposing the danger of *hubris* and the necessity of collective practical wisdom (*phronèsis*; Castoriadis, 2008, pp. 140–141). This is of the utmost importance to Castoriadis: as there is no transcendent source of meaning concerning political affairs; the Athenian political community is completely responsible for its choices. In this way, *hubris* must be understood as the breaking of limits which, in a self-governing democracy, were not pregiven, as a result of the incapacity of self-limitation (Castoriadis, 1997, pp. 282, 286). That is why the ontological presuppositions of tragedy provide citizens with a kind of political education (*paideia*), showing to them all the fundamental truth according to which being is chaos (Castoriadis, 1997, p. 284; 2008, p. 139; see *Paideia*). Castoriadis has focused his interpretation of tragedy more specifically on certain plays, such as Aeschylus's *Prometheus Bound* and Sophocles's *Antigone* (Castoriadis, 2007a, pp. 1–20, 25–31; 2007b, pp. 102–103). Comparing these two plays, Castoriadis shows that in less than a generation the imaginary representation of humankind shifted to embrace the idea of its own self-creation (Castoriadis, 2007a, p. 20).

However, while indeed stressing the importance of its political dimension, Castoriadis does not deny the fact that Athenian tragedy was a very complex phenomenon altogether: a collective festival, a religious celebration and a work of art (Castoriadis, 2008, p. 226). He also mentions that tragic choruses seem to have existed in Sicyone, a *polis* near Corinth, *before* the institution of tragedy in Athens (p. 137). Nevertheless, Castoriadis understands tragedy as a radical creation *ex nihilo* but not *cum nihilo*: inheriting singing choruses, the Athenians *invented* tragedy, creating it as an *eidos*, understood in the full sense of the word (p. 138; see *Creation* ex nihilo). According to Castoriadis, tragedy is mainly 'a total manifestation of the life of the Athenian community: it is the self-presentation of this community by itself and to itself. Within tragedy, the Athenian *dèmos* watches itself, as well as it asserts and denies itself' (p. 226). Considering more specifically the political dimension of tragedy, Castoriadis warns us that it is not to be confused with the political positions of the poets (Castoriadis, 1997, p. 284). It would also be too restrictive to merely understand Aeschylus's *Eumenides*, for example, as the celebration of the converting of private revenge into public justice (Castoriadis, 1997, p. 284; 2008, p. 139). Indeed, the true political dimension of tragedy lies in its ontological foundation and in its role as an institution of self-limitation for Athenian democracy. Those two aspects are closely linked, as they are both sides of the same reality (Castoriadis, 2008, p. 139).

This ontological foundation relies on the fact that tragedy constantly posits *being* as *chaos*. It does not express it in a discursive or reasoning way but rather makes it visible and emotionally felt by the whole audience. Indeed, terror and pity emerge when the destruction of a tragic hero such as Oedipus exhibits chaos as 'the absence of order for man, the lack of positive correspondence between human intentions and actions and their result or outcome' (Castoriadis, 1997, p. 284; 2008, p. 139). In this sense, tragedy may be considered as a paradigm for any work of art, which Castoriadis defines as 'a window onto chaos' (Castoriadis, 2007b; see the *Creative Imagination*). Contrasting art and religion, Castoriadis considers that religion is always the presentation and simultaneous occultation of the chaos or abyss: 'the sacred is the instituted *simulacrum* of the abyss' (p. 47). Art, however, presents the abyss without occulting it, nor does it resort to any kind of allegorism or symbolization. What about Athenian tragedy then, which was not only an art form but also a religious ritual? Castoriadis considers that ancient Greek religion finds its specificity in not being based on any kind of revelation. As it is not a revealed religion, it has neither dogma nor sacred texts. The 'texts' discussing the Greek gods are the written transcriptions of Homer's and Hesiod's oral poems. That is why it is possible for the tragic poets to transform that inherited poetic tradition without being accused of impiety: Homer and Hesiod were neither considered as prophets nor their words as sacred (Castoriadis, 2004, p. 142; 2008, p. 225; see *Autonomy* and *Heteronomy*).

Indeed, the tragic poets rely on the presentation of the abyss they found in that poetic tradition. Castoriadis considers tragedy to be deeply rooted in the Greek mythical and poetic background. He defends the provocative thesis that Greek myths are true *because* they express fundamental *truths* concerning the world (cosmos), death and humankind (Castoriadis, 2004, pp. 96, 182–184; see also Arnason, 2012; Klimis, 2006). Closely analyzing these myths as found in Homer's epics as well as in Hesiod's *Theogony*, Castoriadis retraces the Greek conception of the cosmos as meaningless because it is founded on chaos, that is, on a fundamentally irrational basis, and also talks about the intertwining of chaos and cosmos (Castoriadis, 2004, pp. 171–179). This cosmos is ruled by the *Moira*: a blind, impersonal law indifferent to human beings and to which even the gods are subject (pp. 109–115). The *Iliad* and *Odyssey* show a hopeless conception of death, without any consolation nor eschatological perspective: the dead within the Hades are nothing but miserable shadows without any memory (pp. 101–104). So that Achilles's ghost answers to Ulysses that he would rather be alive and the servant of a swineherd, than the king of the dead. In that light, Castoriadis synthesizes the ultimate contradiction of the epic conception of human life as follows: 'nothing is worth more than life. But if nothing is worth more than life, than life is worth nothing' (p. 103). That is why Castoriadis considers that the Homeric conception of the world, life and death is tragic, making epic indeed even more tragic than tragedy itself (pp. 97–98).

In *Ce qui fait la Grèce 3*, Castoriadis gives a more accurate description of two different tragic conceptions of the world (Castoriadis, 2011, pp. 120–122). The first one is to be found in Herodotus's sentence: 'those which in old times were great have for the most part become small, while those that were in my own time great used in former times to be small' (Herodotus I, 5 in Castoriadis, 2011, p. 120). Previously, Anaximander had expressed a similar idea of one and the same principle behind the generation and the corruption of everything. So, this first tragic vision of the world assumes its necessary decadence. But there is another form of the tragic, which is expressed in Sophocles's *Antigone* and in Thucydides's *Peloponnesian War*. Sophocles's chorus sings that the human being is the most terrifying and extraordinary of all living beings. Extraordinary, because it has created institutions, techniques, language and will create new ones in an unending progress. Terrifying, because it has a dual nature that is not likely to be changed: 'sometimes it walks towards good, sometimes towards evil' (Castoriadis, 2011, pp. 284–285). So, according to this tragic vision of humankind, there is no ethical 'progress' in human nature towards the Good. On the other hand, there is this tremendous technical and political 'progress' due to human inventions (p. 121). It is important to stress the fact that these two opposite characteristics are expressed by one and the same word: *deinos*. We will see its importance later on, as it expresses the ambivalence of human self-creation. Thucydides also points to a progress in history, due to an accumulation of technical and political 'know-how'. But he insists on certain regularities that will always remain, such as human desire for power (pp. 121–122). Therefore the Greek historian recognizes the possibility of a radical creation, emancipated from a law of necessity and decadence: the expansion of the Athenian empire did not imply its destruction and the Athenians could have avoided defeat against the Spartans (pp. 284–285). But he assumes *at the same time* a kind of 'immanent irrationality' as well as imprevisibility within human nature (p. 122).

The form of chaos exhibited in tragedy is 'the absence of order *for* man, the lack of positive correspondence between human intentions and actions, on one hand, and their result or outcome, on the other' (Castoriadis, 1997, p. 284). Tragedy stages an action project that is supposed to restore order but which will eventually transform itself. For instance, in *Oedipus Rex*, Oedipus sends Creon to consult the oracle, because he wants to get rid of the plague that has befallen the city. It is only in the middle of the play that this project will turn into a desperate and unlimited desire for self-knowledge, and so his initial action project fails (Castoriadis, 2008, p. 139). Thus tragedy teaches us that we are not masters of the consequences of our actions and that we do not even master the *meaning* of our actions (Castoriadis, 1997, pp. 284–285; 2008, p. 140). This essential unpredictability of human action (individual as well as collective) is the crossroad where the ontological presentation of chaos meets the political institution of self-limitation. The essential form of chaos as presented in tragedy is indeed the chaos within the human being, that is *hubris*.

Castoriadis defines tragic *hubris* in two ways: first, as the transgression of limits which were not previously defined. Second, as *monos phronein*, the illusion that one can deliberate by oneself and make the right decision for the common good (Castoriadis, 2007a, pp. 13–14). Those two closely linked definitions of *hubris* cannot be understood outside of the political context of Athenian direct democracy. As an autonomous society, the Athenian *polis* recognizes itself as the source of its norms, laws and values. Thus,

> this society cannot evade the question: Why this norm rather than that? – in other words, it cannot evade the question of justice [. . .] neither can it evade the question of *limits* to its actions. In a democracy, people *can* do anything – and must know they *ought not* to do just anything. Democracy is the regime of self-limitation; therefore it is also the regime of historical risk – another way of saying it is the regime of freedom – and a tragic regime. (Castoriadis, 1997, pp. 282–283)

In an autonomous *polis*, the citizens are completely free and responsible for their choices, as there is no 'transcendent guarantee'. The gods do not interfere with politics. No Greek citizen would consult the delphic oracle in order to ask for a law, says Castoriadis. On the contrary, Athenian decrees and laws were decided by the people themselves. Any citizen could make a proposal for a law at the *ecclesia*. Indeed, Athenian citizens were so completely free that they could destroy themselves as Thucydides demonstrates when he apportions blame to the Athenians to explain their defeat in the Peloponnesian war, despite his praising of *andres gar polis*, 'the city is the men'. This ambivalence of total freedom – the possibility of self-creation as well as of self-destruction – is the 'tragic essence' of Athenian democracy.

Because of this total freedom, Athenian citizens had to create their own institutions of self-limitation. Castoriadis studied two of these: one is a procedure called *graphè para nomôn* (accusation of unlawfulness) and the other is tragedy. The *graphè para nomôn* is the counterpart to the possibility for each citizen to make a proposition of law at the *ecclesia*. Any citizen could bring another to trial and accuse him of inducing the people to vote for an unlawful law. This accusation would be examined and judged by a popular jury drawn by lot. In case of conviction, the law would be nullified (p. 283). Tragedy, on the other hand, brings to light the disaster resulting from the inability to self-limit by representing heroes destroyed by their own *hubris*, as we have previously seen in the general definition of *hubris*:

> *Hubris* does not simply presuppose freedom, it presupposes the absence of fixed norms, the essential vagueness of the ultimate bearings of our actions [. . .] transgressing the law is not *hubris*, it is a definite and limited misdemeanor [. . .] *Hubris* exists where self-limitation is the only 'norm'. (p. 282)

For instance, in his *Trojan Women*, Euripides made the Greeks's *hubris* visible right after the taking of Troy: they killed, raped, desecrated temples . . . with that fiction, he warned his fellow citizens: 'such monsters, we are', staging it one year after the slaughter of the Melians. During the Peloponnesian war, the inhabitants of Melos refused to become part of the Athenian Confederation. In retaliation, the Athenians killed all men and dragged all women and children into slavery (Castoriadis, 2008, p. 140).

Another example is the discussion of power in Aeschylus's *Prometheus Bound*. Showing Zeus's tyranny (through his desire to destroy humankind, and his violent revange against the *philanthropos* Prometheus, bound forever), the poet dared to confront the audience with the tyranny inherent in all established power, as well as with its necessary and intrinsic brutality and injustice. Aeschylus also stressed the transitory nature of power, while speaking about the precarious power of the king and master of the world. In doing so, the poet participated in the institution of the new power of democracy. He showed his fellow citizens that the precarity of power is due to the nature of being: all that exists must be destroyed (Castoriadis, 2007b, p. 102). That is why he warned the Athenians about the dangers of *hubris* and the necessity of self-limitation, as Pericles did, while reminding them their empire was a tyranny, gained by force (Castoriadis, 2008, pp. 227–228).

Following this idea, Castoriadis makes Sophocles's *Antigone* 'the' tragedy of democracy. However, this is not because of an opposition between divine right and human law, as prevailing in many interpretations such as Hegel's or Steiner's. Castoriadis reminds us that the burying of the dead has always been a human as well as a divine law. Especially in Athens, the main religious ceremonies were civic and priesthood was just a political magistrature among others (Castoriadis, 2004, p. 149). Therefore, there can be no gods without a *polis* that institutes rituals to honour them (Castoriadis, 2008, p. 142). Furthermore, Antigone and Creon distort both divine and human laws, rather than merely 'representing' them. Antigone's 'divine' law is the *oxymoron* of a 'law of her own' and not a general law, as it is to bury her own irreplaceable dead brother while the divine law is to bury *all* dead, whoever they are (p. 143). Behind her apparent lawful reason, Castoriadis sees Antigone's claim of the irreplaceability of her dead brother as a sign of her hidden passion for Polynices (p. 144). In this interpretation, he stresses the importance of understanding what he calls the 'psychological motivations' of the tragic characters, while avoiding psychoanalysis applied to text: Castoriadis does not decide if Antigone's love is incestuous or not. He rather wants to show how abstract principles are exploited by the heroes' passions (p. 144). As for Creon, while he rightly says that no *polis* can exist without compliance to laws, this character is actually also motivated by irrational passions (*pathè*), such as the desire for power and unquenchable anger against Polynices (p. 144). So, to

Castoriadis, tragedy teaches us two, crucial, political lessons. The first is that very good motivations of political decisions may be wrong if they are *strictly and only* political. Because '*la politique*' (as 'politics' in a strong and explicit sense) is potentially universal, any just political decision should take into account factors that are *not* political. The second lesson is that even when someone believes s/he has made the right decision, relying on the best of his/her knowledge and judgement, this decision may actually be bad and even catastrophic. Neither the signification nor the consequences of an act will be strictly guaranteed by prior reflection (p. 145).

That is why *Antigone* shows the problem of political action in democracy, even if the hero is a king. Even if one is right, one is actually wrong when only listening to oneself and unable to listen to what is sound in someone else's position. That is what Hemon says to his father: nobody can be wise alone (*phronein monos*). The final lesson of that play is to celebrate *to phronein*: practical wisdom in concrete and practical situations. This *phronein* can only stem from a collective deliberation, given the uncertainty prevailing in the field of action, the perpetual fragility and incompleteness of reasons and grounds on which we base our decisions (p. 146).

As Castoriadis is explicitly calling the self-constitution of the Athenian political community a 'philosophy in action' (Castoriadis, 2004, p. 59), based on a participation in political life seen as a continuous *paideia* (Castoriadis, 1997, p. 281), we can wonder in what sense tragedy is part of this process. Castoriadis does not develop this idea further. Nevertheless, from his collected papers and seminars at the École des Hautes Etudes en Sciences Sociales (EHESS) it is possible to reconstruct the premises of an original reception theory of tragedy seen as a continuing political *paideia* for the citizens through *katharsis/Zauberspiel*.

In *La cité et les lois*, Castoriadis stresses the fact that *philia* and *eleos* (friendship and pity) are two essential democratic affects (Castoriadis, 2008, p. 181). *Philia* is 'the first intersubjective relation that matters in the political life of a collectivity' (p. 180). It depends on the political institution of the *polis*, as *philia* can only exist between equals belonging to a free community, and the *polis* is what provides the political conditions for such freedom and equality. But on the other hand, the *polis* depends on the *philia* between citizens who relate to each other, considering they embody common values and virtues such as the *kalos k'agathos* (p. 181). *Eleos* is an affect experimented towards every human being. Referring to Aristotle, Castoriadis defines *eleos* as 'the capacity to put oneself in the place of someone else and to metaphorically suffer from his suffering, in order not to remain unmoved by his misfortune' (p. 180). This *eleos* is what shows up at the end of *Iliad* between Achilles and Priam (p. 180; see also Klimis, 2003; 2011). Referring to this epic but also quoting Aeshylus's *Persians*, Castoriadis justifies Arendt's affirmation that the Greeks invented impartiality (Castoriadis, 1997, p. 284). Not a word is said against the Persians by the very same Aeschylus who also fought them in Marathon as well as in Salamine. Furthermore, he portrayed the Persian queen Atossa as very wise, venerable and mainly pitiable, like all of the Persian people (p. 284). The tragedy shows their collective doom through the *hubris* of their king Xerxès, Atossa's son (Castoriadis, 2008, p. 140). So we could say that, while arousing pity even for the enemy, Athenian tragedy created *philanthropia*: a strong affect of *philia* for all humankind, based on the collective recognition of human fragility and finitude (see Loraux, 2002; Klimis, 2003).

In *Fenêtre sur le chaos*, Castoriadis provides us with a theory of the reception of the work of art using tragedy as a paradigm. The attitude of the subject in front of a work of art is *Zaubertrauer* (enchantment/mourning) which may be one of the meanings of Aristotle's *katharsis* (Castoriadis, 2007b, p. 133). *Katharsis* is a medical term, referring to the purging of bad moods (p. 147). The tragic *katharsis* takes place when the spectator is affected by terror and pity and feels a certain kind of pleasure as a result of those two affects. According to Castoriadis, this pleasure comes from a certain way of experiencing that 'meaning is meaningless and meaningless is meaningful' (p. 153). He says the cathartic affect is specific and indescribable, but he nevertheless gives an approximate description of it: 'we could say it is a mix of joy and sorrow, of pleasure and mourning, of endless amazement and acquiescence [. . .] it is the affect of the end of desire, and that is precisely the meaning of the *katharsis*' (p. 154).

As we have seen so far, it is of crucial importance for Castoriadis to ground his comprehension of the Greeks on a close interpretation of their texts. This must be further elucidated, to use his word. Castoriadis is equally critical of the three main paradigms of interpretation of ancient Greece: the classical thesis of the 'Greek Miracle', the Heideggerian interpretation and the anthropology of

Ancient Greece founded by Vernant and Vidal-Naquet (Castoriadis, 1997, pp. 267–272; 2004, pp. 40–46; see also Klimis, 2006). Speaking of a 'Greek germ', Castoriadis challenges the thesis of the 'Greek Miracle', refuting any idea of Ancient Greece as an eternal model (Castoriadis, 2004, p. 40). Furthermore, he argues that there is no transition from irrational to rational, from *muthos* to *logos*, precisely because the Greek *muthoi* reveal the truth about the ultimate signification of the world, which is to be meaningless. Castoriadis also criticizes Heidegger for his systematic disergard of the *polis* (for politics and democracy), but also of *erôs* and of the *psychè* (Castoriadis, 1988/1991, p. 15). Missing their central position within the Greek social-historical *eidos*, Heidegger also misunderstands ancient philosophy, which is indissolubly interwoven with democracy and the *polis*, even when it considers them as enemies: indeed, Plato's whole philosophy would be incomprehensible without his persistent struggle against democracy, while Aristotle's political philosophy should be understood as an apology of democracy (Castoriadis, 1984, pp. 283–284; 2004, pp. 38–39; 2007a, p. 3; see also Klimis, 2008). With the French structuralist hellenists, Castoriadis recognizes that Greek culture is not superior to others (Castoriadis, 1997, p. 267). But he considers there is a Greek specificity: it is the Greeks who invented the curiosity and rational/critical inquiry about other cultures, that are concomitant with their critical and rational inquiry about their own culture and institutions (pp. 268–269). For Castoriadis, in studying the Ancient Greeks, we are actually trying to understand and to transform *ourselves*, as we still want the project of autonomy and unlimited interrogation that they have invented (Castoriadis, 2004, pp. 52–53). To Castoriadis, the elucidation of the Greek social-historical creation is especially of crucial importance because of the strong heteronomy that characterizes our capitalist social-historical institution, where the project of autonomy and rationality is 'in eclipse' (Castoriadis, 1983/1991, pp. 82–84).

As the project autonomy is closely linked to the 'discovery' of human self-creation, Castoriadis gives careful consideration to the various 'responses' that the Greek thinkers gave to the question *what is anthropos?* We must stress the fact that those thinkers are the Presocratics, the Tragic poets and Aristophanes, the Sophists and Democritus and the historians Herodotus and Thucydides. For Castoriadis, significantly, Plato and Aristotle do *not* belong to this tradition of thought; although they are closely linked with Athenian democracy, they elaborated their own philosophies *in reaction to it*. That is why Castoriadis considers that, in order to understand ancient Greek philosophy, it is necessary to study poetic, historical, as well as institutional texts, because they provide us with the social imaginary significations underlying the Greek social-historical creation. Those schemes allow us to understand the Greek social-historical *eidos*, while reconstructing the complex network grounded in its imaginary significations and connecting specific aims, institutions and affects (Klimis, 2010a). Considering poetic texts, Castoriadis also speaks about 'the comparative exploration of the expressive resources of languages, an all-important subject for the elucidation of the ways and means of social-historical creation' (Castoriadis, 2007a, p. 38). This assertion is quoted from an unpublished text, 'Notes on some poetical resources', Castoriadis has worked on for over 20 years. The very long period of maturation of this essay shows the importance of this research topic for Castoriadis (Klimis, 2010b). Let us see how it may enlighten the comprehension of the Greek human self-creation.

According to Castoriadis, the indivisible polysemy of words and grammatical cases is the characteristic of Greek language which was used by Greek poets (Castoriadis, 2007a, p. 21). In this regard, the use of the word *deinos* in Sophocles's *Antigone* is paradigmatic, as it condenses his whole anthropology (pp. 12–19; see also Klimis, 2004). This term means, simultaneously, terrible and wondrous. Therefore Castoriadis translates the noun *deinotès* as 'terrifying formidableness' (Castoriadis, 2007a, p. 268). We may notice that, although *deinos* also may means 'sublime' (Longinus), Castoriadis never mentions it, but strangely uses 'sublime' as the translation of *hypsipolis* ('great', 'standing high within one's city') as opposed to *apolis*, an outlaw because of his *hubris* (p. 12). This is surprising because the 'sublime', already in Longinus and afterwards in Kant's famous analysis, precisely condenses the ambivalence of *deinos* as terrible and wondrous at the same time.

Castoriadis emphasizes that *deinos* also refers to an excellence in an occupation or an art, to the point of eliciting terror and wonder (p. 25). The first *stasimon* starts with the chorus singing: 'numerous are the *deina*, but nothing is more *deinon* than man'. An enumeration of all the inventions of humankind follows:

agriculture, navigation, medicine, etc. To understand the *deinotès* of humankind, these are the most important verses: 'the human being has taught himself (*edidaxato*) speech and wind-like thought and the instituting passions (*astunomous orgas*)' (Sophocles's *Antigone* vs 354–356, as cited in Castoriadis, 2007a). Castoriadis discusses the importance of this poetic 'definition' of humankind, stressing the importance of the instituting passions: 'the passionate temper, the dispositions and drives, give laws to cities and so, they institute cities [. . .] We usually think of law and institutions as something absolutely opposed to temper or passion', but Sophocles says something 'profoundly true: there is a prelogical intention and "will" at the root of the primordial institution, and no institution can hold without passion' (Castoriadis, 2007a, p. 17). Both Aristotle and Rousseau will remember this Sophoclean lesson: Aristotle while saying that lawmakers must be concerned above all with establishing *philia*, Rousseau maintaining that 'to institute a people, one must first change its *mores*' (p. 27).

Speech, thought and the instituting passions are the 'essential attributes' of humankind, Aristotle would have said. But they are not 'natural'. The middle voice of the verb *edidaxato* denotes reflexive action. No one has taught *anthropos* anything. He has taught himself what makes him human. That is why human beings are more *deinoi* than all the other living beings. All animals are what they are by virtue of their nature. The Gods are more powerful than human beings, but they also are what they are by their 'nature' (p. 16). Only the human beings have *created* their own nature. According to Castoriadis, Sophocles therefore expresses the essence of *anthropos* as self-creation: the human being creates his essence and this essence is itself creation (of techniques, speech, etc.) and self-creation (p. 16). This self-creation is what makes humankind's *deinotès* and its self-limitation necessary. The *deinotès* reaches its summit and self-destruction in *hubris*, when a human being becomes *apolis*, 'unable to interweave the laws of his city with the justice of the gods guaranteed by oaths' (p. 12). That incapacity, due to the belief to be the only one who thinks 'right' (*monos phronein*), has destroyed both Creon and Antigone. But the play raised the 'instituting passions' of the spectators. Through terror and pity, the tragedy encouraged them to create their own way to become *hupsipolis*, 'sublime in the city', by exercising together *to phronein* in their everyday citizen life.

Note

1 The three volumes of *Ce qui fait la Grèce* have not been translated
   in English yet. They follow seminars Castoriadis gave at the EHESS
   in Paris in the early 1980s. They have been published posthumously.
   Volume 1 (2004) deals with the 'Greek creation' from Homer to
   Heraclitus. Volume 2, *La cité et les lois* (2008) is mainly devoted
   to the political institutions of Athens, with special attention to
   the works of the historians Herodotus and Thucydides, and some
   excursus about Greek tragedy, Socrates and the quarrel between the
   Ancients and the Moderns. Volume 3, *Thucydide. La force et le droit*
   (2011), focuses on Thucydides' *Peloponnesian War.*

References

Arnason, J. (2012), 'Castoriadis as civilizational analyst: Sense and non-
   sense in ancient Greece', *European Journal of Social Theory*, 15, 3,
   pp. 295–311.
Castoriadis, C. (1991 [1983]), 'The Greek polis and the creation of
   democracy', in D. A. Curtis (ed.), *Philosophy, Politics, Autonomy.
   Cornelius Castoriadis*, New York, Oxford: Oxford University Press,
   pp. 81–123.
—. (1991 [1988]), 'The "End of Philosophy"?' in D. A. Curtis (ed.),
   Philosophy, Politics, Autonomy. Cornelius Castoriadis, New York,
   Oxford: Oxford University Press, pp. 13–32.
—. (1997), *Castoriadis Reader*, D. A. Curtis (ed. and trans.), Oxford:
   Blackwell.
—. (2004), *Ce qui fait la Grèce, 1: D'Homère à Heraclite*, Paris: Seuil.
—. (2007a [1999]), *Figures of the Thinkable*, H. Arnold (trans.).
   Stanford, CA: Stanford University Press.
—. (2007b), *Fenêtre sur le chaos*, Paris: Seuil.
—. (2008), *La cité et les lois. Ce qui fait la Grèce, 2. La création
   humaine 3*, Paris: Seuil.
—. (2011), *Thucydide, la force et le droit. Ce qui fait la Grèce, 3. La
   création humain IV*, Paris: Seuil.
Klimis, S. (2003), *Archéologie du sujet tragique*, Paris: Kimé.
—. (2004), 'Antigone et Créon à la lumière du terrifiant/extraordinaire
   (deinotès) de l'humanité tragique', in F. Ost and L. Couloubaritsis
   (eds), *Antigone et la résistance civile*, Bruxelles: Ousia, pp. 63–102.
—. (2006) 'Explorer le labyrinthe imaginaire de la création grecque:
   un projet en travail. . .', in S. Klimis and L. Van Eynde (eds),

L'imaginaire selon Castoriadis. Thèmes et enjeux, Cahiers Castoriadis, 1, Bruxelles: Publications des Facultés Universitaires Saint Louis, pp. 9–46.

—. (2007), 'Décrire l'irreprésentable ou comment dire l'indicible originaire', in S. Klimis and L. Van Eynde (eds), *Psyché. De la monade psychique au sujet autonome*, Cahiers Castoriadis, 3, Bruxelles: Publications des Facultés Universitaires Saint-Louis, pp. 25–54.

—. (2008), 'Platon, penseur de l'autonomie ? Castoriadis sur *Le Politique* de Platon', *Cahiers Critiques de Philosophie*, 6, 115–132.

—. (2010a), 'Créer un eidos du social-historique selon Castoriadis', in R. Gély and L. Van Eynde (eds), *Affectivité, Imaginaire, Création Sociale*, Bruxelles: Publications des Facultés Universitaires Saint-Louis, pp. 13–42.

—. (2010b), 'La musicalité sémantique du penser-poème grec. Pour une eidétique du prattein-poiein dans le langage', in S. Klimis, P. Caumières and L. Van Eynde (eds), *Castoriadis et les Grecs. Cahiers Castoriadis, 5*, Bruxelles: Publications des Facultés Universitaires Saint-Louis, pp. 173–243.

—. (2011), 'Individualité et subjectivation dans l'*Iliade*', in C. Dumoulié (ed.), *La Fabrique du sujet. Histoire et poétique d'un concept*, Paris: éd. Desjonquères, pp. 21–28.

Loraux, N. (2002 [1999]), *The Mourning Voice. An Essay on Greek Tragedy*, E. Trapnell Rawlings and P. Pucci (trans.), Cornell Studies in Classical Philology, New York: Cornell University Press.

INDEX